ALSO BY TODD GITLIN

*The Bulldozer and the Big Tent: Blind Republicans,
Lame Democrats, and the Recovery of American Ideals*

The Intellectuals and the Flag

Letters to a Young Activist

*Media Unlimited: How the Torrent of Images and Sounds
Overwhelms Our Lives*

Sacrifice (novel)

*The Twilight of Common Dreams: Why America Is
Wracked by Culture Wars*

The Murder of Albert Einstein (novel)

Watching Television (editor)

The Sixties: Years of Hope, Days of Rage

Inside Prime Time

*The Whole World Is Watching: Mass Media in the Making
and Unmaking of the New Left*

Busy Being Born (poetry)

Campfires of the Resistance: Poetry from the Movement (editor)

Uptown: Poor Whites in Chicago (with Nanci Hollander)

ALSO BY LIEL LEIBOVITZ

Lili Marlene: The Soldiers' Song of World War II (with Matthew Miller)

Aliya: Three Generations of American-Jewish Immigration to Israel

The CHOSEN PEOPLES

America, Israel, and the Ordeals of Divine Election

TODD GITLIN
AND LIEL LEIBOVITZ

Simon & Schuster

NEW YORK · LONDON · TORONTO · SYDNEY

Simon & Schuster
1230 Avenue of the Americas
New York, NY 10020

First Simon & Schuster hardcover edition September 2010

SIMON & SCHUSTER and colophon are registered trademarks
of Simon & Schuster, Inc.

For information about special discounts for bulk purchases,
please contact Simon & Schuster Special Sales at
1-866-506-1949 or business@simonandschuster.com.

The Simon & Schuster Speakers Bureau can bring authors to your
live event. For more information or to book an event contact the
Simon & Schuster Speakers Bureau at 1-866-248-3049
or visit our website at www.simonspeakers.com.

Manufactured in the United States of America

1   3   5   7   9   10   8   6   4   2

Library of Congress Cataloging-in-Publication Data
The chosen peoples : America, Israel, and the ordeals
of divine election / Todd Gitlin and Liel Leibovitz.
         p.   cm.
"Simon & Schuster nonfiction original"—T.p. verso
Includes bibliographical references and index.
1. Jews—Election, Doctrine of. 2. Palestine in Judaism.
3. Zionism—History. 4. Arab-Israeli conflict. 5. Nationalism—
United States—History. 6. Political messianism—United States.
7. Manifest Destiny. 8. United States—Relations—Israel.
9. Israel—Relations—United States. I. Leibovitz, Liel. II. Title.
BM613.G58 2010   296.3'1172—dc22   2010011181

ISBN 978-1-4391-3236-4

To our wives, Laurel Cook and Lisa Ann Sandell,
who had the grace to choose us

*Now therefore, if you will obey my voice indeed, and keep
my covenant, then you shall be a peculiar treasure unto me
above all people: for all the earth is mine: And you shall be
unto me a kingdom of priests, and a holy nation.*

EXODUS 19:5–6

*. . . I shall be most happy indeed if I shall be an
humble instrument in the hands of the Almighty,
and of this, his almost chosen people . . .*

ABRAHAM LINCOLN, ADDRESS TO
THE NEW JERSEY STATE SENATE,
FEBRUARY 21, 1861

Contents

Introduction

THROUGHOUT THREE MILLENNIA of striving and suffering, vast portions of humanity have been stirred, galvanized, burdened, and molded irreversibly by the extraordinary idea that one nation, alone of all mankind, has been singled out by God to be His chosen people.

Oliver Cromwell declared himself an Israelite and the English "a people that have had a stamp upon them from God," their nation called upon by the Almighty "to rule with Him and for Him." Ireland's Protestants couldn't disagree more—they knew that *they* were the ones chosen by God, that they were, in the words of one Gaelic poet, the true "Children of Israel once in Egypt, / under the oppression of the strength of the enemies of God."

Those other rebels against the British Empire, the Boers, laid claim to the same exalted status. In 1885, Paul Kruger, the president of South Africa, had no doubt on which side of heaven that nation's founding fathers stood. "When we think of the former emigrants," he said, "the Voortrekkers of yore, it is then revealed unto us how God, in his divine providence, dealt with them, even as He dealt with the Israelite nation of old. . . . He summoned them to the same task: Canaan was inhabited by heathens alienated from God. . . . Israel was bidden make it the Lord's dwelling place."

Dostoyevsky found signs of God's favor among the long-suffering Russians, who were, as one of his characters proclaims in *The Possessed,* "the only god-bearing people on earth, destined to regenerate and save the world." Similar sentiments were preached from pulpits and shouted on battlefields in France and Germany. For the past century, Saudi Arabia has staked out its own claim. Then again, the Qur'an can be quoted in support of the proposition that it is all

Muslims everywhere who constitute God's people. Monotheism in particular cultivates the conviction that one's own people have been, and continue to be, chosen by a God who is not only their God but everyone else's as well. But even without believing in a single god, the Chinese and Hindus have their own versions. The name that the Navajo use for themselves means "the people."

Amid an epic history of claims to heaven-sent entitlement, only two nation-states stand out for the fundamental, continuous, and enduring quality of their convictions and the intense seriousness (and hostility) with which others take their claims: the United States and Israel. Alone among the families of women and men, each took the idea of chosenness as a cornerstone for a newly founded identity. Each felt it as inspiration, consolation, and reward all at once, and each has been guided, saddled, and haunted by it—even as many citizens of these nations have disputed their claim to chosenness. Even as unbelievers railed against their presumption, each people fashioned a belief in divine election first into a banner and then into a republic. Each began as refugees and became battling pioneers. Each planted the idea in the fertile soil of statehood, where its fruit could nourish—even invent—the national culture.

The settlers who founded America and Israel abandoned their homes and set sail to promised lands in order to fulfill providential fates. They claimed common inspiration and hurled themselves into the future as God's elect. Myths grew into facts on the ground. However startling the foundational story, however downright peculiar or even absurd it may seem, their successors—even the disbelievers among them—felt like its inheritors, curators, and custodians. The story lived in their emotions. It shook them. How could they shake *it*?

They could not. They did not wish to. They sensed that the idea of chosenness was not merely a quirk of fanatics but a potent, luminous, tangled, living complex of ideas; that it descends to earth with a sword; that the very expression *chosen people* by turns ennobled, encouraged, and perplexed those who believed themselves chosen;

that it conferred fortitude, dignity, pride, and anxiety all at once; that it granted gifts, shed blood, and imposed ordeals. Sometimes they blinded themselves to the ordeals. Flattering themselves, they often refused to notice how their claim evoked rivalry, exasperation, and loathing in others. Yet they were often aware that the belief in chosenness calls forth the most profound achievements of human beings as well as the most bitter conflicts—in short, that it makes history. If chosenness is a conceit, it is not an idle one. Embrace it, scorn it, despise it, doubt it, or tolerate it, you have to admit that it is responsible for much of the best as well as the worst that the two nations have accomplished, and aim to accomplish, in the world.

Even when disavowed or reinterpreted, some such idea has infused Judaism and the Jewish people from their beginnings. Its theological roots, albeit often unacknowledged, run deep, and even secular moderns do not disown them at will. The founding fathers of the first Jewish state to materialize in two millennia were moved by a secular idea of the nation, not by an explicit bow to God's will, but they still sought justification from a book hailed to be of divine inspiration, a book that they believe records their divine origin. Even as the majority of Israelis sought, and continue to seek, nothing more than a prosperous, peaceful, and dignified existence, undercurrents of chosenness have rattled the ground beneath them. Even as they fiercely disputed policies, identities, all manner of things, a spirit of chosenness inhabited them, and continues to do so.

So, too, for Americans. Starting with the pious men and women who sought to fulfill their religious passions on the New World's wild shores, Americans have long understood themselves as dedicated to liberty. But however paradoxically, they have felt appointed to liberty from on high. American history is driven by a vision of a territory stretching from sea to shining sea, and a nation built thereon, not as an ordinary country but as God's land, a republic placed on earth by the Almighty to shine the light of freedom into a benighted world. In its youth, whatever the explicit wishes of its founders, the republic mushroomed into an empire. It grew in size, in might, in ambition.

It interpreted its trajectory as clear proof that the divine promise was on its way to fulfillment. On the tongues of some presidents and clergymen, the language of divine election curdled into jingoism, racism, and belligerence. In the minds of others, a chosen people were mandated to create a just and peaceful society apart from—or as a beacon to—the rest of the world. These worldviews clashed bitterly, but they started from the same notion: America was a nation unlike others, uniquely blessed by the God who created the world.

Frankly, when we embarked on this book, the two of us were ourselves inclined to consider it a scourge, if a durable one, to claim that God ever plucked a favored nation from the loins of Abraham—archaic, outrageous, destructive, crazy making, and ripe for iconoclasm. Surely a belief so presumptuous, so absurd, was mismatched to the needs of the living. Surely, if not uprooted, it would bring disaster to Jews and Americans alike. Our task, we thought, was to deflate it utterly, to apply all the sobriety and reason we could muster to overcome this historic misapprehension.

History is a wilderness—"a land not mine, still forever memorable," in the words of the great Russian poet Anna Akhmatova. As we wandered and explored, to our surprise, the complications of chosenness came to feel less bewildering and its logic—unearthly but not inhuman—oddly less alien. In the sermons of preachers and the pronouncements of leaders, in the clarion calls that sent millions to sea or to battle, we found the pure, mad, burning essence of that ancient human quest, the search for deep meaning. For all that the notion of divine election still strikes us as bizarre and incredible, the more we traced its vicissitudes, the more we came to understand its multiple uses. We began writing this book wishing to put out the fires of chosenness, but completed it thinking that—however dangerous they are if allowed to rage out of control—they are here to stay and just might light a way forward. We came to think that the way out of the seminal quandary might be further in—to take the unexhausted tradition of chosenness seriously. Was Israel the Jewish state? Then let it be a *Jewish* state, distinguished not only ethnically but ethically as well. Did America fancy itself a city upon a hill under the eyes of the world? Then let America, in Langston Hughes's words, "be America again."

When you play for such stakes, chutzpah is tempting. At every turn, grand claims scream out that they are meant to be swallowed whole—or renounced absolutely. Nevertheless, we shy away from stone-graven conclusions, rigid interpretations, or party platforms. Instead, we seek to engage readers of various stripes—as the two of us engaged ourselves—in meditating on the origins, attractions, implications, and contradictions of a powerful and intoxicating idea.

It is beyond our powers to deliver doctrinal tablets, but neither are we detached. We are acutely mindful that we live in a world where Jews are all too often despised for being Jews, and where the Jewish state comes under harsh scrutiny far more than others. We are equally well aware that the United States is cheaply condemned as a Great Satan and assigned demonic powers. We refuse to sign on to the prosecution teams. Yet neither are we satisfied to compose briefs for the defense. Rather, we aspire to ruminate and to understand: to excavate the idea of chosenness at work in the two peoples' histories; to explore the reactions of their neighbors, admirers, and adversaries; to see what underlies their affinities as well as their divergences—and to plead for a fresh look.

We could hardly fail to acknowledge that the questions we explore have been contentious for centuries—indeed, for millennia. In fact, the disputes surrounding these questions are among the most interesting things about them. For good reason have they been the quarry of myriad specialists. For our part, we are well aware that we are meddlers and not experts—not theologians, not credentialed historians of either nation, although (and therefore) we are indebted to the work of many scholars. We enter some theological thickets—not painless work for secular, skeptical intellectuals. The biblical conceits are staggering; we both marvel and bridle at them. The capacity of human beings to imagine the world supernaturally is astounding, and we have struggled not to be overwhelmed by the immensely audacious—or presumptuous—idea that a particular group of human beings has been singled out for a magisterial destiny by a supernatural spirit. Still, we have strived not to limit ourselves to the preoccupations of specialists any more than to those of politicians, journalists, or diplomats. These questions are too important to be left to specialists.

It would be unwise to allow sole custody over the volatile idea of divine election to zealots of any persuasion—or to jeerers who believe themselves entitled to take sole possession of the human predicament. The historical hour is much too late for anyone to wish chosenness away. The idea is too deeply ingrained in the two nations to be overlooked, patronized, or definitively repealed. Whether or not we believe that the descendants of Abraham were singled out, in perpetuity, by God; whether or not we believe that the United States of America has a distinct mission in history; whether or not we find these to be outlandish, if not offensive, notions—we must grapple with them, for they are, behind our backs, grappling with us.

The
CHOSEN
PEOPLES

1. "A Stiff-Necked People"

ISRAEL, WITH A population smaller than New York City's in a territory the size of New Jersey, has obsessed the world from the moment of its founding in 1948. Indeed, for millennia, the Jewish people have obsessed not only themselves but much of mankind—often enough with suspicion and lethal fury. Why should such a tiny nation command such a vast fascination?

An obvious prologue to an answer is that the book that narrates the Jews' official story also launches the official story of the vastly more popular Abrahamic religions that trace their origins, too, to the ancient patriarch of the Jews. At its core, the immensely influential Hebrew Bible is a story of a people who believe themselves to have been chosen by God—chosen, moreover, to live in a particular land. The notion of being chosen, whether a gift or a burden, is what fashioned them into a people, revived them in exile, demanded interpretation, and repeatedly plunged them into danger seemingly from the beginning of recorded time. It was this extraordinary belief that impelled Abraham to leave his home and trek to a faraway land he had never seen. The same belief united the Israelites as they received the Torah during their flight through the Egyptian desert. The same belief inspired hope for generations of Jews scattered into one exile after another, and promised a meaning for their suffering across thousands of years. The same belief propelled some of them to advocate and organize a return to Zion.

Indeed, the Jewish people are the product of a single, more or less continuous idea, one of the oldest and most enduring in recorded civilization: divine election. But to be chosen by God turned out to be less a solution than a problem—in fact, one problem after another. What exactly did this exalted position *mean*? Nothing simple.

1

At the core of the history of the Jews has been the ongoing conundrum of what to make of their singular calling.

According to the Scripture, the story of Jewish exceptionalism is a story of covenants with God that made them simultaneously a people, a nation, and a religion. From God's first appearances, as recorded in the Bible, through the twists and turns of exile, slavery, kingdom, war, dispersion, persecution, migration, and gathering, Jews struggled mightily to work out just what it meant to have been chosen, what their mission required of them, and, specifically, what connection they were to have with the land that God had promised. Over the ages, many factions of Talmudic scholars, Hasidim, messianists, assimilationists, and reformers propounded their respective answers. What none of them could do was duck the question or the book that engendered it. Eventually, Zionism propounded yet another answer: return to the land.

Zionism was ostensibly a secular movement for the creation of a modern nation in a world of nations, but Zionism, too, planted a foot in what most Jews understood to be a divinely ordained past. To build a Jewish state meant to fashion a contemporary vessel for the spirit that had inhabited its people from their origins. Once the state was established, its messianic ideals could not be suppressed. The fateful occupation of the West Bank and Gaza, beginning with Israel's military triumph in 1967, was rooted in the nation's far older conviction—the defining conviction that the Jews were the people chosen by God—and the zealous emotions that accompanied it. Zionism's inability to shake the messianic ideal became manifest in the hold that the West Bank settlers exercised on the conscience of the whole nation—as well as its prime ally, another, vaster nation possessed of its own messianic past. Israel's will—even eagerness—to collaborate with a messianic idea became dangerously intertwined with a sort of counter-messianic idea: the Muslim world's vivid sense of humiliation, and its fantastical desire to rescue itself by undoing Zionism. The two missions gripped each other in reciprocal antagonism, an apparently endless dance of mutual menace and injury.

The story that the Jews told about themselves engendered the story that much of the non-Jewish world told about them, the story of an idea by turns thrilling, dangerous, exalting, reckless, potent, ennobling, and virulent—the idea of a people's belief in their divine designation. It seems extraordinary, even bizarre, that the dilemmas of a contemporary state should be so deeply rooted in biblical stories of impossible missions. But the idea of a people called by God is extraordinary from the start.

Chosen by God, chosen for the land: the tallest of orders. To fathom the bloodshed, the wars and rumors of war, the supercharged passions, the wounds and the controversies, not least about the Jewish settlements implanted among Palestinian Arabs—to understand the obsessions of insiders and outsiders alike, the deep anxiety, hatred, and ecstasy evoked by Israel—it is with an ancient and astonishing idea that we must begin: that somehow, millennia ago, on the foothills of a mountain in the Sinai desert, the Almighty, sole God of the universe, singled out a small and insignificant people for some special purpose and promised them a land wherein to enact it. So our exploration of what it means to believe you are chosen must begin with the book that led the Jews to believe it—not least, with the complexities of what it says and does not say.

God's Choices

The book begins with a sequence of covenants that God enters into with human beings. The first is with Noah (in Genesis 8), whom God orders to produce progeny, with the promise that "every beast of the earth" shall fear them. God's covenant with Noah, however, is fundamentally different from the ones to follow, for one main reason: it is not exclusive. Rather than singling out Noah and his descendants for prominence in a future divine plan, God stresses instead the universal nature of His promise; the covenant, He says, is "between me and all flesh that is upon the earth."

God has a different idea for Abram, who abides in the Mesopotamian town of Ur. To Abram God reveals Himself no fewer than five times. First, God commands him: "Leave your country, your people and your father's household and go to the land I will show you." He gives no reason why He is speaking to this man in particular. But He promises to make Abram into a "great nation" and bless him. Abram does as he's told, building an altar to God and taking leave of Ur for Canaan. Once in his new homeland, Abram is reassured that the land is his to inherit: "Lift up your eyes from where you are and look north and south, east and west," God tells Abram. "All the land that you see I will give to you and your offspring forever. I will make your offspring like the dust of the earth, so that if anyone could count the dust, then your offspring could be counted. Go, walk through the length and breadth of the land, for I am giving it to you."

The third divine appearance communicates the covenant in a strikingly different way: via dialogue. For the first time, Abram speaks: "O sovereign Lord, what can you give me since I remain childless?" God again promises Abram a multitude of descendants, and demands the sacrifice of a heifer, a goat, a ram, a dove, and a pigeon. Abram obeys, but that night, God speaks to him in a dream and strikes a more somber tone. "Know for certain," he tells Abram, "that your descendants will be strangers in a country not their own, and they will be enslaved and mistreated four hundred years. But I will punish the nation they serve as slaves, and afterward they will come out with great possessions. You, however, will go to your fathers in peace and be buried at a good old age. In the fourth generation your descendants will come back here, for the sin of the Amorites [a Canaanite people] has not yet reached its full measure." For the first time, there is a clear statement that chosenness is comparative. The Jews have been chosen in contrast to the Amorites, who have not been chosen. The Jews' reward is somehow proportionate to the Amorites' sinfulness. God is universal, not local or tribal—He is not only the God of the Hebrews but the God of Gods—yet He plays favorites.

Two crucial themes emerge here for the first time. Chosenness will be paid for with exile and suffering, both of which shall be inflicted on Abram's descendants through no apparent fault of their own. And the chosen Israelites are counterposed to the sinful Amorites. God retains the initiative. He chooses, though for reasons He leaves obscure.

The fourth and fifth statements of God's covenant with Abram are simpler, and they are accompanied by clear calls to action. The fourth time God appears to Abram, He changes the man's name to Abraham and orders circumcision for him and every male in his household. In return, He promises a specific prize: a son to be named Isaac. Abraham at first doubts God's promise, but falls to the ground in prayer and obeys the divine command. The child in question materializes and serves as the locus of Abraham's fifth, and last, encounter with the Lord. After he is found willing to sacrifice the son he so deeply craved, God once again promises to bless Abraham's seed: "I swear by myself, declares the Lord, that because you have done this and have not withheld your son, your only son, I will surely bless you and make your descendants as numerous as the stars in the sky and as the sand on the seashore. Your descendants will take possession of the cities of their enemies, and through your offspring all nations on earth will be blessed, because you have obeyed me."

Herein lies a departure from all former covenants. Whereas in the course of Abraham's first four encounters with God the divine promises are delivered unconditionally, without regard for any action on Abraham's part or, indeed, any reference to his personal merit, this fifth covenant is presented solely as a reward for his willingness to blindly obey the Lord.

The final covenant is delivered through Moses to the entire people of Israel at Mount Sinai, and although tradition upholds it as the most meaningful, it is noteworthy more for what it lacks than for what it offers. Despite the momentous stature of the occasion—after all, this is the moment when God binds Israel to Him for all eternity, a moment so singular that some observant Jews believe that each and every Jewish soul ever destined to take corporeal form was present on the foothills of Sinai—the Bible offers no single passage, no climactic moment, in which we finally learn the full scope of the divine plan. Instead, Moses dawdles, the people sin, the tablets are smashed, and the whole ceremony must be repeated. God tells the Jews that He has set them apart, though he is not clear about what His unique blessing entails. "Although the whole earth is mine," He declares, "you will be for me a kingdom of priests and a holy nation."

What are we to take from these divine revelations?

For one thing, mysteries. Inevitably, the Jews, bound to the never-ending practice of reading, and striving to make sense of, an exceedingly complicated book, will proceed to spend millennia in a wilderness of perplexity and dispute. If the covenants were self-explanatory, centuries of Talmudic argument could have been avoided. But the covenants are neither straightforward nor, for that matter, consistent. Contrast, for example, the first covenant to the others. Addressing Noah, God delivers a set of commandments that partly prefigure those delivered on Mount Sinai. Why the repetition? In the covenant with Noah, God delivers universal laws that concern "all flesh that is upon the earth," yet He nonetheless sees fit later to deliver another set of laws, this time to a specific people. Why, having addressed a set of general guidelines to the entirety of mankind via Noah, does God later feel the need to choose a specific people as the guardians of His morals? Why choose Abraham, a man of no discernible stature, or the Jews, a nation the Lord himself, not too amused, will call a "stiff-necked people"? Why promise a specific land? Why that particular one?

God has His unfathomable ways, of course, so perhaps such questions are meant to be unanswerable—the ultimate mind-bending brainteasers. Perhaps election is to be understood not so much as a divine obligation, or a reward, as a nation-building principle; to wit: God didn't reward the Jews, or charge them, He *made* them. Divine election planted the seed of peoplehood, later sanctified in a text and enshrined in rituals. In other words, perhaps the Jewish people weren't chosen by God because of who they were, or what they came to be, but rather they came to be because they were chosen by God. He made them stiff-necked in part, at least, because He was patient and preferred to craft a work in progress rather than a final achievement.

The trials and torments that escort the Jewish people from the loins of one man, Abraham, to the foothills of Mount Sinai, where they will encounter God and receive His laws, are integral to the story. God could just as easily have flicked his omnipotent fingers and willed himself a perfect people, but that would have been to defy human nature. To be human is to err, to revolt, to doubt. For limited minds to make sense of an idea as vast as chosenness, a learning curve is necessary. It is little wonder, then, that chosenness begins with an ordinary man, permitted to become the father of a nation only once he learns to overcome his ordinary and flawed self.

Unlike Noah, who, we are told, was "perfect in his generations" and "walked with God," we hear little of Abraham before he appears in Genesis as the recipient of a divine command. We can only assume that he must be stunned to hear from a God of whom he seems to have had no forewarning, of whom he (and, it would seem, the rest of his clan) has never heard, who does not provide any reasons for singling him out among all other human beings—and so imperiously at that, commanding him to leave his country, his people, and his father's household for some faraway land he has never seen. If Abraham has any doubt that the true Divinity is speaking to him, Genesis does not record it. He obeys. Abraham in his unreflective obedience opens up, to anyone who reflects, a long, continuing line of perplexity: what to make of the fact that Almighty God selected him; what to do about being both graced and burdened, with deliverance to come, if ever, only at the far end of many ordeals?

So far as Genesis says, Abraham is undistinguished in character, quality, physique, achievement, or any other way from the rest of Noah's descendants. Why, then, was he chosen?

This is not exactly a necessary question. Divine election can simply be accepted at face value. A man who is chosen must be, by definition, worthy of having been chosen. Has not God spoken? End story. Besides, aren't gods always arbitrary? Is not arbitrariness, the transcendental release from the cage of reason, a characteristic of godliness? Why does the God who speaks to Abraham need reasons? But if you are inquisitive—if you go looking for reasons—sooner or later you will be drawn into the search to interpret. Abraham might take it on faith that God must have chosen him for good reason, even though God's reasons are not fathomable to human beings (despite the fact that they were created in God's image and therefore, presumably, with God's deductive powers). He might pull himself together, accept his good fortune, and determine to follow God's directions on the assumption that he would someday understand why he was singled out. Abraham might also wonder why God does not simply deliver the promised results without going to the trouble of speaking at all. Surely the Almighty can bring about whatever earthly events He chooses without having to make promises first. If Genesis means to teach the responsibility of free human action—a reasonable premise—there is no evidence that Abraham himself understands that lesson. Not yet.

Why Abraham?

The authors of the Bible realize that, to this point, the story of Abraham refuses to speak for itself. It continues to baffle. The idea of chosenness is so mysterious as to generate a tradition and a profession—interpretation. God Himself is the first interpreter. Thus, God later declares that He had a purpose for choosing Abraham: "For I know him, that he will command his children and his household after him, and they shall keep the way of the Lord, to do justice and judgment; that the Lord may bring upon Abraham that which he hath spoken of him." That is, God reveals that He chose Abraham *for a specific purpose*—to bring righteousness into the world. But His statement still fails to explain why He chose *Abraham* in the first place. If He chose him to spread righteousness, what (if anything) was uniquely promising about him as a conduit—particularly coming on the heels of the distinguished Noah, the Lord's previous partner in covenant? Or did He choose Abram/Abraham at random, simply to make the point that God was so powerful that anyone would do? But in that case, why reserve the status of chosenness for the descendants of one arbitrarily chosen man? God's choice of Abraham does not offer a knock-down reassurance—certainly nothing reassuring enough to people who might, from time to time, across many generations, wonder whether they had really been specially graced because their ancient ancestor had been called by God for no particular reason. *Explain this!* some of them must have demanded. *Give us reasons that a human being can understand!*

In the eyes of Islam, Abraham's piety was a reason, or *the* reason, for God's choice. Some Jews, too, presumably troubled, would later gravitate toward a similar explanation. Rabbis produced an interpretation, or Midrash, according to which Abram's father, Terah, who sold idols, once went away and left him in charge. When a woman brought flour to Abram, requesting of him that he offer it to the idols, he grabbed a stick and smashed all the idols but one, leaving the stick in the hand of that one. When Terah returned and asked for an explanation, Abram told him that the idols had quarreled over the flour, whereupon the largest idol had destroyed the others. His father thought Abram was mocking him, and turned him over to the king, who threw him into a furnace, from which God delivered him. But the idol story emerged centuries after the compilation of Genesis. We remain without a satisfying answer to the question *Why Abraham?* To anyone who inquires deeply, it is the blunt fact of God's message that stands out. God spoke to Abraham; He had His reasons; it is not for human beings to know them.

To be chosen, in other words, invites incomprehension, skepticism, and obstreperousness. The Almighty has arranged that humanity should be free, not a set of lifeless pawns in the hands of a bored deity. God may be omnipotent, but paradoxically Man has one power over Him: the power to choose not to believe. Obviously we have the making of an uneasy relationship. God appears, speaks, promises, chastises, threatens, punishes, and smites. Humans, for their part, fret, doubt, and scramble for reassurance. Even those who hear God's words and behold His signs tremble with uncertainty and require confirmation.

Consider that during his third encounter with God, Abraham asks, "What can you give me since I remain childless?" Only when God takes him outside and points to the stars is Abraham willing to take it on faith that his descendants will be numberless, although at the moment he remains without a single child. Even then, God will issue His promise again and again. The authors of Genesis—and God Himself, if you believe the story—take Abraham's skepticism seriously. They understand that a man chosen for great things—and great upheavals—will harbor recurring doubts. So, too, Abraham asks for reassurance that he will gain possession of the land—land that God has already promised him twice. Reassurance about the land comes hard: it requires the sacrifice of animals, and even then, God must come to Abraham in a dream, and the promise of land must also be repeated twice more.

If Abraham (still known as Abram) is anxious and skeptical even when God speaks to him—directly and repeatedly—it is all the more likely that when the founding beholder departs the earth, flickers of doubt will spread among his descendants. Humans are insecure. Even Abraham wants concrete results. Evidently God's promises will take some getting used to. Genesis knows this. It also knows that, in the fullness of time, the descendants of Abraham will increasingly question the meaning of these tales. If Abraham had to struggle to interpret the word of God that he heard with his own ears, how much harder will his descendants have to work to make sense of it! The People of the Book will have to become a people who strive to interpret.

Readers of Genesis may have doubted that Abraham understood matters correctly. They might have wondered, for example, about the precise boundaries of the Promised Land, since they are not clearly defined until much later in the biblical narrative. They might well have wondered, also, whether a promise made to an ancestor, generations earlier, remains binding on—and for—his descendants.

Questions of this sort point to the enduring indeterminacy of all religious belief and the deep reason why belief requires some sort of transcendent faith. Only with faith can the Jews claim to know exactly what God had in mind for them: what God said to Abraham, or why Abraham thought that what he heard was in fact the voice of God; how to make sense of God's different formulations; and then, what Abraham's wife Sarah, his sons Ishmael and Isaac, and so on, made of the story. The closer we look, the more faith is required: to know what the story meant to these figures; to know how the generations who wrote down the words of Genesis, or assembled it from fragments, which in turn might have followed from oral traditions lasting centuries, made sense of it—or whether they made sense of it at all, or whether the way they made sense of things was the way we make sense of things. After all, is the Genesis story meant to be a literal account of facts and events, comparable to "My mother is Sarah" or "That rock fell off the cliff" or "This deer is dead"? Does the "said" in "God said" mean the same thing as the "said" in "Abraham said"? Perhaps the scribes simply recorded what they understood as a fable; perhaps they were unsure how to interpret what they wrote down. Perhaps the scribes discarded, or suppressed, reports of those who believed alternative stories or confessed to being willing to live with a certain vagueness. To cope with such questions, faith steps in.

Faith would seem to render questions about the literal truth of the scriptural stories unnecessary, even petty. Faith accepts that the stories are passing strange. In fact, it celebrates strangeness. That the book's revelations surpass understanding must mark them as transcendent. Only barely comprehensible prophesies could be adequate to the immensity of God. Faith makes it unnecessary to ask whether the ancients imagined the Bible as a sort of blur of beliefs, a hodgepodge of hunches, intuitions, just-so stories, and rumors that could

11

never be unraveled into distinct, definitive strands that could be said to be undeniably true. Faith will not be obstructed by observed facts. Perhaps, then, the chosen people are those who embrace faith.

Yet Genesis records that over and over, faith breaks down. In this sense, at various junctures, the chosen people have chosen to resign their commission—chosen not to be chosen. In which cases, faith has proved not to be a reliable answer to the riddle of chosenness. And yet, the riddle is inescapable. Even—or especially—when faith wanes, prophets and others continue to show up to tell the biblical Israelites that they are still bound by their covenant with God. However feeble, however bewildering, however violated, however incapable of inspiring righteousness, the idea of divine election endures. The Jews will take many chances in its name. They will remember that their forebears took risks in its name, and take courage from memory. Even as they dispute its meaning, chosenness is the concept that will bind this people together, even against their own rebellions and transgressions. A powerful idea, to be invoked perennially by its failures!

If it is absurd to think that we, in the twenty-first century, can arrive at definitive answers about why God elected Abraham for extraordinary treatment (even if we grant that the question of why God does anything makes sense), or why Abraham chose to accept God's mission, or indeed what he understood it to be, it is no more possible to establish the manner in which anyone in antiquity understood what they read or heard about Abraham and his encounters with God. The apparently straightforward text is riddled with puzzles. Possibly, though, this is one of the Bible's most compelling features. The openness of the text, its incompleteness and indeterminacy, its susceptibility to questioning and doubt, endow it with an aura of transcendent strangeness, of doors that open only to reveal other doors. Perhaps inexhaustible strangeness is the portal to sacredness. The mystery concentrates attention—again and again the curious reader must search for clarification. With the primal text in crying need of amplification, no wonder the rabbis will find steady employment. No wonder thousands of pages of the Talmud will be overstuffed with rival interpretations—more hints, more guesses, more outlandish mysteries.

So many questions, so few answers. We moderns believe ourselves more comfortable with doubt than our ancestors were—and so we may well be. God, too, may be understood as not only a rulemaker but also a true modern who embraces doubt, welcomes dissent, and expects disobedience. Abraham hesitates, Sarah laughs, the Israelites stray, and still, God is determined not to choose another people. Rather, it is precisely through doubt that his emissaries—ordinary human beings without any inherent distinction—acquire the grandeur required to play their part in the divine plan.

Consider, for example, Abraham's conversation with God concerning the impending destruction of Sodom and Gomorrah. The Lord is about to strike down the sinning cities, but Abraham is moved by mercy to intervene. In one of the most astonishing passages in an astonishing book, Abraham for the first time starts to sound like a man of justice. Now that his destiny for justice has been broached, he resolves to act as if it already applies. He challenges God's absolute authority. He demands of the Almighty, whose writ extends beyond the need for justification, that He justify His decision. "Will you sweep away the righteous with the wicked?" Abraham asks, indignant. "What if there are fifty righteous people in the city?" Abraham implores and insists. He *shames* God. And God concedes: He will spare all of Sodom for fifty righteous men. But Abraham refuses to pocket his victory and go home. Taking heart from his initial success, though confessing his fear that he is pushing God too far, he proceeds to bargain the Lord of the Universe down to forty-five. Again, God concedes. Abraham bids God down to forty, thirty, twenty, and eventually ten, and each time God concedes.

Abraham has now crossed a threshold and entered into what the philosopher Susan Neiman has called "resolute universalism," for "the Abraham who risked God's wrath to argue for the lives of unknown innocents is the kind of man who would face down injustice anywhere." In his willingness to stand up for people who are not his own flesh and blood, righteous ones whom he does not know and of whose existence, in fact, he can only speculate, people who, taken one at a time, mean nothing to him *but for their righteousness*—people who are, in the cynic's terminology of casual dismissal, "abstractions"—he is the model of an Enlightenment hero. He is interceding in the lives of men as God intercedes in the lives of men. He is standing up to God. God has created the threshold by taking Abraham into His confidence, but it is Abraham who has walked in.

It is at this moment that Abraham suggests some of the complexities of having been chosen. He rises above the patriarchal deference that his contemporaries practice. Abraham is far better known, of course, for being willing, later on, to sacrifice his beloved son strictly because God decides to put him to a test. At that justly famous juncture, God's commandment—*Obey!*—becomes sufficient reason for an unspeakable act, and Abraham wordlessly complies. Perhaps he tells himself that because Isaac, whom he loves dearly, would not have been conceived without the intervention of God, God still owns him, in some sense. To use contemporary parlance, God has moved the goalpost, and Abraham does not dispute His right to do so. On this occasion, God does not renew His promise of numbers or land or blessedness before issuing his command, and Abraham refrains from asking for any renewed promise of a quid pro quo. It is only after the ram arrives to substitute for Isaac on the altar that the angel of God speaks up with a repeat promise of divine bounty for Abraham's offspring. Whatever you want to say about Abraham's morals at the time of the Isaac test—Kierkegaard was neither the first nor the last to argue that Abraham's greatness lies in his understanding that religious reason is higher than ethical reason—it is the Sodom and Gomorrah story that places Abraham squarely in the history of justice. By confronting God, Abraham acquires the distinction that might have warranted his divine election.

But note: he does so only retroactively, after he has gotten to know God and after God, more to the point, has gotten to know him. Which leads to another serious question about chosenness. If

Abraham, the founding father, could tolerate the burdens of divine election only after engaging in a prolonged dialogue with the Almighty, how might his descendants, who lack firsthand knowledge of God, react to the notion that they have been singled out by virtue of descent? What is Isaac to make of this story, or Jacob, or the sons and grandsons and great-grandsons of Jacob, or the others in turn? In times of tribulation, how will Abraham's descendants take courage? How will they revive the sheer impact of God's start-up command, the unprecedented enormity of an event they did not witness with their own eyes and ears?

These are not rhetorical questions. From Sinai onward, when God's contract with a handful of chosen men makes way for a contract with the entire nation of Israel, the Jews are afflicted by a conceptual plague. The word of God does not wear well, and the people, accordingly, repeatedly, are flooded with doubt. Two questions gnaw at them: How do they know that they—not only their ancestor Abraham but they themselves—have been chosen? And what follows as a result?

The first question is, in principle, easier to answer: God says so to Moses during the Exodus. The trumpet sounds as God descends in fire at Mount Sinai. Smoke rises. The very ground trembles from the presence of the Lord. And still, as Moses delivers God's commandments, he cautions the Israelites against thinking that God chose them for any good and particular reason. "The Lord," he tells them, "did not set his love upon you, nor choose you, because you were more in number than any people; for you were the fewest of all people." They were few, then, but perhaps they were also righteous? No such luck: "Not for thy righteousness, or for the uprightness of thine heart, dost thou go to possess their land: but for the wickedness of these nations the Lord thy God doth drive them out from before thee . . ." Your virtue, in other words, is that you lack the others' vices. You are only the lesser evil—"stiff-necked," in fact.

How fully the Israelites live up to their reputation! Again and again, their faith crumbles and they transgress. The Jews, who were supposed to have been the deliverance of all mankind, turn out to be fearful and faltering. No matter that God leads them in a pillar of cloud by day and a pillar of fire by night—they grumble, or worse. When God speaks to Moses at Mount Sinai, reinstates the covenant, and for the first time issues specific instructions to tell the descendants of Abraham, Isaac, and Jacob about the splendors He has in mind for them, He says this: "Now, therefore, if ye will obey my voice indeed, and keep my covenant, then ye shall be a peculiar treasure unto me above all people: for all the earth is mine: And ye shall be unto me a kingdom of priests and a holy nation." The Israelites, in unison, shout out their acceptance in no uncertain terms: "All that the Lord hath spoken we will do."

But they will not. They are laughably unreliable. It would seem to be in their nature to be unreliable. Having watched Moses climb the mountain, having seen him there wrapped in a cloud that they have learned to recognize as the very garment of God, they still cannot bring themselves to behave properly. The very presence of God seems not to matter in the slightest. They refuse to be bound by their own pledge.

Is there no end to the iniquity of the chosen? They are always in a hurry to forget. They are fickle and impatient. They are, the Bible says, "corrupt," "utterly corrupt," "warped and crooked," "foolish and unwise," "a perverse generation, children who are unfaithful," "a nation without sense." While Moses is receiving the Lord's commandments, his people are already in the market for new gods. Bluntly rejecting God's explicit instruction, Aaron casts for them a golden idol in the shape of a calf. Whereupon God commands nothing less than total destruction of this stiff-necked people. Moses, like Abraham before him, intercedes, and God relents; in the end, He is satisfied with the slaughter of a mere three thousand—*three thousand*—sinners. As if this is not enough, God proceeds to visit a plague on the survivors. He threatens them and their descendants with earth-devouring fires, pestilence and more plague, slaughter and terror, untold calamities. It would seem that the Jews are forever

16

in arrears. To be chosen, it seems, is not to understand. It is to rebel, transgress, and be punished.

The Torah throughout is a chronicle of miseries and defeats punctuated by miracles and epiphanies of resolution. After Moses dies, God repeats His instructions to Joshua, and again the Israelites pledge obedience: "Whatever you have commanded us we will do, and wherever you send us we will go. Just as we fully obeyed Moses, so we will obey you." Still, the Israelites suffer from paralysis of the will. They refuse to bind themselves. They might almost be defined as the people who forget. Memory is a wasting asset. No matter how many times they swear allegiance to God, no matter how many rituals they perform to keep God close, the Israelites will "prostitute themselves to . . . foreign gods." The covenant would seem to be self-canceling—it foresees its own demise. It is always on the verge of expiring. Payment on the debt is never-ending.

What Was Promised?

What is chosenness good for, then? This inexhaustible question forces itself upon the Jews.

During the circuitous route to the Promised Land, Moses accuses the Israelites: "You rebelled against the command of the Lord your God. You grumbled in your tents and said, 'The Lord hates us; so He brought us out of Egypt to deliver us into the hands of the Amorites to destroy us.'" In other words, you, the chosen people, fear that God does not protect you unconditionally. Chosenness is no comfort. To the contrary: it feels like a sentence. It invites perpetual failure, permanent indebtedness to God, and anxiety in the face of God's wrath. You will never be done trying to satisfy Him. There will be more curses than blessings. No wonder you rebel and are arrogant. You may go so far as to think that the Lord chose you in order to see you destroyed. Better—you might think—not to have been chosen at all.

In his closing testament to the Israelites, Moses cannot even bring himself to declare that the chosen people are a superior people. Or rather, if they are to prove themselves superior, the proof is deferred until an indefinite future. For they, like Abraham, were not stamped with this value from their origin. Even on the verge of the Promised Land, God saddles the Israelites with the knowledge that they did nothing to warrant their special status.

In the course of the Exodus story, then, the mystery of chosenness only deepens. Chosenness, it turns out, is not automatically renewed. As the covenant had to be restated for Abraham and then again for his descendants at Mount Sinai, it has to be renewed yet again for them, and on behalf of all their descendants, by proxy, in a sense, in perpetuity: "Neither with you only do I make this covenant and this oath; But with him that standeth here with us this day before the Lord our God, and also with him that is not here with us this day."

The same logic of intergenerational membership in the covenant informs the Passover Haggadah, the religious text that retells the story of the Exodus. One of its high points is the story of the Four Sons, representing four distinct approaches to the difficult question of how one can know for sure that one has been chosen. Most instructive is the tale of the Wicked Son, who issues this challenge: "What is this service to you?" The text is fierce in response: "He says 'to you,' but not to him! By thus excluding himself from the community, he has denied that which is fundamental. You, therefore, blunt his teeth and say to him: 'It is because of this that the Lord did for me when I left Egypt'; 'for me'—but not for him! If he had been there, he would not have been redeemed!" In other words, the wickedness of the Wicked Son lies in his failure to see that the covenant is actually an eternal recurrence that binds him as surely as it did his forefathers who received the covenant at a specific moment in human history on a specific mountain in the desert. Every Jew, the Haggadah tells us, must consider himself to have been redeemed personally from the house of bondage. Every Jew must see himself as standing at the foot of the mountain, receiving the covenant first-hand. Even if we reject the metaphysical claim of Orthodoxy—that all Jewish souls who would ever inhabit the earth were present at Sinai—the Haggadah affirms that by retelling the story of the Exodus and the covenant each year and passing it along from generation to generation, Jews confront the problem of chosenness in the present tense and are repeatedly given the chance to imagine themselves in their ancestors' place, free to accept or reject the word of God.

The more difficult question is about what chosenness actually entails. Looking back at the Sinai covenant offers little help. God makes a deeply vague promise to the Israelites, telling them they were selected to be a holy nation and a kingdom of priests. He fails to explain why they were chosen, nor does He remind them, at that solemn moment on the mountain, of His long-lasting relationship with their ancestors. He never elaborates on the responsibilities that divine election may carry with it. There is the benefit of the Promised Land, yes, but the Israelites are not to know just when it will be delivered to them or under what conditions. At the pinnacle of their peoplehood, at the peak of their historical national narrative, the Israelites are confronted with vagueness. If the Bible is a creation myth, it is an amorphous, confusing one. The least ambiguous thing to say about it is that God realizes that chosenness cannot come through a onetime command; it must be a back-and-forth, two-sided process permitting dubious humans to take the initiative.

At its core, the Sinai covenant offers two distinct rewards. On the one hand, there will be a Promised Land overflowing with milk and honey. On the other, the Israelites will be a holy nation and a kingdom of priests. According to many Torah scholars, this dichotomy makes perfect sense: to the masses, God offers a material reward, and to the vanguard—Moses and the Levites, the newly arisen voluntary class of holy men—He offers a spiritual bounty. But this interpretation is problematic. A vanguard elevated above the common and uninspired masses, even protecting them from themselves, has a Leninist streak. It seems to oppose the spirit of the divine promise—

that there will be an entire nation of holy men and women, a nation with no need for an elevated vanguard class of priests.

The dichotomy, however, is still instructive. As the political theorist Michael Walzer notes, the phrase "ye shall be unto me a kingdom of priests and a holy nation" provides no geographical reference but rather a temporal one. The verb forms of the promise are conditional or future-minded, suggesting that holiness, derived from obedience to God's laws, remains to be achieved. In Walzer's phrasing, "holiness lies ahead in time as Canaan does in space." The people need both, crave both, and are torn between them.

Chapter 11 of Numbers makes clear the mercurial nature of chosenness. Once again, the Israelites are malcontents, sitting in their tents and complaining about their hardships. God loses His temper and sets fire to the outskirts of the camp. Moses, like Abraham before him, begs the Lord to act mercifully. The fire dies down, but not the Israelites' disgruntlement. Although the Lord has sent them manna from heaven to save them from starvation, they reminisce about Egypt's cornucopia. "If only we had meat to eat!" they cry out. God grows "exceedingly angry." Moses must intervene again. But he, too, is weary. "Why have you brought this trouble on your servant?" he confronts God. "What have I done to displease you that you put the burden of all these people on me? Did I conceive all these people? Did I give them birth? Why do you tell me to carry them in my arms, as a nurse carries an infant, to the land you promised on oath to their forefathers? Where can I get meat for all these people? They keep wailing to me, 'Give us meat to eat!' I cannot carry all these people by myself; the burden is too heavy for me. If this is how you are going to treat me, put me to death right now—if I have found favor in your eyes—and do not let me face my own ruin."

Listening to his servant, God decides a demonstration is in order. He commands Moses to select seventy elders and bring them to the Tent of the Meeting outside the camp, where the tabernacle had been established as the seat of divinity several months earlier. God promises to infuse some of His spirit into the elders, so that Moses will not have to execute the divine will by himself. God promises He will give Israel enough meat for an entire month. But Moses is still exasperated: "Here I am among six hundred thousand men on foot, and you say, 'I will give them meat to eat for a whole month!' Would they have enough if flocks and herds were slaughtered for them? Would they have enough if all the fish in the sea were caught for them?" But God is in no mood to argue, and Moses obeys, collecting the seventy elders in the meeting tent so that the spirit of God may descend on them.

Then something curious happens. Two men in the camp, Eldad and Medad, feel themselves touched by the spirit and begin to prophesy. This is not a matter to be taken lightly. Just a few months earlier, Moses and the Levites had slaughtered thousands of their brethren for disobeying religious commands. Now, with the tabernacle in place and the Levites consecrated as clergy, it would seem that Eldad and Medad are asserting the right to channel God's spirit independently, bypassing the entire theocratic hierarchy, overriding Moses's authority, and violating his system of organized worship. This, at least, is the opinion of Moses's lieutenant and eventual successor, Joshua, who cries out: "Moses, my lord, stop them!" But Moses will not. "I wish that all the Lord's people were prophets and that the Lord would put His Spirit on them," he tells Joshua. To Moses, Eldad and Medad represent a future in which the divine promise will be fulfilled by the whole of Israel, a holy nation moved by God and directly connected to Him.

Throughout the Exodus story, it would seem that Moses, like God, is conflicted about who is chosen and why. When the spies he sends to Canaan come back with unfavorable reports, questioning the value of the Promised Land as a palpable reward with which to entice the people, Moses slaughters anyone who stands in the way of his mission. But he is reluctant to assume control over the nation, and only after much prodding does he agree to set up a system of governance. He looks forward to the day when the people can transcend their pettiness, their stiff-neckedness, their ingratitude, and live up to God's lofty vision; but he also well understands that until that day, they remain flawed people who require constant gratification, constant goading, constant discipline.

Which may be why the encouraging story of Eldad and Medad, two ordinary men who transcend their ordinariness, is followed directly by God's punishing the multitudes who fail to transcend. Angrily, without warning, God begins to rain down quail from the heavens—so many birds that the Bible tells us each man stood covered to his chest in birds. The people are delighted—here at last is meat! Yet as they sit down to eat, with the flesh of the quail stuck between their teeth, the Lord strikes them with a severe plague. The spot where this bit of divine retribution occurs is named Kivrot Ha'ta'avah, the Graves of Craving. The message could not be clearer. Those who pursue spirituality will be forgiven even the most grievous transgressions. The materialists, those who chase after earthly rewards, will be struck down.

And yet, if chosenness is to be an ordeal, the Bible is suggesting that it must be leavened with rewards. Humans being human, they cannot be expected to undergo such an immense undertaking as the Exodus without material compensation. The promise of Canaan's land isn't enough to assure the errant Israelites that their saga will have a happy ending. Indeed, when they reach the Promised Land and vanquish their enemies, they discover that Canaan is nothing like the paradise overflowing with milk and honey that inflamed the imagination of their ancestors in the desert. The spies Moses executed were telling the truth after all. Canaan is just another unremarkable, arid swath of land whose inhabitants do not welcome the insolent nation that claims their home for itself. Quickly the Israelites seek material compensation elsewhere. They retreat further from the Sinai covenant. They refuse the burden of becoming "a holy nation and a kingdom of priests."

Several generations after taking the land, they go to the prophet Samuel and ask for a king "such as all the other nations have." Fearful of the ordeal of chosenness, they seek uniformity. Samuel is heartbroken and seeks comfort with God. The Almighty is displeased, but He understands that the nation is not yet ready to pay the spiritual price of living up to the covenant. He concedes and, in sadness, instructs Samuel to appoint a king to rule over Israel.

Within a few generations, however, the Israelites are once again sinful, coveting, warring, and worshipping false idols. For their sins, they are exiled. They repent, return to the land, build the Second Temple, sin again, and are exiled again. They learn, in Michael Walzer's words, that "the land would never be all that it could be until its new inhabitants were all that they should be." The more deserving Israel is, the more observant of God's laws, the more fully the land will live up to its promise. Conversely, the Israelites may be chosen, but there is no duty-free delivery.

Herein lies the deep power and exquisite beauty of the idea of divine election. It is not a free ticket to glory. It is not an invitation to superiority. Even in its most straightforward practical manifestation—the Promised Land itself—the divine reward is not a magical moment of redemption but a process dependent on the people's ability to live up to their potential. Unlike Christianity, Judaism doesn't require a figure to descend from the heavens and redeem his followers. The Jewish idea of the Messiah is, in fact, quite the opposite. As Walzer writes, God will not "send the messiah until the people are ready to receive him. But when they are ready, it might be said, they won't need a messiah." The emphasis is on human responsibility and obedience to the laws of the Torah. There is no End of Days. Chosenness is a slow and harrowing process of self-discovery and social repair, a process by which God's favorites, chosen to serve as a model of righteousness, slowly learn to resist the temptations of material well-being—fleshpots and Promised Lands alike—and instead embrace the divine laws, which alone are eternal. We are all, then, like Abraham—at first chosen for no apparent reason, and later permitted to prove ourselves worthy.

In this case, the logic of chosenness and the sequence of covenants makes sense if we grant God the right, and time, to change

His mind. After God laid down the foundation of universal morality with Noah, He realized that He needed to set an example—to show the world that a specific people, living in a specific land and adhering to a specific scripture, could survive when mighty empires had not survived; indeed, could thrive despite being few and stiff-necked. For that purpose, He not only elected the Jews but *created* them, planting the seed of peoplehood in the aged and barren Sarah. At Sinai, and in the desert, He let them discover exactly what chosenness meant. The Israelites, alone of all nations, were required to transcend their base instincts and to adhere to a long and restricting list of arbitrary-seeming commandments, in return for which they would be rewarded with nothing terribly measurable or comforting—just the fleeting satisfactions of living piously.

Far from a catbird seat, chosenness was an ordeal, closer to a curse than to a blessing. The Jews were chosen to serve. They were, in a way, designated martyrs. They would be only scantly rewarded for their efforts. But perhaps, if we understand chosenness in this light, its profound merits begin to disclose themselves. Allowing for the fact that they were written millennia ago, the laws that Israel received at Sinai are remarkably progressive. The letter may be arbitrary, impenetrable, but the spirit has a clear agenda. Cruelty is forbidden. Labor must not be too arduous. Business transactions must be fair. Justice must be dispensed meticulously and with care. Six of the Ten Commandments pertain to how human beings should relate to one another. This is a foundation for a decent society. The Supreme Being would seem to believe that the relationship between Himself and His followers depends heavily on how human beings treat one another. If they conduct themselves properly, they can deliver a measure of justice. The choice is theirs.

God's promise is, then, metaphysical. Material rewards are not the point. Power, land, and money come and go. But the rewards of conscientiousness are everlasting. Justice is eternal. Pursue the former, God intimates more than once, and you shall be punished, exiled, hurt, even destroyed. Pursue justice and your life shall be truly rewarding. Fulfill your end of the Sinai covenant, keep the laws—at least in spirit—and you shall discover that the world can become more civil, more pleasant, more perfect. The chosen people have the power to make sure the Promised Land lives up to its billing. If it doesn't, Canaan degenerates into Egypt.

Exile: The People Who Wait

The Israelites learned that lesson acutely in 70 C.E., when, after four years of revolt against the Romans, they surrendered, suffered the destruction of the Second Temple, and succumbed to exile. Unlike the first exile, in Babylonia, this one did not end after five decades. It lasted for centuries. Stripped of sovereignty, dispersed from the Promised Land, the Jewish people were bound to rethink their chosen status. The theological principle that had guided them out of the wilderness and into their ancestral home—and self-governance—had to be reconstructed in order to generate solace and hope for a community of vanquished people in foreign lands.

While they no longer possessed the holy land, the Jews did possess the holy text, or texts—the Torah, the rest of the Hebrew Bible, and the commentaries of the Talmud. From Talmudic times—more than a decade after the exile—three times a day, at the end of each service, they recited the Aleinu prayer, which thanked God for setting them apart, for bestowing upon them the Sabbath and the Torah. The Aleinu prayer insists on chosenness, which it understands not as a gift but as a duty, for which the divine benefactor must be thanked:

> It is our duty to praise the Master of all, to ascribe greatness
> to the Molder of primeval creation, for He has not made us
> like the nations of the lands and has not emplaced us like the
> families of the earth; for He has not assigned our portion like
> theirs nor our lot like all their multitudes.

Under the delicate conditions of exile, a return to the Promised Land was almost unimaginable. Even to broach the possibility too flagrantly would suggest disloyalty and threaten the precarious position of the Jewish minority. Even if a messianic scenario of return and redemption were imaginable, it would be accompanied by a long and terrible period of violence and upheaval. In the words of Gershom Scholem, the great modern expounder of Jewish messianism, it would have a "catastrophic character." But unless the Jews kept alive the hope of returning from exile, how could they remain distinct—distinct but nonthreatening? The answer was, they would make the most of their weakness. While they waited, they would do what they knew how to do best: sustain themselves by living apart, enfolded in the thick web of laws prescribed in the texts. They would regulate their communal life, suppressing the apocalyptic strain in Judaism, muting their messianic hope, and, for the most part, dismissing unruly thoughts that there was anything they could do to bring the Messiah. The mechanics of ritual would take priority over the maelstrom of ingathering and redemption.

Accordingly, the Jews developed a theology that kept them more or less autonomous, even hopeful, yet at minimum risk—an adaptive theology of righteous separatism. Piety would bring the Messiah, and the Messiah would herald a return to the Holy Land, whereupon the destiny of Jewish history would be resumed—but later, much later. Generations of Jews would preserve their spiritual well-being by keeping the ember of nationhood smoldering even while postponing the promise of redemption, reserving it for an indefinite future. However isolated, however persecuted, the Jews could live within Judaism, a prelude of sorts to salvation, assuring them that life in exile was in some way temporary, even if nothing could be done actively to end it. The reward lay not in salvation but in the persistence of a pious people. In the words of the scholars who, between 200 and 600 C.E., compiled the Gemara, a compendium of rabbinical commentaries: "Let him [the Messiah] come, but let me not see him in my lifetime!" The Jews could not reach

Jerusalem, but they could long for it. They would be the people who wait.

Still baffled by their exceptional status, Jewish thinkers found a way to make sense of their condition as an oppressed minority remote from the Holy Land and presumably at risk of losing their chosen status just as arbitrarily as they had been granted it in the first place. To make the most of their delicate position, they tempered their affirmation of chosenness. They revised the Aleinu, for example, omitting a sentence (from Isaiah 45:20) that praised the Lord for setting the Jews apart from the other nations who "carry their wooden images and pray to a God who cannot give success." Without scriptural backing, a rabbinical theory was floated: it was not so much God who chose the Jews as the Jews who chose God. (In her great proto-Zionist novel, *Daniel Deronda,* George Eliot re-created the thought thus: "The sons of Judah have to choose that God may again choose them.") According to this theory, God was rejected by all other nations until He finally found an attentive and devout audience among the Jews. This made divine election more comprehensible to living generations, since it was not the result of an ancient arrangement between God and Abram; rather, each Jew was free to choose in the here and now by following the rituals and being good. This was Maimonides' view in the twelfth century c.e.: "He who sets oneself apart to stand before, to serve, to worship, and to know God . . . is consecrated to the Holy of Holies, and his portion and inheritance shall be in God forever."

Questions remained. What would prevent non-Jews from inheriting their own portion in God? What would befall those descendants of Abraham who chose *not* to set themselves apart, serve, worship and know God? Still, for centuries, choice through piety was the prime way to live out the idea of chosenness. The Jews had not been chosen once and for all; rather, the covenant had to be renewed perennially. Each generation was threatened in Egypt; each had to wander in the wilderness before entering the Promised Land.

The yearning for Zion persisted even when Jews found themselves living through periods of relative tolerance and grace. Consider the so-called Golden Age of Jewish culture in Spain, ranging for about 350 years from 711 C.E. onward. Even though the Spanish Jews were in some ways subordinated to the ruling Muslims, they were also protected. Jewish physicians served in the court of the Muslim caliph; Jewish intellectuals stood out as diplomats, ministers, poets, and philosophers. But even under these largely favorable circumstances the idea of chosenness did not wither away, and when persecution revived, so did yearning for the Promised Land, along with a theory that placed God's choice of the Jews at the center of history. This original choice awaited completion in the literally Promised Land. In this spirit, while living in Spain, the widely read poet-philosopher Yehuda Halevi (c. 1075–1141) lamented: "My heart is in the east, and I am at the edge of the west. . . . It would be easy for me to leave behind all the good things of Spain; it would be glorious to see the dust of the ruined Shrine." The dust of the ruined shrine was chosen dust. The Jews themselves, carriers of divinity, were destined for an early return to Zion. Halevi set sail for Palestine and was presumably still there when he died.

Judaism's messianic impulse, usually obscured by the mainstream rabbinical tradition that urged Jews to make do with traditional rituals, was still irrepressible. In the mid-seventeenth century, it erupted in a mass movement of Middle Eastern and European Jews who lined up behind an erratic, wild-eyed mystic from Smyrna named Sabbatai Zevi, who claimed to be the Messiah, reveled in violating the laws of the Torah, and proposed to restore the kingdom of Israel. Another revolt against the rabbinical status quo was the Hasidic movement of the eighteenth century. For the Hasidim, direct contact with God, more than ritual observance, was the essence of religious life. Yet for all their departure from conventional religious practice, they agreed that the life worth living took place in the present tense, here, on this earth, not later in a faraway land. Rabbi Yisrael Ba'al Shem Tov, their founder, expressed his deep belief in the divine election of the Jews shortly before his death in

1760: "Every Jew is a limb of the [Divine Presence]." According to him and his successors—and in contrast with the Jewish majority—even Jews who were unschooled in the Torah and the intricacies of Jewish law should nevertheless regard themselves as holy. They would return to the Lord in ecstasy on the strength of the ancient covenant with the people as a whole. One day, the Messiah would shepherd the scattered Jews home to the Promised Land, bringing about peace on earth and justice for all. But in the meantime, ghettoized and *shtetlized,* they lived in their own unpromised, compromised world.

Emancipation and Redemption

The Hasidim, for all their radical departures, continued to believe that Jews must be "separated" and "severed . . . from other people." The real rupture in the Jewish theological fabric came with the Jewish Enlightenment (Haskalah) of the late eighteenth century, a movement among European Jews who strived to break out of the ghettos, to take full part in the wider Enlightenment of France, Germany, and Great Britain, to enter on equal terms into the secular world. Many Jews now abandoned their ancestor-bound lives, lives that felt to many of them cloistered, parochial, airless. To those who writhed under the yoke of tradition, who hated—like the closeted Jewish mother of *Daniel Deronda*—"living under the shadow of [their fathers'] strictness," who "wanted to live a large life, with freedom to do what every one else did, and be carried along in a great current," the Enlightenment was radiant with possibilities.

However unevenly realized, the new dispensation threatened what had been the foundation of chosenness for millennia: separateness. Emancipation—which gave Jews a host of rights—was for *me* more than for *us*. By definition, the promise of equal rights and citizenship undermined the separateness of an entire world-unto-itself. The emancipated would trade in their yearnings for a faraway

Israel that, in their eyes, would never amount to more than an un-redeemable past. In the words of one Jewish liberal, the great German-Jewish philosopher Moses Mendelssohn, "The messiah, for whom we prayed these thousands of years, has appeared and our fatherland has been given to us. The messiah is freedom, our fatherland is Germany." To be sure, Jews could practice their faith in the privacy of their own homes, but when they stepped out into the street they would leave faith behind and join their Gentile countrymen. Assimilating Jews, *modern* Jews, contributed willy-nilly to the rapid disintegration of Jewish nationhood itself. With the walls of the ghetto torn down and the Jews living among the goyim, not only did the cohesive communal structure that had contained Jewish life for more than a millennium collapse, but Judaism itself underwent a drastic transformation. Distinct denominations arose, and not just in Europe. In particular, a Reform movement arose within Judaism, finding fertile ground in Germany and in the United States. The 1885 Pittsburgh Conference of the American Reform movement declared: "We consider ourselves no longer a nation, but a religious community, and therefore expect neither a return to Palestine, nor a sacrificial worship under the administration of the sons of Aaron, nor the restoration of any of the laws concerning the Jewish state."

But the new denomination was never free to adapt peacefully. Emancipation was painfully incomplete. Legal rights did not always translate into actual rights. Moreover, in order to accommodate the Gentiles, to appear nonthreatening and, above all, loyal to the state, Judaism had to undergo fundamental transformations. As early as 1783, Moses Mendelssohn wrote that "the hoped-for return to Palestine" was reserved only for synagogue and prayer, and "has no influence on our conduct as citizens." Some Jews experienced such changes as curtailment or a theological warp. When, in 1807, Napoleon summoned the major rabbis of Europe to Paris—part of his mad dream of reviving the Sanhedrin, the supreme religious council of the ancient Jewish nation—Jewish leaders realized full well that Emancipation would come dearly. When the rabbis prostrated themselves before Napoleon, writes the rabbi-historian Arthur Hertz-berg, they were in effect "proclaiming that the civil law of the state, and its military needs, were to override all contrary prescriptions of Jewish religious law and ritual. . . . [T]he Sanhedrin insisted that it was granting away only the political laws of Judaism, 'which were intended to rule the people of Israel in Palestine when it possessed its own kings, priests, and judges,'" and not the religious laws, which were absolute. But even then, the Jews' legal rights were less than equal. Accommodating Paris, Berlin, or Vienna meant abandoning the promise of Jerusalem—but for what?

For a while, Orthodox rabbis such as the German-Jewish Samson Raphael Hirsch struggled to reconcile Judaic tradition with the stric-tures and sensibilities of modernity and nationality. More straight-forward and influential was the solution offered by the Reform movement. If the Reform leaders were to accommodate the Christian majority, the Promised Land could not be allowed to remain even "a pious dream" (Arthur Hertzberg's words), for even the dream might call into question the loyalty of the Jews to their native states. Instead, Reform Judaism preached "the mission of Israel," a belief that the Jews were dispersed among all the nations of the world to guide hu-manity toward biblical ideals of justice and peace, an idea in which Christians, themselves believers in the Old Testament, could share. In theory, Christians would no longer be threatened by Jews who had relinquished any claim to their own nation. Hannah Arendt summed up these theological tremors as follows:

> The Jewish intelligentsia was exposed also to the influences of the Jewish reformers who wanted to change a national re-ligion into a religious denomination. To do so, they had to transform the two basic elements of Jewish piety—the Mes-sianic hope and the faith in Israel's chosenness—and they deleted from Jewish prayer books the visions of an ultimate restoration of Zion, along with the pious anticipation of the day at the end of days when the segregation of Jewish people

from the nations of the earth would come to an end. Without the Messianic hope, the idea of chosenness meant eternal segregation; without faith in chosenness, which charged one specific people with the redemption of the world, Messianic hope evaporated into the dim cloud of general philanthropy and universalism which became so characteristic of specifically Jewish political enthusiasm.

Without chosenness, Zion, or the Messiah, the Jewish people were deprived of the very elements that had made them a people, informed their faith, and bound their community. The French Revolution, wrote David Ben-Gurion in 1961, "gave the Jews the first impetus to emancipation and equality of rights. But this revolution demanded of Jewry the obliteration of its national character. Many Western Jews willingly succumbed, and an assimilationist movement arose which threatened to overwhelm the Jewish people." An "overwhelmed" people were left with the ephemeral goodwill and vacillating spirit of liberalism, which, despite many victories won for Emancipation, began yielding to the vicious vitality of nationalism. Many Jews joined left-wing movements that aspired to achieve universal redemption, as if all of humanity might yet be chosen. But the progress of these movements was halting and reversible.

Meanwhile, European persecution did not disappear. To the contrary: millions in the Diaspora found it reasonable to conclude that persecution was the baseline fate that, despite pauses and deviations, Christian Europe had chosen for a people repeatedly damned for the death of Jesus, the slaughter of innocents, the wealth of some and the backwardness of others, the depredations of capitalism and the surge of radicalism alike. Whatever troubled the sleep of Christians, the Jews were the usual suspects whose destiny was to be rounded up, expelled, insulted, banned from regions, professions, and property-holding, and otherwise discriminated against—as well as, from time to time, murdered en masse. In the late nineteenth and early twentieth centuries, Russian rioters descended on Jewish shtetls to kill thousands, and rape and injure many thousands more, in marauding expeditions for which a distinctive term was devised: *pogroms*. Czarist Russia saw the worst outrages, but the prosecution of France's Captain Alfred Dreyfus and the upsurge of anti-Semitic leaders and parties in, among other countries, Germany, the very center of Emancipation, sent strong signals that the Jews were living on the edge of a volcano. Evidently Enlightenment would not "solve" the "Jewish problem." Even without the benefit of post-Holocaust hindsight, it was scarcely irrational to think that Christian Europe would never be reconciled to the presence of a people whose very existence, at least in their midst, seemed an intolerable offense.

Under these conditions, Zionism erupted from Europe's soil. The spirit that had guided Jewish thought from roughly 200 C.E. until the middle of the nineteenth century was not obliterated by the Enlightenment and the Emancipation, but rather repressed—only to return in the bright and intoxicating form of Zionism, which once again interpreted Judaism in the framework of nationhood, yearning to make whole that which had been torn asunder.

Not that the early Zionists were explicitly religious. Neither Moses Hess's *Rome and Jerusalem: The Last National Question* (1862) nor Theodor Herzl's *The Jewish State* (1896) was interested in chosenness, or even in scriptural reference. Hess and Herzl were exceedingly practical men, more comfortable with Marxism and liberal nationalism than with the Torah or Talmud. (Indeed, Hess was a friend of Karl Marx.) Neither believed that Israel's national revival was required by divine will. For both, the urgent need for Zionism derived from modern anti-Semitism, which they did not see as an ancient and irrational religious hatred, but rather as the product of economic upheavals caused when the Emancipation introduced the Jews to the workforce—in a sort of perverse class struggle. For both men, the Jewish homeland would be more than a refuge for Jews and a site for the revival of Jewish nationhood. It would be an experiment in social justice.

But however secular its arguments, Zionism came with a penumbra of distinctly religious overtones, particularly in the work of two precursor rabbis, the Serbian Judah Alkalai (1798–1878), who is thought to have had a significant impact on Herzl's grandfather, and the Prussian Zvi Hirsch Kalischer (1795–1874). Alkalai, a student of the Kabbalah, or Jewish mysticism, was convinced that the Jews' messianic redemption would begin in the year 1840, and called for the Jews to prepare actively—to pray in behalf of Zion and to tithe themselves to support those Jews who already lived in Jerusalem. Kalischer, mindful of how many eastern European Jews were homeless, and how many in the Promised Land were reduced to begging, campaigned for agricultural training and military security in Palestine. While the two rabbis claimed a theological foundation for the ingathering of the Jews, their approach was evolutionary rather than revolutionary. It was wrong, they claimed, to see the coming of the Messiah as a singular event in which a man would descend from the heavens on a fiery horse-drawn carriage and gather the Jewish nation back to its Promised Land. Instead, they promoted a gradual and practical progression to return Jews to their homeland, an "awakening from below" that would bring about "an awakening from above." In their most famous postulate, teshuva (Hebrew for "repentance") meant shiva (Hebrew for "return," understood as the return to Zion).

Kalisher and Alkalai found supporters mainly among religious Jews, though also among the newly organizing, largely secular proto-Zionists who dubbed them "Harbingers of Zion." But the Orthodox establishment railed against them and their idea. Orthodox rabbis were quick to remind their flocks that according to the Talmud, three prohibitions forbid attempts to return to the Promised Land before the divinely appointed time. First, Jews were prohibited from "ascending the wall," meaning returning to the land in an organized fashion, as a single people. Second, they were forbidden to "hasten the end," namely, to try to bring about the coming of the Messiah. Third, they must not rebel against the nations of the world. It was evident to the Orthodox that the Harbingers of Zion were violating all three injunctions. Writing in 1899, the Lubavitcher rabbi Shalom Dov Baer Schneersohn best crystallized the Orthodox objections to Zionism. "We must not heed them [the Zionists] in their call to achieve redemption on our own," he wrote, "for we are not permitted to hasten the End even by reciting too many prayers, much less so by corporeal stratagems, that is, to set out from exile by force." Kalischer and Alkalai argued in response that while the final act of redemption—the actual coming of the Messiah—was in the hands of God, the necessary preparation was in the hands of the Jews themselves.

Among the eastern European Jews who paid close attention was a Lithuanian rabbinical prodigy named Abraham Isaac Kook. In 1897, just after the first Zionist Congress brought together ardent proponents of the nascent ideology, he wrote a pamphlet on the question of Zionism—still an uncommon topic for most serious Jewish scholars—endowing the new political program of Herzl and his followers with a messianic spark: "Nothing in our faith, either in its larger principles or in its details, negates the idea that we can begin to shake off the dust of exile by our own efforts, through natural, historical processes. . . . We have a sacred duty to try to do so by whatever means are at our disposal."

This essay and its successors propelled the author to the forefront of religious and Zionist thought. Following Kalischer and Alkalai in arguing that (in the historian Aviezer Ravitzky's formulation) "the Messiah is not to be understood as the driving force behind the historical process but as its outcome," Kook interpreted the "Messiah" to mean not a single, miracle-making man but a process in which the sages of Israel would once again be enthroned in Jerusalem, the Sanhedrin would once more have arisen, and the law of the Torah would govern the Jews in the Promised Land. Kook wrote: "Holiness will return to its rightful place in our national Zionist movement for only with it can we gain the source of life. . . . And this will be our way of return which will heal all our ills and will bring near the complete redemption, speedily in our days, Amen."

Within the movement, Kook fought uphill. The cosmopolitan writer Max Nordau, second only to Herzl in the nascent movement and, like him, converted to Zionism in reaction to the Dreyfus affair, declared that "Zionism has nothing to do with theology; and if a desire has been kindled in Jewish hearts to establish a new commonwealth in Zion, it is not the Torah or the Mishnah that inspire them but hard times." Early rabbinic supporters of Zionism took Nordau to be saying, "Zionism has nothing to do with religion," a sentiment that drove many of them away, finally leading Herzl—eager not to alienate religious Jews—to disassociate himself from his zealous deputy, with whom he fully agreed. Kook was still inconsolable, and wrote sharply against the Zionists. As long as the Zionist leaders remain avowed secularists, went one of his typical sermons, and "do not draw near in their deeds to the Torah and the commandments, do not glory in the faith of Israel or relate to the Lord God of Israel, this movement will cause much immorality." Torn between the spiritual and the political, Kook decided to resolve his inner conflicts by moving to Palestine, settling there in 1904.

During his three remaining decades, Abraham Isaac Kook became one of Judaism's most complicated and fascinating figures. He identified Herzl with the Messiah Ben Joseph, a dark figure who, according to Jewish apocalyptic literature, fights the final battles of time to prepare the ground for the End of Days and who precedes Messiah Ben David, the final redeemer who brings peace to earth. To Kook, the early Zionists, no matter how unorthodox their behavior and secular their outlook, nonetheless—objectively—brought forth the *Atchalta De'Geula,* the beginning of redemption. Witnessing the early Zionist immigrants firsthand, he gradually became emboldened, abandoning his earlier belief in the need to draw the Zionists ever closer to traditional religion in favor of a radical new notion: "There are times," he wrote in 1934, just before his death, "when laws of the Torah must be overridden, but there is no one to show the legitimate way, and so the aim is accomplished by a bursting of bounds. . . . When prophesy is blocked, rectification is achieved by a sustained breach, outwardly lamentable but inwardly a source of joy!"

To Kook, this invitation—or, at the very least, permission—to override the divine rules was not as radical as one might think. He firmly believed that Israel was unique among the nations because of its inherently religious quality. Unlike the biblical prophets, convinced that the Lord would abandon His people if the people were to abandon the Lord's commandments, Kook believed that the nation and the Creator were eternally, unconditionally bound. "It is established as a covenant for the Assembly of Israel," he wrote, "that it will never be utterly defiled. The spirit of the Lord and the spirit of Israel are one!" Whereas ultra-Orthodox rabbis disdained Zionism, Kook declared that "the light of holiness dwells also in secular Zionism which is founded upon the love of Israel and of its land."

For Kook believed that the chosen people drew their very life from an eternal, indestructible bond with God. Even when they defiled the Sabbath, ate forbidden foods, and transgressed against most of the Torah's laws, the early Zionists remained holy by virtue of living in and working the Holy Land. There, he wrote, ideas are "influenced by the very air," making even the most profane thoughts of the most fiercely irreligious pioneers somehow sacred and wholly Jewish.

As Kook rose to prominence, other religious figures also struggled to reconcile the ancient messianic yearning with the modern nationalistic movement. Foremost among them was Rabbi Isaac Jacob Reines, the Lithuanian father of the Mizrachi (Religious-Zionist) movement, who argued for severing Zionism from the messianic idea. One of Zionism's first rabbinical recruits, Reines regarded Zionism solely as a practical solution to anti-Semitism. "Anyone who thinks the Zionist idea is somehow associated with future redemption and the coming of the Messiah and who therefore regards it as undermining our holy faith is clearly in error," read a pamphlet he and his followers published in 1900, adding that the Zionists "saw that the only fitting place for our brethren to settle would be in the Holy Land. . . . And if some preachers, while speaking of Zion, also mention redemption and the coming of the Messiah and thus let the abominable thought enter people's minds that this idea encroaches upon the territory of true redemption, only they themselves are to blame, for it is their own wrong opinion they express." In so writing, Reines and his colleagues were echoing Herzl. Zionism, they agreed, was nothing more nor less than a practical doctrine interested primarily in the physical well-being of the Jews.

This notion of a separation of realms—Zionism providing shelter from persecution in this world while not concerning itself with the next—was exceedingly popular at the time, corresponding as it did to the Zionist founding fathers' perception of their movement as a modern, secular entity. But both Herzl and Reines underestimated Zionism's greater depths. The movement flourished, in fact, precisely because it could attract many varied strands of Jews, each seeking to fill it with its own grand, universal meaning: Marxism, socialism, and utopianism for leaders such as Nachman Syrkin, Ber Borochov, A. D. Gordon, and Berl Katznelson; culture for the poet Hiam Bialik and the essayist Echad Ha'am; religion for thinkers such as Samuel Mohilever, Shlomo Pines, Judah Magnes, and, to some extent, Martin Buber; forceful national revivalism for Vladimir Jabotinsky, the founder of Revisionism and a staunch supporter of Jewish self-defense.

But for all Zionism's polyphony, there resounded within it a recurrent, audible hum of messianic yearning personified in Abraham Isaac Kook. Even those Zionist leaders who were careful to excise any trace of religiosity from their writing often revealed a sliver or more of that ancient theological framework that has sustained Jews for millennia: belief in divine election and fervor for redemption. Receiving the Balfour Declaration of 1917, for example—the official letter from the British foreign secretary stating that the British government "view[ed] with favour the establishment in Palestine of a

national home for the Jewish people"—the chemist and avowed sec-
ularist Zionist leader Chaim Weizmann couldn't help but revert to
an old-time religious frame of mind. "When I had the Balfour Declaration in my hand," he later wrote, "I felt as if a sun ray had struck
me; and I thought I heard the steps of the Messiah." Even Herzl
himself, careful to present his own Zionist awakening as a practical response to anti-Semitism, was more than a bit inflamed by the
religious spirit. In the first biography of Herzl—published in 1919,
fifteen years after his death—the author quoted Herzl talking about a
dream he had had as a twelve-year-old boy, a dream, Herzl said, that
sparked his interest in the cause to which he devoted his life: "[The
Messiah] took me in his arms and carried me off on wings of heaven.
On one of the iridescent clouds we met Moses. . . . The Messiah
called out to Moses, 'For this child I have prayed!' To me he said,
'Go and announce to the Jews that I shall soon come and perform
great and wondrous deeds for my people and all mankind!'" And
yet, Herzl told his biographer, he kept the dream to himself "and did
not dare tell anyone." One need not be a Freudian to see in such a
dream, and in Zionism itself, a return of the repressed.

Whatever else it might have been—a rescue operation, a defense,
a nationalist rally—Zionism was surely also a movement to repair a
major fracture in Jewish history by restoring the Jews' vital link to
their origin as a chosen people.

In the second half of the twentieth century, the most influential version of this act of restoration was promoted by Rabbi Zvi Yehuda
Kook (1891–1982), the son of Abraham Isaac Kook and the animat-
ing spirit of the West Bank settler movement. Kook the elder had for-
mulated the unity of the national and the divine; Kook the younger
added a crucial component that for his father had been minor—the
sanctity of the land. Kook the younger believed that Zionism could
not fulfill its true calling until the holy trinity of land, people, and
faith came together with the founding of the Jewish state.

This view he shared, of course, with generations of secular Zionists, for whom the land itself had already become central as they settled in Palestine. Not least among them was the hardheaded David Ben-Gurion, who still waxed poetic in 1944 about the Jewish people's "prophetic hopes," adding:

> What Israel gave the world when it lived in its own land was achieved not by those Jews who served Egypt, Babylon, and Rome, but by those who remained faithful to our own identity. If we are destined to make a contribution once more to the totality of human civilization, that will be done only by those who keep faith with the Jewish revolution and the Jewish spirit. One Degania [a Jewish settlement in Palestine] is worth more than all the "Yevsektzias" [the Jewish wing of the Soviet Communist Party that fiercely opposed Zionism as a bourgeois nationalist movement] and assimilationists in the world.

The undeniable leader of the Jewish community in Palestine was declaring that the Jews—*all* the Jews—must accept the centrality of Israel to Jewish life. He was affirming the younger Rabbi Kook's view that the greatness of the Jews could be realized only if Jews returned to their ancient homeland and rebuilt it. Outside the Promised Land, Ben-Gurion said later, Jews were "a mixed multitude of human dust without a language, without education, without roots, and without any roots in the nation's tradition and vision."

On the ground, the Zionist movement was reinventing itself, laying claim to a reverberation from the divine election. Messianic yearnings had churned under the surface for two millennia, and now Zionism transposed divine election into a sort of nation-building principle, a force to gather the Jews once more in the Promised Land. If the Promised Land had stamped the Jewish people in the first place, it was only fitting that the Jewish people establish (or reestablish) their nationhood there. Settling the land, the Jews would confirm their biblical—that is, divine—origins. In effect: the first time chosen, the second, choosing. Whether the ideological re-unification of people, religion, and land was Zionism's inevitable trajectory is unknowable. What is clear is that, in the wake of the Holocaust and the creation of the Jewish state, a consensus formed in Israel to the effect that the actually existing Israel represented *some* kind of extension, or resumption, or redemption, of chosen nation-hood. Eventually, Israel's Chief Rabbinate would cease recognizing even Orthodox conversions performed in the Diaspora, while a sec-ularist such as the novelist A. B. Yehoshua would maintain that not Judaism but only the state of Israel could ensure the survival of the Jewish people. When the land, the people, and the religion were re-united in Zion, they seized the collective Jewish imagination—even that of most American Jews, who, for all their dissent from Isra-el's theocratic elements, could agree that Israel was the center of the Jewish world and Jewish destiny.

1967: The Hastening of the End?

All the elements for a fusion of people, religion, and land were as-sembled in the Promised Land, but it was only in 1967, with the stunning—some claimed miraculous—victory in the Six-Day War, the reunification of Jerusalem, and the acquisition of some of Juda-ism's holiest places, from Hebron to the Wailing Wall, that another stage of Zionist thought and action became possible.

This development owed more to the younger Kook than to any-one else. Where most of international Jewry saw the Holocaust as a horrific reminder of the need for an independent Jewish state, Kook interpreted it largely as divine punishment for the Diaspora Jews' unfaithfulness to the land of Israel—"a type of heavenly surgery . . . a deep and hidden purification from the impurity of exile." He hard-ened his father's positions, swept away ambiguity, and demanded immediate action. As Aviezer Ravitzky notes: "Among Zvi Yehuda

Kook and his followers the elder Kook's optimistic expectation and messianic faith are turned into absolute certainty about the future. In their view, there can be no going back now that the redemption of the Jewish people has begun to unfold." To them, the unfolding redemption becomes manifest first in the birth of the Jewish state, and then, even more, in the liberation of Judaism's most holy sites. Kook the younger interpreted this moment in history not as the end of the beginning but as the beginning of the end. "We are not hastening the end," he is famous for saying, "but the end is hastening us." Convinced that a redemptive process had begun—a process that would lead to the End of Days—Kook urged his disciples to take action, lest they prove unworthy of their historical moment. In that remarkable sequence characteristic of millenarian movements, certainty about the direction of history sparks not fatalism but action. Eager activists work tirelessly on behalf of their cause and then present the consequences of their actions as further, irrefutable evidence of God's will.

Kook the younger took his father's theology further. "The State of Israel is divine," he proclaimed shortly after the 1967 war. "Not only can/must there be no retreat from [a single] kilometer of the Land of Israel, God forbid, but on the contrary, we shall conquer and liberate more and more. . . . Heaven protect us from weakness and timidity. . . . In our divine, world-encompassing undertaking, there is no room for retreat." In Kook's understanding Judaism (a religion), Israel the state (a political entity), and Israel the land (a geographical entity, however indefinite its boundaries) were interchangeable.

Only a small minority of like-minded fanatics wholly endorsed Kook's fusion. How, then, were the settlers and their allies able to acquire so much leverage in an Israel that was mostly secular? On the surface, this should have been a Herculean task.

In the standard account, the success of the settlers is a story of a brilliant political maneuver by the few combined with the political inertia of the many. A forty-year-and-counting occupation can be explained as the victory of settler verve and tactical genius over secular opportunism and timidity. In this interpretation, Kook's enthusiasts settled the West Bank, camouflaging their constructions as military when they were patently civilian (and therefore explicitly forbidden by international law, as the foreign ministry legal counsel Theodor Meron informed the Israeli government in a September 1967 memorandum). Labor governments thought they would hold on to the Occupied Territories as bargaining chips, eventually to be traded. Through no fault of their own, they lost the initiative. They failed to bring their bargaining to a successful conclusion. Inertia took care of the rest.

This interpretation is not false, but it is inadequate. To grasp the tenacity of the settlers, and the willingness of secular governments to accommodate them even at immense cost to Israel's international position, requires a deeper explanation, one of a different order. There was a momentous convergence. The secularists yielded to the messianists because they sensed, even if they couldn't admit, that the messianists expressed some deep Jewish truth—hidden, essential, eternal. Israel's leaders from 1967 onward, often men and women of Labor who declared their commitment to peace with the Palestinians, not only allowed Kook's disciples and the rest of the settlement movement to flout the law, dictate international policy, and, in the process, jeopardize Israel's security, but did so willingly—out of a peculiar, if elusive, sense of identification.

This odd ideological trajectory can be traced back to Zionism's birth. Side by side with Kook (*père et fils*) and the other believers in Zionism's messianic destiny, many of the movement's founding fathers set themselves up in fierce opposition to the idea of divine election. A people chosen by God, they argued, were a people perpetually at His mercy, never free to make their own way and forge their own fate. They shared the sentiments expressed by Nachman Syrkin, a leader of Socialist Zionism, when he wrote that the Jewish religion was "not a religion but a tragedy"—it bound the Jews to a divine, incomprehensible plan. Eager to assert their independence, many of them drafted essays, manifestos, and poems that celebrated their newfound freedom from the messianic yearnings of millennia. Ber Borochov, for example, a prominent Marxist Zionist and labor leader, appropriated the Passover Haggadah, praising the Wicked Son—the one we are told is punished for distancing himself from the true believers—for rejecting freedom if it came with divine strings attached. The Wicked Son, Borochov wrote, insisted on securing his own freedom himself, and was therefore the true spiritual father of the Zionist pioneers. Likewise, a popular song in the *yishuv,* the pre-state Jewish community in Palestine, put a twist on the traditional story of Hanukkah. In the original story, the Maccabees, Jewish warriors fighting off the Greek occupiers, find a small can of oil that miraculously lasts for eight days. The song, however, presented a far more grim account: "No miracle happened to us," it lamented, "we found no can of oil." The moral was clear—the Zionists were *not* those ancient Jewish heroes whose duty it was to carry out a divine plan. In Palestine, scoffed the Zionist pioneers, there were no miracles, only blood and sweat and soil.

Still, even while rejecting the messianic tradition in the most vehement terms, its detractors nonetheless spoke the language of that tradition fluently. Borochov may have preached a thoroughly secular ideology of liberation, but he did so while remaining firmly in dialogue with the ancient Jewish texts. The authors of the Hanukkah-themed song played on the holiday's lore; they were unable to imagine any other point of departure. Even as these early Zionists marched under the banner of anti-messianism, the dark matter of Jewish history always loomed just above their heads.

The messianic idea's gravitational pull wasn't lost on some of Zionism's more nuanced leaders. After all, Herzl and the movement's other founding fathers were well aware not only of Zionism's force as a practical solution but also of its deep roots in the spiritual traditions and yearnings of the Jews. Zion was to be not only material balm but also a reward for the spirit. The flight from Egypt would be recapitulated. The Promised Land would be not only home but also deliverance. A few generations later, however, with a substantial Jewish community thriving in Palestine, another point of view—call it materialist—became dominant. The land itself was the point: the physical land that embodied the age-old Jewish dream. Not only had the Jews seen the establishment of the first Jewish homeland in Canaan in two millennia—barely half a century after Herzl first began prophesying, and at a time when the ovens of Auschwitz had barely cooled. But then, during the Six-Day War, a small and proactive Jewish army launched a surprise attack and crushed its numerous enemies in less than a week, recapturing the Wailing Wall, Abraham's tomb, and other biblical landmarks. Israelis could hardly be blamed for believing that they were living in miraculous times, that God was palpably on their side, and that He had expressed His gratitude for their efforts with an indisputable gift—the remainder of the Promised Land, indeed the part where Israel's scriptural triumphs had taken place in all their glory. Even those who, following Syrkin and Borochov, abhorred the idea of miracles now felt something like the hand of God.

This messianic zeal was even more pronounced given the particular ideological environment in which it was nursed. After 1948, having achieved its worldly goals with amazing speed, the Zionist movement had to find a way to channel its revolutionary energies into the duller enterprise of running a modern nation-state. Ben-Gurion was pivotal in this transition. As enamored of governing the nation as he had been of driving the world-historical process that brought it to life, he replaced the tentative coalition that had formed the earliest nucleus of the Zionist movement with a single party. He signaled to Jews everywhere that their aspirations and religious sensibilities were marginal to the only important thing in Jewish life: the state of Israel. The state was not an intimation of unrealized spiritual achievement, not an instrument of justice, not a flawed human contrivance required to choose among policies. It was a solution to the problem of Jewish dispersal, a necessary redoubt for the Jews' defense against anti-Semitism. If the Jews failed to defend themselves with a state, they had only themselves to blame. In fact, he wrote in 1944, "The Jewish people erred when it blamed anti-Semitism for all the suffering and hardship it underwent in the *Diaspora*. . . . The cause of our troubles and the anti-Semitism of which we complain results from our peculiar status that does not accord with the established framework of the nations of the world. It is not the result of the wickedness or follies of the Gentiles which we call anti-Semitism."

So the Jewish state rectified the anomaly in which the Jews had been a landless nation adrift. But it was also a miraculous fait accompli, a virtual object of worship in itself. It was as if the spirit of Hegel had returned to proclaim again: "The State is the divine Idea, as it exists on earth."

Divinely ordained victory or historical redemption, or both at once—the themes merged in the triumph of 1967. Both religious and secular Israelis swooned in the aftermath of swift and overwhelming victory. The teachings of the younger Rabbi Kook found ready ears. His yeshiva became a popular and influential seminary, training the best and brightest sons of religious Zionism. "The end" was "hastening" them. Their state was "divine." It required "conquest." There was "no room for retreat." The onrush of the End of Days, the sanctity of the land, the elimination of doubt: these credos of Kook's were alive in the hearts of his followers.

Never mind that they flew in the face of a conception of chosenness as an ongoing, never-ending process driven by the judgment and decency and audacity of humans, not God. They reverted to a more apocalyptic, unreflective notion of chosenness as a linear process that cascades toward a once-and-for-all end. The settlers who were eager to reclaim Hebron or the Nablus-area village of Sebastia as Jewish obscured the historical fact that when these places were Jewish before, it was spiritual—not military—weakness that brought about their downfall. The religious settlers insisted, contrary to Exodus, that the land was inherently great, even sacred.

This was, and remains, at best insufficient. The only thing that

Judaism holds to be truly holy is time. When He creates the world, God sanctifies a day, the Sabbath, a courtesy He never extends to any strip of earth. (How hard would it have been to add an Eleventh Commandment declaring the inherent holiness of the Promised Land?) But for Kook's true believers and their successors and enablers, the material land is an icon of worship: even a golden calf. All-important doubt, the doubt that haunted Abraham and Moses, Sarah and all the heroes among the Israelites, has dissolved. For Kook and his followers, doubt is weakness, obedience virtue, and the arduous passage from one to the other, the passage traversed by Abraham in fear and trembling, is obsolete.

The appeal of this steely resolve goes a long way to explain the uncanny ability of Kook's disciples to shape Israeli politics over the past four decades. Settler certainty outfoxes and outlasts secular uncertainty—a spirit actually closer to the puzzle of chosenness if deeply understood. To these zealots, the settlements look like a historical inevitability, anchored, first of all, in biblical Israel, then resumed in the arc from Herzl to Ben-Gurion, now far along toward the final reawakening of the divine promise—the implantation of the Jewish people everywhere in the Promised Land. By the ordinary logic of events, the West Bank was not a destiny but (in the journalist Gershom Gorenberg's phrase) an "accidental empire." Israel until 1967 made do with the narrative that depicted it as a righteous David besieged by the malicious Goliaths of the Arab world. With its unanticipated victory, Israel basked not only in the proof of its own military might but also in an occupation of land that carried obvious historical and spiritual significance for even the most adamantly secular Israelis. To be confronted with such an immensity was an astonishment that virtually no one was prepared for. As Akiva Eldar, one of Israel's most prominent journalists, and Idith Zertal, one of its leading historians, write in their *Lords of the Land: The War Over Israel's Settlements in the Occupied Territories, 1967–2007,* the newly acquired territories "confronted Israel's political leadership with dilemmas beyond its capacities." Too big and also, perhaps, too fundamental. It is one thing to feel hastened by the end; it is another to rule an occupied territory.

The major conundrum—what to do with the land and its Palestinian residents—was entrusted by the Labor-dominated government of Prime Minister Levi Eshkol to a committee of four respected military intelligence officials. On June 14, 1967, only a few days after the war's end, the committee released a short document detailing its findings. Titled "A Proposal for a Solution to the Palestinian Problem," the paper is striking in its simplicity. It is written in the laconic, bullet-pointed style common to armies everywhere. There is nothing transcendental about it.

"Principles in Approaching the Solution," the paper's main section, enumerates two principles and two alone: "the security of the state of Israel" and "achieving peace." "The ideal solution to achieve both security and peace," it says, "is the establishment of an independent Palestinian state, under the auspices of the Israel Defense Forces, and in agreement with the Palestinian leadership." Under another heading, titled "Borders," the experts advise a withdrawal to the 1949 armistice lines, though with a few minor alterations. In other words, they propose abandoning the lion's share of the newly acquired territories—with the exception of East Jerusalem. In an unlikely departure from the document's dry tone, the authors conclude: "We repeatedly emphasize that if we wish to arrive at a peace agreement, and an agreement that would last for long, we must be generous and daring as we approach the Palestinians. Any other way—even if it leads to achievements in the present—would only sow the seeds of destruction in the future."

At first, Eshkol's cabinet, understandably preoccupied with security questions and at the same time progressive in their social agenda, seemed to adopt the spirit, if not the letter, of the report it had commissioned. Their official statement of June 19, 1967, made it abundantly clear that Israel viewed its newly acquired territories mainly as a bargaining chip in future peace negotiations. While the eastern part of Jerusalem—the Jewish people's holy of holies and the nation's capital—would be annexed to Israel, the rest of the West Bank would remain under military governance "as a transitional phase" until a "long-term constructive solution" emerged. At the same time, the government had a solution in mind—a deal with Jordan's King Hussein entailing the king's patronage of Palestinian self-governance in the West Bank. Even without the sharpness of the military intelligence recommendations, the government still appeared to be headed toward disengagement from both the lands and the people over which it had won sovereignty in battle. It understood that its security and future well-being depended on a quick and peaceful resolution that took into consideration the national aspirations of its neighbors.

Other factions, however, had other designs and took other initiatives. On August 16, with no major decisions yet made about the West Bank, a delegation of religious Zionists arrived at Eshkol's office and pleaded with him to allow Jewish resettlement in Gush Etzion, a group of Jewish villages on the northern part of Mount Hebron, many of whose inhabitants had been massacred by the Arab Legion during Israel's War of Independence in 1948. The prime minister, with his hangdog face and his tendency to see every conceivable side of every argument, muttered a host of indecisive, jumbled apologies. "I haven't yet visited there for certain reasons," he said cryptically. "What's the rush?" "The government is still debating this matter," he added, "and within a short period of time we will reach a decision as for what to do with the territories. There's no point to hold them now and and let go of them later."

The followers of the younger Rabbi Kook couldn't wait. With the help of their Knesset representatives, the members of the National Religious Party, they pressed the prime minister. The mild-mannered Eshkol dressed and sounded like an elderly European clerk, and his political capital was severely depleted. In the weeks leading up to the war, as Egypt's President Gamal Abdel Nasser closed the Straits of Tiran and signaled that war was inevitable, Eshkol had been heavily criticized for lack of resolve. In a radio address a week before the war, the hapless Eshkol had misread his own text and stammered badly as a result. An elderly civilian who had never quite shaken the faint accent of his Russian youth, Eshkol was seen as a relic unfit to command. The Israeli daily *Ha'aretz,* for example, editorialized that "the government in its present composition cannot lead the nation in its time of danger," and called on Eshkol to resign. His larger-than-life predecessor, David Ben-Gurion, technically retired but still very much an active force in Israeli politics, didn't trust him. The next generation of leaders, soldiers such as Moshe Dayan and Yigal Allon, were heroic and accomplished veterans of Israel's armed conflicts. Forced to concede the position of minister of defense to Dayan only days before the war, Eshkol—who, following Ben-Gurion's example, had served as both prime minister and minister of defense—was too weak to deny any request to assert Jewish ownership over the liberated lands. Certitude overcame waffling. The pressure was too much to withstand.

The generation gap in Israeli leadership is not irrelevant to this history. Israel's founding fathers, men such as Ben-Gurion and Eshkol, grew up in eastern Europe, while their successors-in-waiting, men such as Dayan and Allon, were sabras raised in the nascent farming communities of pre-state Palestine. Ben-Gurion and Eshkol were fundamentally pragmatists. Documents show beyond doubt that Ben-Gurion vigorously pursued peace with Israel's Arab neighbors in the 1920s and early 1930s, before he became convinced that war was inevitable. Dayan and Allon, on the other hand, were reared in a society gripped by the need to fashion itself as a community of New Jews and enamored of robust physicality and force.

A popular story about the young Yigal Allon illustrates the new attitude. When Allon turned thirteen in Palestine, he spent the morning of his birthday reading the Torah, as is customary for all Jews who celebrate their Bar Mitzvah. But the religious ceremony wasn't the real rite of passage. As soon as he was done with the Torah, his father, Reuven Paicovitch, called him out to the barn. Writing years later, Allon recalled his father's words verbatim:

By putting on phylacteries [black leather boxes containing parchment inscribed with biblical verses that practicing Orthodox Jews wrap around their arms, hands, and head daily in remembrance of the covenant with God] you still do not satisfy *all* the main commandments; today, you are a man and, from now on, you will have your own weapon.

With this, Paicovitch pulled out a semiautomatic Browning rifle and handed it to his son.

The young Allon was thrilled, but his excitement soon turned to fear. A few hours later, his father summoned him again and told him to take his new firearm and walk to the village's farthest field, where he was to stand guard all night. If any of the neighboring Arabs tried to steal any wheat, Paicovitch told his son, the boy was to aim his rifle and shoot. At nightfall, Allon marched for more than three miles to the faraway spot. Every sound, every crackle, made him jump. He held his weapon tight. Silently, he wished for a quiet night. His wish was not granted. Just after midnight, three Arabs from nearby villages rode their horses into the field, dismounted, and began filling their burlap bags with the harvested wheat. Allon recalled his father's commands: first allow the bandits to begin stealing, then surprise them by shouting out words of warning in Arabic, and only then fire a few shots in the air. He should aim at the bandits only if directly attacked and in mortal danger. "I followed all the instructions," Allon recalled years later. "I got over my fright."

The bandits were unimpressed. Hearing Allon shout and cock his gun, they did the same, shouting back at him and threatening to attack. The young Allon stood paralyzed. Should he run away? Shoot to kill? Shout more? Just then, his father appeared, screaming and shooting like an avenging angel. Terrified, the Arabs mounted their horses and rode away. The young Allon was thrilled. Not only had he passed his test, but his father had witnessed his bravery. He had become a man.

Such rites of passage were common among men of Allon's generation. In the words of the Israeli historian Anita Shapira, Allon's biographer, they perfectly captured the difference between Ben-Gurion's generation and Allon's. Men of Allon's generation, she wrote,

> were raised to believe that one must fight for one's being and for one's honor. This was no abstract principle, like the sort expounded by most men of the Second Aliyah [Ben-Gurion's generation], but something concrete that was immediately translated into physical contact. That was the way of life in the Wild Galilee, where anyone who isn't ready to fight and holds back on beating and getting beat up is doomed.

Ben-Gurion's generation had their great achievement—the State. They had, in a sense, completed Zionism by establishing it in the Promised Land. What could anyone do for an encore?

On September 22, a second group of Gush Etzion advocates came to appeal to Eshkol. These were muscular, assured young men, perfect sabras, native-born Israelis whose mighty hands had evidently reclaimed and rebuilt the Promised Land. The visitors, refugees who had fled Gush Etzion as children in the late 1940s, informed the prime minister of their "strong desire" to resettle there. Eshkol promised his response within a week. Two days later, Eshkol brought the subject up before his cabinet. Dayan and others were thrilled. To the storied general, any opportunity to reclaim territory was welcome. True, Gush Etzion had not been included in Dayan's "Five Fists" plan of 1967, which proposed that Israel seize control of strong points on the mountain ridge running north-south through the West Bank. Still, the one-eyed warrior had no problem adding the territory to his list. For Dayan, every conquest was a good conquest. Most of the other ministers were opposed to rebuilding Gush Etzion, not necessarily for ideological reasons but because they wanted to see a coherent policy before approving piecemeal settlements. The cabinet released a mild resolution noting the prime minister's statement that a vanguard would soon set up in Gush Etzion.

Eshkol was being less than honest. He knew full well that the young men with whom he'd been negotiating were eager to install their "facts on the ground" as soon as possible. Nevertheless, he refrained from telling his ministers that this vanguard was far more than a theoretical possibility—that it was, in fact, already being readied. For their part, the settlers were ready to establish their outpost with Eshkol's consent or without it. One of the leaders who met with him on September 22, a religious former paratrooper (who had helped seize the Temple Mount) and future Knesset member named Hanan Porat, was fond of saying that the new community in Gush Etzion would rise either with the blessing of the government or with the blessing of the Lord.

In those days, Porat would often shut his eyes and mumble, as if in a trance, *"Hineni,"* "Here I am"—exactly what Abraham said to God when God called him to sacrifice his son. Writing years later, Porat expanded on this theme: "Here I am—for the priesthood, for the kingdom, to kill, to be killed. O Lord, here I am . . . this is how I understand the true meaning of the word *pioneer*." In 1967, no disobedience was necessary. Porat and his men were granted a permit. The first settlement was established cavalierly, without serious debate over general settlement policy and its political consequences. Two months later, testifying before the Knesset Foreign Affairs and Defense Committee, the weakened Eshkol betrayed his confused state of mind. "I didn't want to approve their setting up a vanguard, but I didn't want to refuse their request." Pressed on his use of the term "vanguard"—or, in Hebrew, *he 'achzut,* meaning literally "holding on to the ground"— the prime minister smiled wearily and said: "We are talking about a vanguard, but I know that, with time, kids turn into goats."

Promised Land and Conquered Land

Gush Etzion was a precedent for many religious settlements to come, but its story is significant for another reason as well. Already at its founding there erupts the fundamental question of why a co-

alition dominated by a left-of-center Labor Party with strong socialist roots, led by a man who abhorred the idea of settling the West
Bank, prodded by his top military analysts to pursue peace through
the establishment of a Palestinian state, allowed the construction of
a major Jewish settlement that, many times multiplied, would stand
in the way of Israel's chances for peace. This question launches a
second: Why did settlements expand not only under right-wing governments that ardently embraced them but also—if more quietly—
under Labor-dominated governments and their successors that ruled
for ten continuous years after the 1967 war and then, intermittently,
for some eight years thereafter? Did this happen, as a Victorian historian once said of the British Empire, "in a fit of absence of mind"?

Nations are gripped by emotion. Collective postwar euphoria
certainly led most Israelis to ignore long-term implications. For the
Jews to reclaim the ancient biblical lands felt like another transcendental turn, an embrace of the same divine spirit that had made it
possible for Israel to crush a host of Arab armies *in six days*—no more
than God had taken to create the world. But responsibility for the
birth of the settlement movement is more complicated, resting as
it does on two complementary forces. Obviously the first includes
Hanan Porat and his fellow followers of the younger Rabbi Kook.
Porat lifted *"Hineni"* away from Abraham's experience of wrestling
with doubt and converted it into the zealot's unquestioning action.
He confounded the priesthood with the kingdom. He brought to his
willfulness a passion for martyrdom.

But still: Why the continuing support, encouragement, and tolerance for the settlements and their expansion by one Israeli government after another, even governments headed by otherwise
moderate and sensible men? Why did the shrewd tactician Moshe
Dayan assent to the settlement of Gush Etzion even when he had
not included it on his "Five Fists" list of strategically important locations? Why did Yigal Allon, who shortly after the Six-Day War
promoted a peace plan advocating rapprochement with Jordan and
partition of the West Bank, support settlements that would surely

stand in the way of such a plan? Why the *consistency* with which secularists have yielded to religious, millenarian settlers, even, at times, against strong opposition from the left?

The answer must have something to do with the spiritual hold exercised by the settlers. These zealots who longed to work the liberated soil of "Judea and Samaria," as they like to call the West Bank, held an unspoken allure for Labor Zionists who also grew up believing devoutly in mixing their labor with the soil. Was this not the very identity of the State of Israel in the first place—the land of the kibbutz and the moshav, of hard-won irrigation for communities in the desert? Labor Zionism was of the earth—in a way, it was the Middle Eastern version of Jefferson's ideal of a nation forged by and for yeomen. Now Labor's men could feel moved by the spirit of pioneering and self-creation, glorying in a connection with a past that they themselves were reviving. Somehow, in the utopian designs of the religious settlers, the whole Zionist ethos was at stake—or could be made to appear so. This was the unstated logic of the collaboration between religious and labor Zionists.

We have argued that Zionism emerged not only as a protective strategy but as a cure for the ailments of the Enlightenment and Emancipation; that, having severed the time-honored bond, to paraphrase Hannah Arendt once again, between messianic hope and divine election, between the Promised Land and the chosen people, and having replaced ancient theological yearnings with the paltry prize of citizenship, Jews found themselves afflicted by a gaping spiritual void, one that might well be built into secular modernity. Zionism had replaced the complex transcendental desires of old with a clear, obtainable goal, namely, the creation of a Jewish state in Palestine. Once the Jewish state was firmly established in its land, its secular adherents had to adapt. Just as some religious Zionists moved, within a few generations, from timid flirtations with the idea of returning to the Promised Land before the coming of the Messiah to a full-blown belief that the End of Days was approaching, thanks to the faithful, so did most secular Zionists feel the rapture of the land.

They had their own versions of the younger Rabbi Kook, men who preached uncomplicated sermons about the utmost import of land. One such materialist was Yitzhak Tabenkin, a staunch socialist who had been one of the founders of the kibbutz movement as well as a colleague of Ben-Gurion in the founding of Labor. Tabenkin believed that Zionism's primary goal was the expansion of the boundaries of the land of Israel. In 1966, he said that "anywhere war will allow us, we will restore the country's [territorial] unity."

Among the Israeli-born generation who took Tabenkin as their leader was Yigal Allon. Lacking the messianism of Kook's followers, they were nonetheless entranced by Kook's ideas and his unhesitating style. In moments of clarity, these men realized full well that a peace agreement with the Palestinians and the abandonment of the West Bank and Gaza was the only viable long-term solution that could guarantee Israel's well-being and security. But what drove them more than farsighted clarity was the appeal of combat against their enemies. Reasonable calculations were for marginal people, losers, not winners. Dispassionate arguments smacked of the ghetto. Addressing the Knesset early in 1970, Allon expressed this position, albeit clumsily, when he referred to the massacre of Hebron's Jews four decades earlier: "We must never come to terms with the fact that because of a murderous pogrom in 1929 we, out of our free will, will make Hebron clean of Jews."

He was speaking in support of the newly established Jewish settlement in a city "ethnically cleansed" of Jews forty years earlier. Surely Allon, a master tactician, knew that establishing a small Jewish community of uncompromising messianists in the heart of a large and bustling Palestinian city was, to say the least, problematic. Surely it was detrimental to the security of actual Israelis. His own plan for peace and security, the Allon Plan, would actually have ceded Israeli control over the city where Abraham and Sarah were buried. Yet here he was, however haltingly, embracing fanatics who had defied his government to settle in Hebron, apparently to stay.

Men like Allon, Dayan, and, later, Yitzhak Rabin did not share the settlers' messianic zeal. They opposed it. They *said* they opposed it. They said so often. But they dared not try to stop it. They could not offer an ideological counter.

Now, one may call into question the need for a national ideological design. Why should a modern nation-state support a grand vision at all? Who needs a world-historical view? The state busies itself with governing some of the affairs of its citizens—their collective security and, to varying extents, their collective welfare. And yet, even as David Ben-Gurion tried to empty Zionism of its revolutionary energies and dedicate the Israeli enterprise to the mundane affairs of effective administration, he failed to exorcise the ancient messianic hopes. The existence of the Jewish state was not sufficient unto itself. Many of the diverse factions that had joined to launch Zionism imagined not just a Jewish shelter to protect the persecuted but something of a utopian place that, by means of religion or Marxism or *something,* would serve as a beacon of justice in a darkened world. In this sense, the establishment of a Jewish state in the Land of Israel was never the ultimate goal of Zionism. Permeated by the wild energies the Emancipation unleashed when it upset the social and religious structures that had kept Jewish life intact for millennia, Zionism has always been a messianic movement at heart. Even its secular leaders acknowledged, however vaguely, the mission articulated by Isaiah and other prophets: ushering in peace and justice for all. That is why the movement remains so popular with Jews the world over.

Survey Italians today, a century and a half after Garibaldi, and even the republic's staunchest supporters are unlikely to define themselves as followers of Italy's original unification movements. Insofar as they identify themselves with the nation, they know themselves as *Italians.* Israelis, on the other hand, as well as a large swath of Jews globally, identify strongly as Zionists. Considering that Zionism is a late-nineteenth-century movement founded to establish a homeland for the Jews, and considering that that goal was achieved with Israel's Declaration of Independence in 1948, this self-identification may appear strange. Why not simply be *Israelis*? Why not inter the Zionist movement in the history books and turn to the governance of an ordinary state in a world of states?

The answer is obvious. Israel is not, has never been, and can never be an ordinary state. Its existence relies on an otherworldly premise: having been promised by God to His chosen people thousands of years ago. As much as it was a modern nationalist movement, Zionism carried in its heart the longing for a de facto return to this same divine promise—a future commensurate with its past. It was predicated on a quivering hope for a glory not yet delivered. Is it not evident that this promise has not been fulfilled, and that contemporary Israelis have failed to learn the lesson their ancestors learned: that the land was not inherently sacred, that its value rested on the people's commitment to God's commandments, that the land was theirs only so they might strive to become just? Is this not a time to recall that Israel's first two historical sojourns in Zion ended in exile, with the Lord displeased with His people's transgressions, their greed and idolatry?

Contemporary Israelis groan beneath the ancient burden, compelled to make sense of chosenness, queasy about unchecked territorial expansion, bereft of a spiritual understanding, unsure which course to take. As opinion polls show time and again, the settlers' solution—the continuing occupation of the West Bank and the construction of Jewish communities in biblically significant locations—does not appeal to the majority of secular Israelis. But neither does normality: Israelis still overwhelmingly support the Law of Return, which grants immediate citizenship to any Jewish immigrant, and object to any measure designed to make the state less Jewish by nature, such as the revision of the flag, the national anthem, or any of the state's official, and deeply Jewish, symbols. Fearing a militant theocracy on the one hand, most Israelis reject pure Western democracy on the other, fearful that it would usher in the end of the Jewish state.

Baffled, disgruntled, torn between contradictory desires, the nation succumbs to political paralysis. Most of its citizens support peace initiatives. Most of its citizens enthusiastically support every war it wages on its neighbors, no matter how misguided or cruel. Its citizens lose faith in the political system, giving their votes to one whimsical party after another—like the anti-religious Shinui Party in 2003 and the Retired People's Party in 2006—looming up in one election cycle and utterly vanishing by the next. Wisps of smoke from the old dream engulf the culture in a haze of confusion. Writing as early as 1982, Amos Oz, the prominent Israeli novelist, captured this state perfectly: "Perhaps we bit off too much," he wrote. "Perhaps there was, on all sides, a latent messianism. A messiah complex. Perhaps we should have aimed for less. Perhaps there was a wild pretension here, beyond our capabilities—beyond human capabilities. Perhaps we must limit ourselves and forgo the rainbow of messianic dreams. . . ."

But the rainbow still shines bright, illuminating everything from political speeches to popular songs. Israel still displays vestiges of that old Zionist rejection of divine election—each year, a ceremony commemorating the transition from Memorial Day to Independence Day, symbolically scheduled a day apart, features the old song riffing on the Hanukkah story and declaring that no miracle aided the self-sufficient founders of the modern Jewish state—and yet when Israelis speak about their economy, education, and politics, the language of chosenness is their native tongue. Debating how to approach the scores of undocumented foreign workers who flood Israel in search of work, many on both sides evoke the idea of divine election. Those against immigration measures justify themselves by claiming to protect the purity of the chosen people, while those who support more lenient measures insist that a nation entrusted with shining a light on a benighted world is morally obligated to treat the impoverished foreigners with dignity and compassion. At the outset of a June 2009 meeting of the Knesset's committee to investigate the problem of undocumented foreign workers, for example, the committee's chairman, Ya'akov Katz, thanked the nonprofit organizations whose reports the committee was considering that day by saying: "In

Israel, we were always experts at being good. We're very happy that there are Jewish non-profit organizations who work hard at being a light unto the nations." Similarly, speaking in 2009 about the importance of his portfolio, Minister of Education Gideon Sa'ar declared that education secures the future better than any tank or plane, and that the goal of a robust Israeli educational system should be no less than rendering the country "a light unto the nations." Even as they debate policy, secular Israelis cast their eyes heavenward.

Such messianic manifestations permeate popular culture as well. Uzi Hitman, for example, a well-loved singer-songwriter and television entertainer, gained much of his renown in 1979 with the hit "I Was Born for Peace." An instant left-wing anthem, it expressed a strong ecumenical yearning: "I was born for the tunes and the songs of all nations," read the lyrics, "I was born for peace, may it come already." Later on in his career, however, Hitman had another success with "A Light unto the Nations," a catchy tune whose lyrics celebrate not universal culture but the specific glory of Israel. "It's up to you and up to me," goes the song, "may we live to see how the Jewish light shines a light unto the nations." Hitman saw no contradiction between the sentiments expressed in the two songs; in his heart and mind, as in the hearts and minds of most Israelis, the cosmic stirrings of left-wing politics and the particularist tones of Jewish messianism coexist, however uncomfortably.

This confusion has been well described by David Grossman, one of Israel's leading novelists. Speaking at a massive 2006 rally in Tel Aviv marking the eleventh anniversary of Prime Minister Yitzhak Rabin's assassination, Grossman, who had recently lost his soldier son in Israel's invasion of Lebanon, said that the crisis Israel was facing was larger than the sum of its parts. "The death of young people is a horrible, ghastly waste," he said. "But no less dreadful is the sense that for many years, the State of Israel has been squandering, not only the lives of its sons, but also its miracle; that grand and rare opportunity that history bestowed upon it, the opportunity to establish here a state that is efficient, democratic, which abides by

Jewish and universal values; a state that would be a national home and haven, but not only a haven, also a place that would offer a new meaning to Jewish existence; a state that holds as an integral and essential part of its Jewish identity and its Jewish ethos, the observance of full equality and respect for its non-Jewish citizens." Grossman's speech became an instant media sensation. The consensus was that the writer had eloquently pinpointed the sense of purposelessness that drives most Israelis to question the future of their national enterprise.

Grossman's speech, however, illuminated not only the problem but also its possible solution. In a manner uncommon in Israeli public discourse—usually dominated by clipped sentences about concrete details—Grossman intimated that a resolution might have little to do with the specifics of security and everything to do with the stirrings of the soul. The path out of the quagmire, he suggested, involved looking not so much to Israel's hazy future as to its glorious past, and seeking there the religious and spiritual and ideological inspiration that could once again reintroduce Israel to its historical trajectory.

What this trajectory might be, Grossman didn't say. He spoke of Jewish existence, Jewish identity, and Jewish ethos, but refrained from using the word without which these three concepts can barely be understood: *chosen.* Jewish existence owes everything to the unfathomable and in so many ways implausible belief that the Jews became a people because God made a covenant with Abraham. Like it or not, Jewish identity rests on the premise of having been singled out and entrusted with alleviating the world's sorrows, whereupon an ordeal ensued, with the Jews again and again falling short and the enemies of the Jews again and again refusing to accept their right to be who they are. The prayers, the theology, the philosophy, the culture of the Jews, their history from the Exodus to the Holocaust and beyond, are the record of an ordeal that began with chosenness. Wherever you look in Jewish history, chosenness is there.

Still, as formative as the idea has been, most Israelis and secular

Jews dismiss it as irrelevant to their future—even an embarrassment. Chosenness would seem to be the exclusive domain of the bearded maniacs who shoot up mosques and set up bristling outposts on barren, windswept hills in the West Bank, assassins who believe in the literal truth of the Bible's archaic narratives. In Tel Aviv, Haifa, and Be'er Sheva, in universities and high-tech firms and sidewalk cafés, the Bible is not an acceptable blueprint.

For the biblical literalists, and the secular Jews who accommodated Kook's wild simplemindedness, chosenness brings concrete rewards. Kook revered the land because he thought it sanctioned by God, Tabenkin because he thought it sacred by virtue of having been a national Jewish homeland for millennia on end. But both religious and secular Zionists adhere to a narrow, materialistic interpretation of chosenness. They reject the ordeal of working toward a more just society in favor of facile striving for territory. Kook and his disciples negated the centuries-long Jewish tradition that warned against such idolatry, discarding the Talmudic warning that the Promised Land can be delivered only by the Messiah, and the Messiah comes only when all Jews, through their good deeds and upholding of the Torah's values, are found worthy. Thus, too, post-state Zionists, Israel's Joshua Generation, have negated the decades-long Zionist commitment to temper sheer land-love with social justice, whether via Marx or Maimonides. Prime Minister Benjamin Netanyahu neatly embraced both Kook's religiosity and Tabenkin's historicity when, during the winter of 2010, he added the Cave of the Patriarchs in Hebron and Rachel's Tomb in Bethlehem to an official list of national heritage sites—never mind that they lie on the occupied West Bank, outside Israel's internationally recognized borders. For Netanyahu and his allies on the Israeli right, the value of heritage is to be itemized on a register of the hilltops, valleys, and ruins of a long-bygone biblical nation.

This territorial mania vies with a wiser, more generous Israeli impulse. Most of the time, most Israelis understand that to climb out of collective confusion, to resurrect an alternative to both the murderous zealotry of Baruch Goldstein—the crazed Jewish settler who opened fire in Hebron's Cave of the Patriarchs in 1994, murdering twenty-nine Muslim worshippers—and the universalist vagueness of Western democracies, Israelis need to resurrect a repressed side of their own past.

The missing alternative is to embrace the idea of chosenness in a different key: to understand it not as a mandate but as a burden to be gladly shouldered—a divine commandment to build a society that treats its sons, daughters, neighbors, and strangers with compassion and grace and at the same time renounces any claim of superiority. This is the idea that God instilled in Moses, in Samuel, and in the later prophets: the notion that the Promised Land cannot thrive without justice; the commands "there shall be one law for the citizen and for the stranger who dwells among you" (Exodus 12:49) and "when an alien lives with you in your land, do not mistreat him" (Leviticus 19:33); the idea that the Messiah will not come until the chosen people mend their ways.

This is, of course, a far more sober vision than the titillating one put forth by Kook's followers. It offers no spiritual surges, no final epiphanies, no heavenly rewards, only the modest satisfaction that comes with slow and steady improvement of entirely earthly affairs. This vision is compatible with the modern needs of a nation-state. It does not presume to guess at the bold strokes of the divine plan. It does not harbor in its heart the fatalistic fear (and pride) that what it was chosen for was embattlement, a state of siege, and endless war. It concerns itself instead with the spirit of earthly life as it breathes through the particulars of social, economic, and foreign policy.

But wouldn't sheer normality be the wiser objective? Is it not time for the Jewish state to lay down the burden of chosenness and take up its legitimate place among ordinary nations, entitled to live and let live, to settle into a comfortable middle age, to be—and to be *permitted* to be—the state of the Jews, just as Denmark is the state of the Danes and South Africa (finally!) the state of the South Africans? Such an ambition would deserve nothing but sympathy. The desire of citizens to live placid lives—not to fear exploding buses or missiles—is surely no more in need of justification than the desire of Palestinians, or anyone else, to lead their own normal existence. Surely the Jews are no more worthy or entitled than the Danes or the South Africans—but no less so either.

If the large majority of Israelis who are Jews identify with their history as seriously as they claim to, they cannot simply shrug off the burden that brought them into being in the first place and sustained them for hundreds of generations of servitude, exile, and persecution—but also into astounding realms of human achievement, not least the plain glories of endurance. Even if it were possible for the Jews of Israel to accept the modest project of living normally, it is hard to see how they can reconcile themselves to the belief that their new mission consists of getting by. Logically possible it might be, but psychologically? Not very likely.

Are we proposing, then, a fantastical metamorphosis of the messianic dream? That would seem not only presumptuous but futile. Inklings of any such visions in Israeli life have been crowded out by the trivia and tumult that preoccupy Israel's exhausted political class. The religious dimension of the Jewish state is largely confined to rituals. But without a sizable leap of imagination, Israelis may be doomed to relive the tragedy Hannah Arendt prophesied: once the idea of the Promised Land is severed from the messianic desire to earn the reward with just deeds, the Jewish people, secular and religious alike, are left with the forceful pursuit of territory.

When the State of Israel gained the West Bank in 1967, blind fanaticism took hold along with relief and ecstasy. There were those, of course, who spoke out against the mindless conquests and the cruelty of imposing martial law on the Palestinians. There were those who opposed the settlements and demanded they be dismantled. But the settlements prevailed, delusory shortcuts to a palpable proof that the Jewish people were truly blessed by God.

These are the afflictions of chosenness; we bear them still.

2. "His Almost Chosen People"

AMERICA IS NOT just "a nation with the soul of a church," as G. K. Chesterton wrote in 1922: it is a nation with the mind of a crusade. Through centuries of change, through huge religious, cultural, social, economic, and political shifts down to the present day, America's leaders and much of the populace have regarded the country as chosen for glory. "Like Israel of old," wrote America's foremost theologian, Reinhold Niebuhr, in 1963, "we were a messianic nation from our birth."

In fact, this understated the case. Messianic ideals long preceded the birth of the American nation; they were present at the nation's conception and long gestation. Christopher Columbus wrote to the Spanish court in 1500: "God made me the messenger of the new heaven and the new earth of which he spoke in the Apocalypse of St. John . . . and he showed me the spot where to find it." Independently, many Puritans took up and applied the older idea that *England* enjoyed a covenant with God—a "covenant of grace," they called it—even if they hesitated at first about whether the Promised Land was to be found in the new England or the old. Even in vastly more commercial and secular Virginia, the English settlers had scarcely arrived before they proclaimed the new land sanctified. "God hath opened the door of Virginia . . . God hath opened this passage unto us, and led us by the hand unto this work," preached the new Virginian Alexander Whitaker in 1613, around the time he converted and baptized Pocahontas. Even colonists who denied that New England corresponded to Canaan defended their territorial claims with reference to Genesis 1:28—"replenish the earth and subdue it." Sometimes the biblical vision was even announced sight unseen, as, for example, when John Cotton preached of the "land of promise" to

John Winthrop's Puritan voyagers aboard the *Arbella* as they were about to set sail from Southampton in 1630, drawing his text from II Samuel 7:10: "Moreover I will appoint a place for my people Israel, and will plant them, that they may dwell in a place of their own, and move no more; neither shall the children of wickedness afflict them any more."

Another sermon preached to the passengers of the *Arbella* on their way to New England is better known: John Winthrop's declaration that "we shall be as a city upon a hill." These words have become more famous still in the version preferred by Ronald Reagan, who gilded Winthrop to say that the "city upon a hill" was "shining." Winthrop, though not Reagan, added immediately: "The eyes of all people are upon us." Winthrop meant that the Puritans stood before the world in full scrutiny. He spoke of both "the duty of love" and the awful price that "the God of Israel" would exact for transgressions. "We are entered into Covenant with [God] for this work," he said, but the covenant was distinctly conditional. For if we can learn to "delight in each other, make others' Conditions our own, rejoice together, mourn together, labor and suffer together, always having before our eyes our Commission," Winthrop said, then "the Lord will be our God and delight to dwell among us, as his own people and will command a blessing upon us." But in the spirit of Old Testament prophecy, Winthrop warned the settlers of what would befall them if they yielded to selfishness, carnality, and hubris and were "seduced" to "worship and serve other Gods, our pleasures and profits": "[I]f we shall deal falsely with our God in this work . . . we shall be made a story and a by-word through the world, we shall open the mouths of enemies to speak evil of the ways of God. . . . We shall shame the faces of many of God's worthy servants and cause their prayers to be turned into curses upon us. . . . We shall surely perish out of the good land."

Like Abraham, Winthrop believed that God had promised a chosen people a land yet unseen. Cotton Mather later likened Winthrop, who "carr[ied] a colony of chosen people into an American wilderness," to Moses—as well as to Nehemiah, who led the Israelites out of their Babylonian exile back to the Promised Land. Salem was named for Jerusalem.

Proclamations such as Cotton's and Winthrop's were not the tossed-off stuff of casual Sunday sermons. They bubbled up from a red-hot cauldron of urgency, hope, and terror. England's Puritans believed, and declared, that the prevailing corruption and signs of Satanic adversity were proofs that divinity was at work; that the Apocalypse was nigh and time was short to found the kingdom of God; that God's covenant with the new Israel was the successor to his covenant with the old Israel.

Decade after decade, all the way to the years of the Revolution, leaders of varying dispositions, ministers and revolutionaries, Congregationalists and Deists, up to and including the Founding Fathers, sought shelter in the idea that the new American population, understood at first as part of England and later as a distinct nation, was destined to continue the work of ancient Israel—specifically, that America was repeating the Exodus and the deliverance unto Canaan. However heterodox their own ideas at times, they lived in a fervently religious country that dreamed world-saving dreams. Consider that on July 4, 1776, the very day that the Continental Congress adopted the Declaration of Independence, Congress was sufficiently mindful of symbolism to instruct Benjamin Franklin, Thomas Jefferson, and John Adams to design a seal for the United States. Even the Deist Franklin harked straight back to Exodus. A few weeks later, Franklin proposed this image (in his own words): "Moses standing on the Shore, and extending his Hand over the Sea, thereby causing the same to overwhelm Pharaoh who is sitting in an open Chariot, a Crown on his Head and a Sword in his Hand. Rays from a Pillar of Fire in the Clouds reaching to Moses, to express that he acts by Command of the Deity. Motto, Rebellion to Tyrants is Obedience to God." Jefferson split the symbolic difference (and foreshadowed subsequent disagreements about who, exactly, was chosen) by suggesting, for the front of the seal, "a representation of the children of Israel in the wilderness, led by a cloud by day and a pillar of fire by night," and for the reverse, depictions of two legendary brothers credited with leading the first Anglo-Saxon settlers in Britain. Curiously, for reasons left unrecorded, Adams, actually the most Christian of the three, selected a pagan image to signal civic republicanism: an allegorical painting of the young Hercules choosing between the flowery path of self-indulgence and the arduous trail of duty and honor. Congress promptly exhibited its own independence by rejecting all three designs.

The nation had been chosen to redeem mankind, but the question of who constituted that nation exactly, and what ought to be done to, or with, those unlucky enough not to belong to it, would roil the country for centuries. Divine election; millenarian hopes snatched from the storms of tribulation; trust that the colonists had a providential destiny; a belief that the rest of the world ought to be grateful: this ideological compound continues down throughout American history, tying together people of many different persuasions. In 1850, Herman Melville wrote that "with ourselves, almost for the first time in the history of earth, national selfishness is unbounded philanthropy; for we cannot do a good to America but we give alms to the world." In 1878, the elderly Emerson declared that "this country, the last found, is the great charity of God to the human race." Accepting the Progressive Party nomination in 1912—the theme song was "Onward, Christian Soldiers"—Theodore Roosevelt closed his speech with the words "We stand at Armageddon and we battle for the Lord." There is surely a straight line connecting TR (as well as his victorious rival that year, the still more fervent Christian Woodrow Wilson) with the George W. Bush who declared in his First Inaugural that God's "purpose is achieved in our duty" and that "an angel still rides in the whirlwind and directs this storm."

Other claimants to world-historical leadership have invoked one or another sort of divine or otherwise transcendent supervision at times—imperial Rome, Napoleon's France, Victoria's Britain, Wilhelm's Germany. But the others had to abandon their hopes as their nations suffered defeat and decay, whereupon a certain modesty became mandatory. By contrast, America's history has never worked out so unpleasantly as to dash our millennial dreams altogether. Not that the coloration of the American spirit is fixed for all time. Two original biblical themes—Americans' identification with the ancient Israelites, and the belief that they have a leading role to play in preparing the kingdom of God—were sometimes mixed together with the idea of Anglo-Saxon racial superiority; sometimes with a defense of democracy on biblical grounds; generally with the idea of America's mission to spread democracy and freedom. In the course of the past century, suffering has receded as a sign of America's exceptional designation, replaced by good cheer. But even as the pain of tribulation is no longer required as proof of our destiny, dreams of a redemption to come remain the shank of an unending saga in the American imagination.

They also remain the butt of ongoing skepticism and downright opposition, as expressed, for example, in 1898, a year of millennial extravagance, when the best-selling satirist Finley Peter Dunne had one of his characters mouth Rooseveltian bombast with the words, "We're a gr-reat people," to which Dunne's mouthpiece Mr. Dooley replied: "We ar-re that. An' th' best iv it is, we know we ar-re."

A Wilderness of Anxiety

The Israelites always believed that God had chosen them *as a whole people.* When they doubted God, which they frequently did, they turned to the rituals of Moses, who, they thought, had direct contact with Him. The new Americans found matters more complicated. The Puritan leader Peter Bulkeley claimed the Israelite heritage for his people when he declared in 1646 that the colonists were "the children of Abraham, and he is our father, because we are of the same faith with Abraham, and under the same covenant." Yet even so, the Puritans thought that it was each individual's chore to work his own arduous way into salvation. The marrow of the Puritans' exceptionalism was a strenuous individualism. Bulkeley wrote: "God conveys his blessings only by covenant, and this covenant must every soul enter into, every particular soul must enter into a particular covenant with God; out of this way there is no life." The Puritans, good Calvinists, felt called, chosen, to bear up *as individuals* under the weight of election. No Puritan could ever be certain of personal salvation. The pressure to prove oneself would weigh on everyone, one soul at a time. The collectivity of the pure would come to the aid of the weak-willed. Confronting insufficiently pure others, the new Israelites would lash them as well.

In the words of the literary historian Perry Miller, the Puritans believed that God was "hidden, unknowable, unpredictable." But under difficult circumstances, such thoughts could not fully assuage their bouts of disbelief. If the will of God could not be divined, then the Puritans needed to focus their energy on the City of Man, which was the work of a church or a godly people. Their credo was millennial hope, but their experience, especially in the first generation, was anxiety. For what were they chosen? What discipline was required for survival? The New World was not so hospitable. Roaming from provisional settlement to provisional settlement, hunting for the most auspicious places to plant roots, suffering from what Anne Hutchinson would call "the meanness of the place," beleaguered by natives and unsure whether to face them as missionaries, conquerors, neighbors, or admirers, many wondered whether they truly belonged in New England or back in the Old, thinking that salvation might break out there after all.

The hope of redemption in the mother country held an understandable appeal. With the persecution of Europe's Protestants still fresh in the colonists' minds, the feeling of chosenness was a sort of compensation. *Foxe's Book of Martyrs,* a huge compendium of persecution stories first published in London in 1563, remained a best-seller for centuries. And it was not only English Puritans who had been scarred by Catholic oppression. The memory of the St. Bartholomew Day's Massacre of 1572, when thousands of Huguenots were slaughtered in France, was deeply engraved; German immigrants were reeling from the slaughter of the Thirty Years' War. Though refugees from France and Germany to the New World were few in number, they tugged at the conscience of other Protestants. The Quaker leader William Penn intended Pennsylvania—"the seed of a nation"—to be a refuge for persecuted Christians from all over the world. To be chosen, in other words, was associated with victimhood, and not only in New England.

But New England's Puritan clergy in particular clutched at the conviction that they were retracing the wilderness ordeal of the Israelites fleeing Egypt, as well as the devil's tempting of Jesus. Their troubles were, after all, evidence that they had been chosen for great things. If life got too comfortable, these could not really be the End Times. But the settlers remained uncalmed by the lineage they claimed. As they prospered, they worried whether they were being drawn back toward the dog-eat-dog mentality they had fled. "After twenty years of being American," writes the literary historian Andrew Delbanco, "the first-generation [Puritan] leadership . . . were, like many immigrants after them, more bewildered than revived." In the early generations, many migrated back to England—all told, about half of New England's educated males between 1620 and 1660.

As long as the Puritans believed themselves living in the End Times, on the brink of apocalypse, ministers were powerfully motivated to scourge their flocks to purify themselves of sin and fortify themselves against Satan and auxiliary devils. They topped off their chronicles of tribulation with invocations of the redemption to follow, leavening dread with what would become the most American of redemptive styles: optimism. They thundered about the prospect of divine retribution but found something to celebrate. They came to believe that God's punishments would correct them, not destroy them. In the popular form of state-of-the-covenant address that the literary historian Sacvan Bercovitch has called "the American Jeremiad," they sermonized that "His vengeance was a sign of love, a father's rod used to improve the errant child."

The Puritans' millenarian impulse flourished, even as, by the 1630s, schismatic Protestants were gravitating to divergent views of who would be saved during the End Times. Anne Hutchinson's breakaway rebels upgraded women, downgraded the clergy, and thought they could identify the elect; Roger Williams's Baptists proposed a "wall of separation" between church and state; the Quakers strived to see something of "God in everyone." As hopes for a millennial upheaval in England waned, the providential spirit shifted westward with invocations of an exceptional American destiny. In 1653, Edward Johnson of Massachusetts published *Wonder-Working Providence of Sions Saviour in New England,* arguing that the saints had to emigrate to the New World when England, infested with "Popery," "began to decline in religion." Johnson, typical of Puritan historians, drew parallels between biblical days and the Puritans' own redemptive age. The colonists, he wrote, "forerunners of Christ's army," had already become, in some sense, a divinely favored Nation unto themselves. In 1676, the prominent minister Increase Mather, also of Massachusetts, called for the compiling of a "record of the providential Dispensations of God" in the form of a history of New England that would match the Bible's providential histories of Israel. In 1702, his son Cotton would comply, publishing *Magnalia Christi Americana,* a treatise describing "the *wonders of the CHRISTIAN RELIGION, flying from the Depravations of* Europe, to the *American Strand,*" where "His Divine Providence hath *irradiated* an *Indian wilderness,*" and God's actions "exceeded all that has been hitherto done for any other Nation."

The Christian-Republican Marriage

Colonial ministers reached deep into the well of apocalyptic imagination to summon the vast, emotional religious revival movement of the 1730s and 1740s, known as the Great Awakening. The same Jonathan Edwards who terrified slackers and backsliders in his famous, ferocious sermon of 1741, "Sinners in the Hands of an Angry God," declared in 1742 that "the beginning of this great work of God [the millennium] must be near. . . . [M]any things . . . make it probable that this work will begin in America." To "balance . . . the old continent," which was the source of mankind, "the most glorious renovation of the world shall originate from the new continent"—originate but not end there, for as Edwards had written, when the millennium came, "the absolute and despotic power of the kings of the earth shall be taken away, and liberty shall reign throughout the earth."

In such phrases, what historians have come to call "the Christian-republican synthesis" already sounded. Evidently Edwards felt no contradiction between his antimonarchic passion and his millennial passion. Rekindling the Puritan flame, Edwards not only prophesied the downfall of the Antichrist but resorted to biblical imagery, citing Exodus and Isaiah:

> When God is about to turn the earth into a paradise, he does not begin his work where there is some good growth already, but in the wilderness, where nothing grows, and nothing is to be seen but dry sand and barren rocks; that the light may shine out of darkness, the world be replenished from emptiness, and the earth watered by springs from a droughty desert.

Reviving the Puritans' impassioned, apocalyptic visions as tensions grew between the colonists and the mother country, the spokesmen for the Great Awakening also fed republican fires. Lonely, sin-ridden souls were invigorated when the colonies resounded with the Bible's visionary prophecies. More Christian than Jewish in inspiration, the Awakening's revival meetings offered salvation to the riffraff, to souls who thrilled to feel communion with others. By inviting the personal embrace of Christ, the Awakening movement disrupted the authority of the traditional churches. When the inspirational evangelist George Whitefield preached to thousands of worshippers in the open air, in galloping, repetitive cadences, "Come poor, lost, undone sinner, come just as you are to Christ," he was invoking the need for a sacred community that would spill over the boundaries of any particular church. Elites of the traditional churches quavered.

What would have become of the spirit of the Awakening in the absence of political tensions with London cannot be known. What is clear is that religious fervor migrated from the church to the incipient nation. Even if Whitefield's converts did not in their own persons become the rioters who poured into the streets in 1765, at the time of the Stamp Act, to protest the British imposition of "taxation without representation"—and there is no evidence one way or the other—the Awakening's evangelical, exhortational style helped the more Enlightenment-influenced, increasingly secessionist revolutionaries to mobilize a fighting base of support. Whitefield would have been surprised to be told, before dying in 1770, that he was helping invent the spirit of a nation rebelling violently against the motherland. But it cannot be a coincidence that even as evangelical church attendance ebbed after the Awakening's high tide, evangelicals overwhelmingly supported the Revolution.

The Great Awakening was the New World's first mass movement, sweeping mainly throughout the middle- and lower-class white population. In effect, it undermined religious authorities by inviting believers to find, or found, a social body that would be grander, if more disorderly, than any church. Given the growing disgruntlement with the British, the Awakening undermined monarchy across the board and fueled the passion for a republic. In this way, the evangelical fervors of the Awakening—Perry Miller called them "hysterical agonies"—mutated to serve the cause of independence. "More colonists were prepared for armed resistance by the clergy's Sunday and election sermons and weekly lectures than by the books and pamphlets of a Locke or a Paine," writes the historian Conrad Cherry, estimating that "the more millennialist churches in the late eighteenth century counted perhaps roughly half the population among their adherents." People not only listened to fiery sermons, they read the texts by the thousands. Sermons, devotional tracts, theological treatises, and the like made up the bulk of all printed matter in the colonies.

Stimulated by the literal earthquakes of the 1750s and the British war against Catholic France (1754–63), millennialism went political. Actual bloodshed promoted the apocalyptic temper and the prophetic mood. Surely the end of days was at hand, and then perfection! Ideological themes fused as millennial portents were discerned in westward expansion into "heathen" lands. Ministers frequently cited the prophet Isaiah—who spoke, for example, in what would later reemerge as a Zionist metaphor, of "the desert blossoming like a rose"—and interpreted the French and Indian War as a war against Popery.

In the 1760s and 1770s, political strains with London channeled the millennial sentiment that had previously been divorced from political implications into revolutionary passion. Even outside New England, the insurgent style of the Great Awakening primed the colonies for political and social reform by undermining the habits of deference and civility. Contention became all the rage. Zeal was especially transferable when adroit leaders knew how to shuttle between vocabularies. Militant politics and militant religion blended. Gradually, American writers extracted the idea of providential mission from its previous identification with Great Britain as a whole. Moderate ministers heralded worldly expansion and prosperity, while the immoderate wondered aloud whether this was "the Time, in which Christ's Kingdom is to be thus gloriously set up in the World." In 1765, no less a republican than John Adams deftly argued from the divine anointment of *America* to the divine right of *the people* and against the divine right of *kings,* insisting that the liberty that "we have a right to" was "derived from our Maker," since the "Creator, who does nothing in vain, has given them understandings, and a desire to know"—and moreover, "an indisputable, unalienable, indefeasible, divine right to . . . knowledge . . . of the characters and conduct of their rulers."

Even non- or anti-evangelical leaders of the Revolution, Deists and rationalists as some of them were, used evangelical language in behalf of the revolutionary cause. This may have been partly because they knew that many of their readers were Protestant believers who were shaken and moved by End Times thunderings. But they also sincerely believed in a republican interpretation of the Old Testament. In his electrifying and influential 1776 pamphlet *Common Sense,* no less a Deist than Thomas Paine traced the revolutionaries' ideological lineage back to the ancient Jews who lived in "a kind of Republic" for ages until, "hankering . . . for the idolatrous customs of the Heathens," they succumbed to "a national delusion" and decided to pay "idolatrous homage" by "requesting a king," thereby placing a mere human being on a throne that ought to have been forbidden to anyone but the Almighty. Monarchy was therefore not only a crime but a sin, "a form of government which the word of God bears testimony against, and blood will attend it." Paine called upon the Americans to become a godly nation that, free of kings and lords and priests, rules itself.

A Christian-republican alliance had crystallized, with each theme drawing on the vocabulary of the other. Believers were willing to overlook the religious heterodoxy of the founders, as the founders were willing to use biblical narratives to serve republican arguments. There took place what the historian Bernard Bailyn called a "contagion of liberty"—a current that apparently ran both ways. Revolutionary partisans understood British tyranny as a divine punishment laid upon a sinful people. In revolutionary-era sermons, it was now distinctly the Americans alone, and not the denizens of the mother country, who were held to be bound to God by a "visible covenant." "The day of the American Israel's trouble," of "our declensions and abounding iniquities," was the time of the great test for an overly proud, self-indulgent, pretentious, but still chosen people. The Second Continental Congress of 1775 rehearsed an argument (soon to be promoted by Paine in *Common Sense*) to the effect that God had waited until the colonists "were grown up to our present strength" before nudging them toward breaking the chains that bound them to Britain.

Came the outbreak of armed resistance, clergymen not only sermonized for the patriotic cause, they served in committees of correspondence and safety and enlisted in the army. As the country came to a boil, then, it may seem surprising that clergymen were not prominent in the revolutionary leadership. Only a single minister took part in the Continental Congress and signed the Declaration of Independence—the Presbyterian John Witherspoon, president of the College of New Jersey (now Princeton), who introduced the Scottish Enlightenment into the curriculum, taught Hebrew to James Madison in 1771–72, impressed John Adams as "an animated Son of Liberty," "as high a Son of Liberty, as any man in America," and in 1776 became the first public figure in New Jersey to support the cause of independence, assuring Americans that God was on their side even as they faced a "multitude of opposing hosts."

Witherspoon, a recent Scottish emigrant to the New World, was unique in transferring his religious position into a direct political role; other ministers were inhibited from political leadership by church tradition. Yet this barrier did not hold back the fervent congregations, nor did it prevent millenarian zeal from taking a revolutionary turn in the 1770s. In prerevolutionary Concord, Massachusetts, many of the "embattled farmers" (as well as mechanics, artisans, and others) who "fired the shot heard round the world" had been inspired by the Great Awakening of twenty-five years earlier; they declared themselves against the Crown and enrolled in the Minutemen at a time when the traditionalist elites held back. "Especially in New England, the cutting edge of the revolutionary movement," the historian Ruth Bloch writes, "Manichaean religious assumptions were so deep among ordinary colonists that the objectionable imperial measures were almost immediately presented by patriot publicists not merely as unconstitutional but as demonic."

Without question, the Founding Fathers, frequently Deists or unorthodox Christians, spoke a largely secular language. They were, in the main, Enlightened men who led an army of the Greatly Awakened. They welcomed the clergy's voices in no small part because opposition to the Crown's policies, and the embrace of Enlightenment ideals of liberty, were fully compatible with a God-fearing vocabulary. "Liberty, traced to her true source, is of heavenly extraction," declared the chaplain of the Continental Congress, a Philadelphia Anglican minister, in 1775. "Liberty is the cause of God and truth," preached a Salem Calvinist in a 1777 sermon titled "An Antidote Against Toryism." If liberty was of divine origin, then by Manichaean logic it followed that Toryism was the devil's work. Patriots frequently described their troops as Christian soldiers battling *"all the powers of Hell,"* "the prince of darkness," "the serpent," "the dragon," and "the antichristian beast." Patriotic writings exclaimed that "the great ends" of Providence were at work in the Revolution, which would culminate in "perfection" as God would fulfill His ancient promises to the Jews.

The providential consensus spilled beyond New England, too. A Pennsylvania minister declared in 1782 that "the rankest deist can scarcely deny the hand of Providence in our successes." Newspapers transmitted New England's rambunctiousness throughout the colonies of the Middle Atlantic and South, and beyond the clergy as well. The states organized fast days to underscore their patriotic piety. By 1776, the theme of the divine election of the United States resounded loudly throughout the thirteen colonies, as in these words of the planter-lawyer William Henry Drayton, appointed chief justice of South Carolina:

> The Almighty . . . has made choice of the present generation to erect the American Empire. . . . And thus has suddenly arisen in the World, a new Empire, stiled [*sic*] the United States of America. An Empire that as soon as started into Existence, attracts the Attention of the Rest of the Universe; and bids fair, by the Blessing of God, to be the most glorious of any upon Record.

Other revolutionaries, without going so far as to decree that a new empire was nigh, identified the Americans with the chosen Israelites, especially those who grew disgruntled in mid-Exodus. In a 1777 sermon, Nicholas Street of East Haven, Connecticut, likened backbiting Americans who doubted George Washington and other leaders to the "infidelity, inconstancy, hypocrisy, apostacy [*sic*], rebellion, and perverseness which lay hid in [the Israelites'] hearts" when God kept them in the wilderness as they carped at Moses and Aaron, adding: "The British tyrant is only acting over the same wicked and cruel part, that Pharaoh king of Egypt acted towards the children of Israel above 3000 years ago." Pharaoh was not the only precedent for George III. "[T]he British nation are the rod of God's anger to scourge and chastise us for our sins, as the Assyrian monarch was to God's people of old."

Many of those who expounded on such themes during the Revolutionary War envisioned continental expansion as the proof of America's divinity. On July 4, 1778, in one of the first Independence Day orations ever delivered in the United States, David Ramsay, a Philadelphia doctor who had relocated to Charleston, South Carolina, offered the crowd his prediction that as a result of "the special interposition of Providence in our behalf," the United States was destined to spread across the continent, providing enough land to draw in "thousands and millions of virtuous peasants from Europe" and signaling that "the thrones of tyranny and despotism will totter" everywhere. Decades before the Louisiana Purchase, continental destiny was heartily desired as one more sign of God's grace.

Nor did the millennial theme of God's New Israel fizzle out once the Americans had driven the British out of the New World. Many clergymen published victory sermons heralding the Revolution as the fruit of Providence and the prologue to a future Kingdom of God. Some harked back to the millenarian themes of the previous century, seeking to match present-day events precisely to biblical precedents from the End Times texts of Ezra and Revelation. But increasingly, many argued that faith in Providence would be rewarded in a worldly, indeed territorial fashion. Such was the case with Ezra Stiles, the president of Yale and a leading exponent of the Christian-republican synthesis. Stiles, convinced that "true religion" was necessary to perfect "our system of dominion and civil polity," greeted what he called "God's American Israel," with Washington cast as "the American Joshua," in a sermon on May 8, 1783, titled "The United States Elevated to Glory and Honor." Stiles's text was Deuteronomy 26:19, Moses's declaration that the Lord would elevate his "holy people" "high above all nations." In Stiles's vision, America's ascendancy in world trade would fulfill biblical prophecy. America's grand success would surely prepare Europe for the much-desired "annihilation of the Pontificate," also preparing the way for the twelve tribes of the Jews to "reassemble" in the Holy Land, a necessary prologue to the battle of Armageddon and the second advent of Jesus.

Less grandiosely, in his last address as commander in chief, George Washington in 1783 told a crowd in Trenton he had seen "the Divine Arm visibly outstretched for our deliverance" while modestly acknowledging "my humble instrumentality in carrying the designs of Providence into effect." In 1787, the theological poet Timothy Dwight, grandson of Jonathan Edwards (and himself a future president of Yale), waxed grandiloquent in calling the Americans "this chosen race," which could claim "all the improvements of all lands" for "its base," as "Far o'er the Atlantic wild its beams aspire, / The world approves it, and the heavens admire. . . ."

The Finger of God and the Glory of the Republic

The heavens may have "admired" "this chosen race," selecting it for the great adventure of "improving all lands," but the millennial vision, whether in Christian or republican form, was premature. Still, the revolution in France reignited hopes of a world turning upside down. In the words of Conor Cruise O'Brien, Thomas Jefferson and James Madison spent several years persuaded that the French upheaval was "an angelic auxiliary for the cause of freedom in America." Even in late 1791, Madison could declare that "the revolution seems to have succeeded beyond the most sanguine hopes," and in 1792, that Americans ought to "favor an event so glorious to mankind and so glorious to this country, because it has grown as it were out of the American revolution." But the French Revolution, which in its honeymoon years glowed as a splendid vindication of the American precedent, soon enough lost its luster even in the eyes of its most fervent American partisans. As the guillotines went to work and *sanguine* gave way to *sanguinary,* the fantasy of revolutionary universalism crashed and burned, forcing a reconsideration of America's national destiny. America may have been divinely elected, but its inspirational reach was going to be limited.

In no other individual did the tensions of postrevolutionary aftermath play out so clearly as in Madison's tutor in French matters, Thomas Jefferson, who, unfazed by contradiction, entertained at various times an intense theory of chosenness; a profound suspicion of government; a willingness to exercise arbitrary power; and a vivid ambition for what would later be called America's Manifest Destiny. No wonder a prominent newspaper edited by a onetime admirer of Jefferson wondered aloud after his death: "What *principle* in the political ethics of our country might not be *sanctioned* AND *refuted* by the writings of Mr. Jefferson?"

Even before the colonies broke from the motherland, Jefferson was partial to the idea that America had begun with a sort of virgin birth. In a 1774 pamphlet, he argued that the Saxons of Germany and pre-Norman England were yeomen who had long thrived without kings or lords. (In 1776, he would feature those Saxons in his design for the nation's official seal.) The next year, no doubt casting about for arguments in favor of independence, Jefferson was at pains to argue that the first American settlers had paid their own way to the New World, "unassisted by the wealth or the strength of Great Britain." In 1781, he went out on a limb and produced this more dramatic formulation: "Those who labour in the earth are the chosen people of God, if ever he had a chosen people, whose breasts he has made his peculiar deposit for substantial and genuine virtue. It is the focus in which he keeps alive that sacred fire, which otherwise might escape from the face of the earth." Jefferson hedged his bet on whether a chosen people existed at all, but it is striking that he should adapt the language of "chosenness" and "sacredness" to exalt his "virtuous" countrymen. The Saxons became the yeomen, who settled, in turn, a country uniquely blessed.

In his First Inaugural, in 1801, Jefferson made explicit what had earlier been implicit: he grafted the concept of chosenness specifically onto physical territory. Americans, he said, "possess[ed] a chosen country, with room enough for our descendants to the thousandth and thousandth generation." In his religiously unorthodox manner, he assured Americans that he and they were "enlightened by a benign religion, professed, indeed, and practiced in various forms," all of which "acknowledg[ed] and ador[ed] an overruling Providence." Yeomen required land to fulfill their mission as a people needing neither lords nor kings, and America was blessed with more than sufficient land. Jefferson himself was deeply involved in Virginia land speculation.

It might therefore have surprised literal-minded citizens when, a mere two years later, Jefferson as president seized the opportunity to double the territory of the United States of America with one grand move—the Louisiana Purchase of 1803. Hadn't he just pronounced the United States "room[y] enough"? Why, moreover, was he ready to resort to arms if peaceful negotiations failed to procure New Orleans and guaranteed access to the Mississippi River?

When Jefferson proved willing to exceed his constitutional powers in order to buy Louisiana's hundreds of millions of acres, was he simply availing himself of a stroke of good fortune? Was the erratic visionary overcome by practical temptation? Or, one eye cocked on the "exterminating havoc" of Europe, was he just protecting what would one day be called "national security interests"? After all, in 1803, the United States shared the American continent not just with feeble Spain but with Napoleonic France—which,

Jefferson knew, had by secret treaty taken control of New Orleans and the surrounding territory. The French revolutionary hope had curdled into a potential threat, and as Madison wrote Jefferson in 1800, "the late defection of France [to military rule] has left America the only theatre on which true liberty can have a fair trial." Jefferson, once president, worried that any foreign power that held land east of the Mississippi (i.e., France, supplanting Spain in Florida) would become the "natural enemy" of the United States, and that "there is on the globe one single spot, the possessor of which is our natural and habitual enemy"—the great Mississippi entrepot of New Orleans. In the menacing form of Napoleonic France, Jefferson warned in 1803, a "gigantic force has risen up which seems to threaten the world."

It is true that Napoleon's overreach presented Jefferson with a huge opportunity. Napoleon needed cash to resume his war against England and to open a campaign in Egypt—prospects that enlivened him more than any hypothetical Western Hemisphere base. In the event, any plans he might have had for a French empire in North America exploded when the army he sent to reconquer Haiti in 1801 after its slave revolt—an army he intended to go on to occupy Louisiana—was laid low by Haitian resistance and yellow fever. Unprepared to fight on two continents under these circumstances, Napoleon conceived the masterstroke of disburdening himself, selling not only New Orleans but the entire, immense Louisiana Territory for a pittance—$15 million, or less than three cents per acre.

When so much land came calling, Jefferson must have felt that his transcendent and practical motives had splendidly fused. The practical interest in protecting the national flank matched up with the thrilling promise of vast lands where untold yeomen could settle—even though, in the eyes of Jefferson's unremitting Federalist opponent Alexander Hamilton, it was premature (to put it mildly) to think that the yeoman were getting crowded, since by Hamilton's calculation only one-sixteenth of the land east of the Mississippi had yet been settled.

This offer Jefferson could not refuse, despite his having often declared himself a partisan of small government and a fierce foe of debt. Transcendent opportunities were not to be rejected. He took the plunge in a fit of presence of mind. If the original colonies had been a "chosen country," the Purchase would more than double their divinely sanctioned potential. Americans could now, as the historian Nicholas Guyatt writes, "imagine the glorious colonization of their own continent rather than the redemption of Europe." The Christian-republican synthesis marched on.

And perhaps not incidentally, expansion across the Mississippi offered a bonus—an option for solving the nagging problem of what to do about those recalcitrant Indians who refused either assimilation or surrender. On February 27, 1803, just a few months before purchasing Louisiana, Jefferson had written confidentially to William Henry Harrison, the governor of the Indiana Territory (later to become Indiana, Illinois, Michigan, Wisconsin, and part of Minnesota), of his grand manipulative "system" with respect to those unassimilables: "Our system is to live in perpetual peace with the Indians, to cultivate an affectionate attachment from them, by everything just and liberal which we can do for them within the bounds of reason." But as their game reserves dwindled, the Indians would have to face reality: "[We] wish to draw them to agriculture, to spinning and weaving." They would be forced to give up on their forests and trade them for necessities:

> In this way, our settlements will gradually circumscribe and approach the Indians and they will in time either incorporate with us as citizens of the United States or remove beyond the Mississippi. The former is certainly the termination of their history most happy for themselves. . . . Should any tribe be foolhardy enough to take up the hatchet at any time, the seizing [of] the whole country of that tribe, and driving them be-

yond the Mississippi, as the only condition of peace, would be an example to others, and a furtherance of our final consolidation.

Once, Jefferson had imagined the Indians as potential yeomen themselves. Looking back after his presidency, in 1813, he could still fondly recall his earlier, happier scenario in which the Americans would teach the Indians to farm and practice crafts, to live on private property, and join the chosen possessors of the land after all: "They would have mixed their blood with ours, and been amalgamated and identified with us within no distant period of time." But when the British "seduced" the tribes to side with them during the war of 1812, "to take up the hatchet against us, and [commit] cruel massacres . . . on the women and children of our frontiers taken by surprise," Jefferson explained to his correspondent, the explorer Alexander von Humboldt, the United States was "oblige[d] to pursue them to extermination, or drive them to new seats beyond our reach."

By such a rash expedient Jefferson hoped to slash through the Gordian knot that had bound Americans to the recalcitrant natives for two centuries. In truth, he was following the main line that the colonists had pursued from the seventeenth century on as, like it or not, they confronted the stark fact that their Promised Land was already occupied by peoples whose providential significance was unclear. Were they among the lost tribes of Israel? Were they present-day Canaanites whose destiny was to be removed? Was the proper response to convert them, segregate them, expel them, or kill them? Already, chartering the Virginia Company in 1606, King James had promoted the merits of "propagating of Christian religion to such people, as yet live in darkness and miserable ignorance of the true knowledge and worship of God." The Virginians sustained this intention in their early tracts aiming to convert the Indians. On a parallel track, in 1630, John Cotton was telling Winthrop's Puritans: "Offend not the poor natives, make them partakers of your precious faith." In Massachusetts as in Virginia, few "savages" wished to be converted, at least not if the prerequisite for conversion was that they be inducted into the settlers' idea of civilization. They resisted. A few years later, Cotton was thundering that the savages be "blast[ed in] all their green groves, and arbours."

The settlers seized upon both biblical and political credentials to justify depriving the Indians of the land. God meant the land to be cultivated, and it was on this basis that Carolina, for example, was claimed in the first place, in 1629, as a region "*hitherto untilled* . . . But in some parts of it inhabited by certain Barbarous men." Genesis 1:28 ("replenish the earth, and subdue it") was cited as authority, whereby the Indians, as hunters and gatherers, were held to violate the divine mandate. In addition, a theoretical warrant emanated from no less an authority than John Locke. In 1669, while serving as secretary of the Board of Trade and Plantations for the Lords and Proprietors of the Carolinas, Locke helped write the *Fundamental Constitutions of Carolina,* the chief governing document overseeing most of the territory that lies today between Virginia and Florida; later, in 1682, he took part in revising it. Locke wrote in his *Second Treatise of Government,* around that time, that "God gave the World to Men in Common, but it cannot be supposed he meant it always to remain common and uncultivated. He gave it to the use of the Industrious and Rational (and *Labour* was to be his *Title* to it)." When he wrote the chapter on property in his deeply influential *Treatise,* he knew a great deal about colonial land policy in the New World.

As the colonists expanded, taking lands where the Indians hunted, massacre begot massacre, each one justified as a necessary defense against a ruthless and unremitting foe. Expelling the Indians, pushing them beyond the pale of civilization, seemed the obvious tactic. Both advocates and opponents of Indian expulsion claimed providential warrant for their positions. If Jefferson, in a contemplative mood, saw tragedy in the irresistible flow of civilization—in the same letter to Humboldt in which he took either "extermination" or expulsion to be an American "obligation," he went on to lay the blame on "Anglo-mercantile cupidity"—he was willing to reconcile himself to his role in this destiny, just as, by the relentless logic of history, the Indians would have to reconcile themselves to their own.

Jefferson had to have thought about the meaning of Louisiana for his Indian policy, for his political enemies harbored ideas of their own—harsh ones. In 1803, Federalist New England had no use for a land whose otters, one of them wrote, were better prepared for democracy than what he called Louisiana's "*Gallo-Hispanic-Indian omnium gatherum* of savages and adventures." For Jefferson, all the motives for acquisition converged. The desirability of acquiring an immense wilderness to which to transfer the Indians may not have been uppermost in his mind when he seized upon Napoleon's offer, but he readily realized that Louisiana could also serve as "the means of tempting all our Indians on the East side of the Mississippi to remove to the West." Thus, in the words of the historian Jon Kukla, "the Louisiana Purchase prompted an ominous transition in the government's policies toward American Indians. . . . America's visible first steps along the Trail of Tears were taken in the White House as Thomas Jefferson pondered the implications of the Louisiana Purchase."

But to fully grasp Jefferson's resolve to possess Louisiana, we need to address one of the commanding paradoxes of his career. This master craftsman who delighted in taking command of every detail of every task that stirred his mind—from designing the University of Virginia's rotunda to anonymously writing dozens of resolutions and planting them in state legislatures to ensure the political outcomes he desired—nonetheless had little to say about designing the most Olympian of his projects, the republic of the United States of America.

He was profligate with rhetoric: the empire of liberty, the pursuit of happiness, the sacred fire of freedom. As he knew the yeomen were the heroes of history, he also knew that a government governed best when it governed least. How his gentlemen farmers were to govern a growing nation needful of armies and monies and institutions, Jefferson never thought through. It might be fruitful, then, to investigate not only Jefferson's sphinxlike character but his beliefs—as much as they can be fathomed, at any rate.

This qualification is called for because Jefferson resisted being pinned down, at least partly because the vitriolic politics that prevailed in the late 1790s and into his presidency convinced him that words committed to paper could readily be subjected to gotcha tests. The religious references in his voluminous correspondence were only sporadic, and while often enough declaring himself in sympathy with a Unitarian view of God and a "rational Christianity," he had little patience for formal theology, declaring that "it is in our lives, and not from our words, that our religion must be read." Still, the lion's share of his views are well-known. For all of his inconsistencies, there can be little doubt that he was indeed a trenchant opponent of autocracy and a guardian of freedom. He was consistently as fervent an advocate of religious liberty as he was an opponent of all organized religion. In 1786, for example, he wrote James Madison to herald the erection of "the standard of reason . . . after so many ages during which the human mind has been held in vassalage by kings, priests, and nobles." In 1816, he persisted in insulting the clergy with the declaration that "there would never have been an infidel, if there had never been a priest."

But alongside his private reflections on the nature of God, reflections he was committed to keeping out of public view, there was another enduring, transcendent—and more public—component to Jefferson's thought. He told his countrymen that the republic he was shaping in word and deed was a surge forward not merely in the political evolution of nations but in the destiny of a uniquely, divinely sanctioned chosen people.

During Jefferson's years in the White House, America was experiencing an evangelical boom that came to be known as the Second Great Awakening. The fastest-growing churches were those possessed of the most intense, emotional, missionary energy—especially Baptists and Methodists. (By 1810 there were more Methodists in the United States than in Great Britain.) Protracted revival meetings and voluntary societies mushroomed. Even in the absence of his own complicated and unorthodox religious beliefs, Jefferson would have been mindful of the religious ground moving under his feet.

In his second term as president, when he was less reluctant to irritate his political enemies and more concerned about America's place in the long arc of history, he brought this sense of American chosenness out of the closet. On March 4, 1805, he sounded every bit like a Puritan father when he inserted the language of divine election into his second inaugural address, asking "the favor of that Being in whose hands we are, who led our fathers, as Israel of old, from their native land and planted them in a country flowing with all the necessaries and comforts of life; who has covered our infancy with His providence and our riper years with His wisdom and power." Providence had ushered in not only wisdom and power but land that stretched far beyond the Mississippi. Jefferson found "Israel of old" a usable past for an expanding nation, shielded as it was from the scourges of war-ravaged Europe. Revolutionary universalism contracted into Manifest Destiny, but Jefferson could make the most of that. No longer was it sufficient to be a city visible upon a hill, inspiring others with its example, bound to God by covenant, subject to tribulation; the Louisiana Purchase signaled that it was time to go on the march.

Four years later to the day, upon ending his second term of office, Jefferson addressed the citizens of Washington, D.C., with chosenness again on his mind. This time, however, he expressed a still more somber view of American prospects in a hostile world:

> The station which we occupy among the nations of the earth is honorable, but awful. Trusted with the destinies of this solitary republic of the world, the only monument of human rights, and the sole depository of the sacred fire of freedom and self-government, from hence it is to be lighted up in other regions of the earth, if other regions of the earth shall ever become susceptible of its benign influence.

This was no casual flourish, even if it tailed off into one of those qualifying "if" clauses with which Jefferson liked to hedge his bets. He had already used the phrase "sacred fire." Now he repeated it. Then, a few months later, he delivered to the New York State Legislature a slight variation of his farewell, this time inviting Americans to think of themselves as the "sole depositories of the remains of human liberty."

It may disconcert the prevailing image of Jefferson the empiricist to observe that he also devoted his life to a religious project. But he was, after all, an astute student of the Exodus—recall his proposal for a Great Seal with "a representation of the children of Israel in the wilderness, led by a cloud by day and a pillar of fire by night." President Jefferson learned the same lesson as Moses: a Promised Land would also require governance, even raw power. Fleeing Egypt, Moses, too, dreamed of a people unbound by governors and clerics, "a kingdom of priests and a holy nation." Only reluctantly did he appoint the Levites as guardians of religious duties and customs. Only after observing his charges descend into chaos did he install a governing hierarchy. Then, having ordered the slaughter of tens of thousands of Israelites who had contested his designs for the nation, he watched with relish as two ordinary men, Eldad and Medad, excluded from the ranks of religious officialdom, felt moved by the spirit of God and began to prophesy.

Like Moses, Jefferson erected a steely edifice of government while decrying its necessity. In 1808, this fierce opponent of a standing army dispatched that very army to strong-arm the populace of northeastern ports into submitting to his ill-advised embargo on trading with England. As smugglers defied the law, he went so far as to argue that citizens might be held guilty until proven innocent. Like Moses, Jefferson came to tolerate no divergence from the righteous path, whatever burdens had to be shouldered as God's chosen ones journeyed toward a perfect, exemplary union. Like Moses, Jefferson died without reaching the Promised Land.

Where Jefferson's gift was to summon up a world with words, to thread his way between contradictions on paper, Andrew Jackson's was to slash his way through the world with a sword, to defy the enemy and lay him low. The warrior spoke in the unadorned language of tactics and strategy—whereas when Jefferson practiced his wiles, he had wrapped them (or disguised them, his enemies thought) in vision. In 1824, a political jingle had counterposed "John Quincy Adams / Who can write" to "Andrew Jackson / Who can fight," and in this contrast it was the polymath Adams, not the barely literate Jackson, who stood in the line of Jefferson. Jefferson, after all, wished to be remembered as the author of foundational documents and the founder of a university; Jackson left behind not a single memorable phrase. The aged Jefferson himself is said to have exclaimed in 1824: "I feel much alarmed at the prospect of seeing General Jackson president. He is one of the most unfit men I know of for such a place. He has had very little respect for laws and constitutions. . . . His passions are terrible. . . . He is a dangerous man." Adams captured the elite opinion of the time when in 1833, he boycotted the Harvard ceremony at which an honorary degree was bestowed upon Jackson and labeled him "a barbarian who could not write a sentence of grammar and hardly could spell his own name."

Yet as he galloped his way toward the highest office in the land— he was defeated in 1824 but won in 1828 and again in 1832—Jackson found his political polestar not in George Washington, a fellow general whose pistols, a gift from the Founding Father's family, Jackson proudly hung above his fireplace, but in Jefferson, a William and Mary graduate who never distinguished himself in battle (and whose enemies commonly accused him, in fact, of cowardice on the field). When Old Hickory's supporters called him "the second Jefferson," he mightily approved. Jackson was Jefferson in uniform.

How could this be? Jefferson, the elegant thinker, began his public life arguing from rights to defiance, while the rough-hewn Jackson, the son of an actual immigrant yeoman and a mother who hoped he would enter the ministry, unphilosophical as a point of pride, spoke from experience when he wrote: "Every man with a gun in his hand, all Europe combined cannot hurt us." In 1780, when a British officer drew his sword and struck at the head of the thirteen-year-old Jackson, who had refused to clean his muddy boots, the boy had raised his left hand and suffered a severe gash there and another on his head, whereupon he dared the officer to try again. Expressing visions was not Jackson's game; enacting them was.

Their affinity was in large measure ideological, but this does not mean it was purely intellectual. "I have long believed," Jackson wrote in 1835, "that it was only by preserving the identity of the Republican party as embodied and characterized by the principles introduced by Mr. Jefferson that the original rights of the states and the people could be maintained as contemplated by the Constitution." But there was more. The master of Monticello had never been able to reconcile his passion for a nation of independent and self-governing yeomen with his dedication to a growing republic that needed the guiding hand of a central hierarchy. He was torn between the vision of America bearing a "sacred fire" and the need for a this-worldly state. He never quite succeeded in undoing that Gordian knot.

But Jackson's sword could slice through it. Like Jefferson, Jackson saw the nation as possessed of a transcendental purpose. "Providence," he declared in his farewell address of 1837, "has showered on this favored land blessings without number, and has chosen you, as the guardians of freedom, to preserve it for the benefit of the human race. May he who holds in his hands the destinies of nations make you worthy of the favors he has bestowed, and enable you, with pure hearts, and pure hands, and sleepless vigilance, to guard and defend to the end of time the great charge he has committed to your keeping."

His supporters were singing from the same hymnal. As the great revival movement surged outward, and its missionary campaigns and camp meetings, its "personal decisions for Christ," became all the rage from the "burned-over district" of western New York State down through the Appalachians and across the South, Jackson found ready support for a rekindled spirit of American chosenness. It took the form of a reincarnation of the Christian-republican synthesis of the previous century. During his eight years in office, Jackson pursued the principle that if America was to "defend to the end of time the great charge" that God had committed to its keeping, it had to do so by force. The hero of New Orleans had made his name by inflicting some eighteen hundred casualties on the British—some 40 percent of all the casualties they suffered in the course of the war of 1812–15. When, in 1817, President James Monroe ordered him to lead a campaign against the Seminole and Creek Indians in Georgia, Jackson interpreted Monroe's (perhaps deliberately) vague order to "terminate the conflict" by invading Spanish Florida, which the Seminoles were using as a base to attack Georgia, and deposing its governor.

This particular move could be defended as military necessity, but Jackson as president built on the precedent to plant facts on the ground many times, most brutally in the case of removing the Indians. If Jefferson drew up the blueprint for the Trail of Tears, Jackson paved it. He did so while taking up, though less subtly, Jefferson's patronizing and elegiacal tone. In an echo of Jefferson's 1803 letter to William Henry Harrison, Jackson spoke in his First Annual Message to Congress of a dire "fate" that doubtlessly, but somehow impersonally, awaited the Indians if they were permitted to stay in place, "[s]urrounded by the whites with their arts of civilization which by destroying the resources of the savage doom him to weakness and decay. . . . Humanity and national honor demand that every effort should be made to avert so great a calamity."

To enable the Indians to govern themselves, as the Cherokees in Georgia persisted in wanting to do, would have violated several interests. Even though the Cherokees seemed a very model of assimilation, having given up hunting, taken up agriculture, converted to Christianity, and adopted a constitution patterned on the American one, they insisted on their own sovereignty against the state's wishes—a violation of Article IV, Section 3 of the U.S. Constitution. If ideals were not enough to justify federal intervention, gold was discovered on Cherokee land just a few months after Jackson's inauguration. His goal for the Indians was, he said, high-minded: "to preserve this much-injured race" by transferring the tribes across the Mississippi, where "the remnant of that ill-fated race" would be "placed beyond the reach of injury or oppression, and . . . the paternal care of the General Government will hereafter watch over them and protect them." After Congress passed the Indian Removal Bill in 1830, he uprooted almost forty-six thousand natives and resettled them west of the Mississippi. What a later age would cynically call "ethnic cleansing" constituted, for Jackson, a rescue.

When South Carolina tried to nullify federal law by state fiat in 1832–33, Jackson told Congress that what was at stake was not just the Union as such but what he declared to be the Founders' core commitment: "a Government of laws and a Federal Union founded upon the great principle of popular representation." *Popular representation:* this was Jackson's original note, a striking departure from the sparer republicanism of Jefferson and Madison. He himself represented the people in ways that disgusted the Founder elites. All his predecessors in office were descended from Virginia or Massachusetts gentry, whereas he was (in their eyes at least) crude, and the politics that he preached and practiced—like those of the awakened evangelical Christians who harked to him—took aim at the influence of small and privileged cabals. He fought the absurdly undemocratic Electoral College with all his might—and lost. To strengthen the presidency was in his eyes to strengthen the one institution that best reflected the popular will. If this was self-serving, it was also principled.

So when he addressed the threat of secession by announcing, "I will die with the Union," and promised to mobilize up to two hundred thousand troops unless his native state of South Carolina backed away from the "brink of insurrection and treason," he meant, in effect, that Americans had been chosen for the sake of *democracy.*

It was democracy, albeit for whites, of which he was the strong right arm. Under him, the national government would reaffirm what the American people had been chosen for, even if he used a vocabulary that was usually earthier than it was divine.

Another principle stirred in Jackson, too. This fierce man on horseback leading the people against their enemies, this plebeian yet noble hero who embodied (as he thought) their virtues and (as he didn't think) their vices, was the incarnation of America's vigorous, go-getting, triumphant, and unstoppable individual obeying his own personal call to Manifest Destiny. Later, Emerson wrote: "It is said to be the Age of the first-person singular." For him, this was a mixed curse. "Every Man for himself" was his next line, and it was not complimentary. During the Jacksonian years, the sage of Concord was fervently ambivalent about the Jacksonian America that both exalted and catered to commoners. "'Tis a wild democracy," he said of Jackson's America, and in 1832 he warned straight-out that "we shall all feel dirty if Jackson is reelected." But the barn door was open and a newly revived populace was in no mood to yield to its betters. The "wild democracy" that Emerson half dreaded and half hailed, the democracy that rallied to Jackson, had drunk of the spirit of inspired self-creation. The nation was being swept by the Second Great Awakening and its promise of personal redemption for all comers. Emerson captured the spirit of the time when he wrote: "The Protestant has his pew, which of course is only the first step to a church for every individual citizen—a church apiece." He exaggerated but he caught something profound in the Awakening spirit. Religion was surging. The percentage of Americans who joined Protestant churches increased sixfold between 1800 and 1860.

In Andrew Jackson, awakened Americans saw the secular, national incarnation of the same promise they heard in the passion of tent meetings. He was no Jefferson or Madison or John Quincy Adams, no patrician designated from on high to govern on their behalf, but their bolder embodiment—an impoverished son of South Carolina whose sheer strength of character, bravery, and cunning combined were proof of what could be achieved with fortitude, rectitude, and a swift sword. If the hero incarnated a man's duty to stand strong for an exceptional nation, he could rise to the Oval Office. Later, Herman Melville would capture this mood in *Moby-Dick* with a rhapsody to "immaculate manliness . . . that democratic dignity which . . . radiates without end from God Himself . . . thou just Spirit of Equality . . . thou great democratic God! who didst pick up Andrew Jackson from the pebbles; who didst hurl him upon a war-horse; who didst thunder him higher than a throne!" Jackson bore no small resemblance to Captain Ahab, the wounded, weathered warrior who maniacally, ruthlessly, violently seeks to subdue the natural world. Such an American soul, equally splendid and dangerous, would not have been possible before Jackson.

There remained for Jackson one exceptional moment. After spending the bulk of his 1837 farewell address in prosy denunciations of dissension, nullification, and the "organized money power," he built up to his climax with a thunderous warning against the "cupidity," "corruption," "disappointed ambition," and "inordinate thirst for power" that menaced the republic from within. Then this man whose mother had intended him for the Presbyterian ministry soared: "Providence has showered on this favored land blessings without number and has chosen you as the guardian of freedom to preserve it for the benefit of the human race." The spirit of chosenness lived.

But it kept colliding with recalcitrant others—or perhaps we should say that, unless all concerned act with supreme wisdom, it is in the nature of a nation that believes itself chosen to antagonize the unchosen, to suspect them, test them, encroach upon them, and often enough go to war with them, as those on the other side of the vanishing boundary feel called upon to do the same reciprocally.

For most Americans who left any record of their views, there was no stopping with the Louisiana Purchase. As the market economy flourished, a nation whose citizens were increasingly individualistic would be bound together with an idea of a common destiny, a *manifest* destiny that was (to use an earlier term for America's confidence in its truths) "self-evident"—a destiny that could be read off from the natural wonder on display in American territory. With older denominations spawning schismatic denominations and churches spawning yet newer churches, there was no single all-embracing, all-forgiving church to serve as a solvent for differences. Only a whole nation defined against outsiders could enfold a multiplicity of American ideals that ranged, not least, from slavery to abolition.

After the Louisiana Purchase, the splendors of nature supplied one possible proof of American glory. American nature was somehow the absolute heart of *all* Nature. A romantic celebration of the land united explorers and Transcendentalists, naturalists and devout Christians alike. The Hudson River School of artists flourished. Throughout the early nineteenth century, wrote Perry Miller, "this resurgence of the romantic heart against the enlightened head flowered in a veneration of Nature." American writers celebrated the idea that even amid boisterous growth and growing competitiveness, America remained "Nature's nation." One typical and widely reprinted essay of 1835 declared: "God has promised us a renowned existence, if we will but deserve it. He speaks this promise in the sublimity of Nature. It resounds all along the crags of the Alleghanies [*sic*]. It is uttered in the thunder of Niagara," etc., etc. Eventually, in 1868, even a budding pantheist like John Muir would exult of his first sights of California that the Sierra Maestra flowed "with more of milk and more of honey than ever did old Canaan in its happiest prime" and that Yosemite Valley was a "New Jerusalem."

Many were the motives for expansion, but always shining above the amalgam of democratic, demographic, pecuniary, racist, and anti-Catholic impulses was the idealistic, distinctly Christian sense that God had an interest in the outcome. In a high rhetorical register, the Jacksonian editor John O'Sullivan, usually credited with first publishing the phrase "manifest destiny" (1845), left no doubt that the nation's spirit, origins, and godly inspiration were all of a piece:

We are the nation of human progress, and who will, what can, set limits to our onward march? Providence is with us, and no earthly power can. . . . [T]he nation of many nations is destined to manifest to mankind the excellence of divine principles.

It would be America's "future history, to establish on earth the moral dignity and salvation of man—the immutable truth and beneficence of God." In his potpourri of time-honored American themes, O'Sullivan found so close an alignment between the American and the divine that they were veritable equivalents. He went on: "For this blessed mission to the nations of the world, which are shut out from the life-giving light of truth, has America been chosen."

Why *manifest* destiny, then? Why not a "divinely ordained" or "providential" destiny? "Manifest" meant obvious, incontrovertible. The term distinguished between God's ordination of Israel for unstated reasons of His own—reasons which the Jews spent millennia trying to parse—and, on the other hand, a clear destiny that Americans could readily perceive—our geography, our system of government, our generosity and natural bounty.

Mexico, by contrast, was in American eyes benighted—and some of it was there for the taking. Never mind that the Mexicans, like the Indians, claimed treaty protections against American power. In the dominant American view, just as the Indians wasted good land, so did the Mexicans, whereas by contrast, according to Jackson's protégé Senator Thomas Hart Benton, Americans used land "according to the intentions of the Creator." (Benton called American settlers "children of Israel" who "entered the promised land, with the implements of husbandry in one hand and the weapons of war in the other.")

When, in 1836, rebels in Texas seceded from an unstable Mexican government, and Mexico refused to recognize the breakaway republic, Washington saw its chance. In 1845, Congress resolved to annex Texas, disregarding an 1828 treaty that had accepted Mexican sovereignty there. Later that year, Texas chose to join the United States— as a slave state. To Mexico, not having accepted secession, this was a casus belli. After a series of provocative military maneuvers directed by President James Polk, war broke out in the spring of 1846.

For some in the war party, the war against Mexico was a crusade for freedom, even "nobility"—although the southern planters who supported annexation had their own idea of what American-style freedom in Texas would mean. An editorial in the *Brooklyn Daily Eagle* asked:

> What has miserable, inefficient Mexico—with her superstition, her burlesque upon freedom, her actual tyranny by the few over the many—what has she to do with the great mission of peopling the new world with a noble race? Be it ours, to achieve that mission!

The author of these florid lines was no less a herald of this glorious hour than Walt Whitman, who hailed one of General Zachary Taylor's victories in Mexico as "another clinching proof of the indomitable energy of the Anglo-Saxon character." Whitman was no conventional Christian, but he was not yet the poet of the all-embracing *I.* He was a romantic nationalist who was not averse (at this stage) to displaying a racial tinge in what he professed to be his "lofty views of the scope and destiny of the American Republic," yet in the same editorial insisted that "we do not take [the Mexicans] to be our inferiors in any respect." Yet Mexicans, he wrote, were "an ignorant, prejudiced, and perfectly faithless people." American rule would introduce them to agriculture, commerce, and literate civilization. Evidently their ignorance, prejudice, and faithlessness could be remedied under the proper tutelage. Ultimately, Whitman was confident: "It is for the interest of mankind that [America's] territory should be extended—the farther the better. We claim those lands, thus, by a law superior to parchments and dry diplomatic rules." America's great poet was more than half a century ahead of Rudyard Kipling and "the white man's burden."

Even opponents of the Texas takeover claimed to be on the side of divinity, which they were sure, in turn, was on theirs. Former president and now representative John Quincy Adams, the prime opponent of the Texas acquisition, ordered the House clerk to read from Genesis in support of his view. Adams preferred to assert American "title to the territory of Oregon," using the same argument against the British that he, Jefferson, Benton, and many others had used against Indian land claims—man was meant to multiply and subdue the earth, not just hunt and trap. Adams was no vulgar imperialist. He had strong abolitionist sympathies, and he wished the nation to occupy the city upon a hill, not the fortress on foreign ground. As secretary of state, he had resolutely declared in 1821 that America "goes not abroad, in search of monsters to destroy." He assured his listeners that America "is the well-wisher to the freedom and independence of all. . . . She will commend the general cause by the countenance of her voice, and the benignant sympathy of her example." He was perfectly willing to herald peaceful westward expansion under a Christian as well as a secular standard, and saw no contradiction between them. As he asked rhetorically in 1837:

> Is it not that the Declaration of Independence first organized the social compact on the foundation of the Redeemer's mission upon earth? That it laid the corner stone of human government upon the first precepts of Christianity, and gave to the world the first irrevocable pledge of the fulfillment of the prophecies, announced directly from Heaven at the birth of the Saviour and predicted by the greatest of the Hebrew prophets six hundred years before?

He delivered this oration on the Fourth of July, not Christmas or Easter Sunday.

Such thoughts were common not only among evangelicals—whose sympathizers have been estimated at 40 percent of the population in 1840—but among the most influential Americans of those times. The Puritan idea of a covenant that binds believers to one another was melting away in favor of an assumption that America was privileged by "divine right." Senator James Buchanan of Pennsylvania would declare in 1844: "Providence has given to the American people a great and important mission . . . to spread the blessings of Christian liberty and laws from one end to the other of this immense continent." Senator Sam Houston of Texas declared in 1848 that, just as God had supported the Israelites in their own wars, "the Divine Being has been evidently carrying out the destiny of the American race." In the press, too, the language of regeneration blended with Christian and providential themes. The *New York Herald* declared in 1847: "The universal Yankee nation can regenerate and disenthrall the people of Mexico in a few years; and we believe it is a part of our destiny to civilize that beautiful country." The same year, the *New York Sun,* which wanted the United States to absorb all of Mexico, could see the "finger of Providence uplifted for the salvation of a people oppressed by tyrants and robbers."

In other quarters, too, John Winthrop's reminder that "the eyes of the world are upon us" came up for renewal. When former secretary of the treasury Albert Gallatin opposed the Polk administration's conduct of the Mexican War, he did so in the name of America's *real* providential purpose, "to be the Model Republic." Addressing the House on the annexation of Texas in 1845, the Whig representative Robert C. Winthrop of Massachusetts, a seventh-generation descendant of John, found it "not a little amusing to observe what different views are taken as to the indications of the 'hand of nature,' and the paintings of the 'finger of God,' by the same gentlemen, under different circumstances and upon different subjects." Winthrop quipped that "the finger of God never points in a direction contrary to the extension of the glory of the republic."

His Whig colleague Abraham Lincoln, arriving in Congress after war with Mexico had ensued, did not trouble himself with the providential rhetoric with which many of President Polk's supporters, if not the president himself, had pursued the war. Perhaps because the war was now well advanced, Lincoln confined himself, in detailed, lawyerly fashion, to accusing Polk of "from beginning to end, the sheerest deception." Like other Whigs, including John Quincy Adams, Lincoln thought Polk had provoked the war in order to enlarge the territory open to slavery, and then "trust[ed] to escape scrutiny, by fixing the public gaze upon the exceeding brightness of military glory—that attractive rainbow, that rises in showers of blood—that serpent's eye, that charms to destroy."

"This Almost Chosen People"

Lincoln, who would preside over America's bloodiest war, had no millenarian illusions—not in the name of military glory, not in the name of the national mission, not even with respect to whether he himself was, as he wished to be, God's instrument. America, he believed, took its identity and its meaning from a foundational covenant called the Declaration of Independence, in which he discerned more than ringing words about self-evident rights and equal creation. He discerned there a motif of national modesty.

It was—and remains—easy to miss the second half of the Declaration's opening sentence, the half in which the new nation arrogated to itself not only the right to "dissolve the political bands which have connected them with" Great Britain but "to assume among the powers of the earth, the separate and equal station to which the Laws of Nature and of Nature's God entitle them." *Equal,* not *superior.* America, which stood for equality, renounced any claim to be anyone else's overlord. The American people were not inherently graced, but rather, their *political* status entitled them to take their place among other "powers." The Declaration, in Lincoln's view, in effect renewed John Winthrop's reminder that "the eyes of the world are upon us." After Winthrop, as we have seen, those words had become muted for two centuries, not least because of America's exquisite successes and the plenitude of her bounty. America was simply too splendid, too intoxicating, to be taken as anything less than spectacularly entitled.

But Lincoln only once spoke or wrote the phrase "chosen people," and on that single occasion—tantalizingly, subtly, mysteriously—he qualified it. On February 21, 1861, making his slow way from Springfield to Washington to be inaugurated as president, he spoke to New Jersey's State Senate, and being in Trenton, he said, put him in mind of his boyhood reading of Parson Weems's *Life of Washington,* from which he had learned of Washington's crossing the Delaware, his battle against the Hessians, and the "great hardships endured at that time":

> I recollect thinking then, boy even though I was, that there must have been something more than common that those men struggled for; that something even more than National Independence; that something that held out a great promise to all the people of the world to all time to come.

He had imbibed the absolute maximalist meaning of the United States, in short—its unbounded promise to everyone, everywhere, forever. It was not the nation's territorial integrity alone that Lincoln now pledged to retain:

> I am exceedingly anxious that this Union, the Constitution, and the liberties of the people shall be perpetuated in accordance with the original idea for which that struggle was made, and I shall be most happy indeed if I shall be an humble instrument in the hands of the Almighty, and of this, *his almost chosen people,* for perpetuating the object of that great struggle. [Italics added.]

Lincoln knew his King James Bible. He was steeped in it. He knew it precisely, knew its rhythms, and took them into his own. He must have chosen this coinage, this original phrase, deliberately—to signal his understanding that the American mission was not consummated at birth. Its chosenness was incomplete. Perhaps, Lincoln seems to have been suggesting, it depended on whether the country was finally ready to admit black people into the company of the chosen—to rectify the awful refusal to have done so from the moment the nation was born. In other words, in a foreshadowing of the Gettysburg Address, Lincoln seems to have broadly hinted that "the original idea for which" America had pursued its "great struggle," that "something even more than National Independence," that luminous "great promise to all the people of the world to all time to come," was the idea of equality before the law.

Chosenness, in other words, depended upon what the Union would do for itself. America was not for all time chosen but was instead a *choosing* nation, making itself up as it went along—not fully built up in the past, a complete achievement to be conserved, but flawed, imperfect, its shape left to the future. As for Lincoln himself, he *hoped* to be "an humble instrument in the hands of the Almighty," as well as of "his almost chosen people," but he could not be sure matters would work out that way.

As he speechified his way toward Washington, Lincoln invoked "Divine Providence," "the Providence of God," "that God who has never forsaken this people," "the Divine Power, without whose aid we can do nothing," "that Supreme Being who has never forsaken this favored land," "the Maker of the Universe," and "Almighty God." He must have liked the ring of "this favored land," for he used it again in his inaugural speech. But perhaps his enigmatic "almost chosen people" had too much the ring of heresy, for this phrase he did not reuse. He did, however, extend the modesty motif when he addressed the members of the Pennsylvania delegation who congratulated him after the inauguration, urging them not to "insult" or "irritate" the people of other states, "so that we may not, like Pharisees, set ourselves up to be better than other people."

As for the question of whether he would "be an humble instrument in the hands of the Almighty," his uncertainty on this score would deepen during the course of the war. In the spirit of jeremiad, he would deplore the shortcomings of the people he had considered "almost chosen." Proclaiming a National Fast Day in 1863, he suggested, in full prophetic voice, that the awful calamity of civil war, which now desolates the land, may be but a punishment, inflicted upon us, for our presumptuous sins, to the needful end of our national reformation as a whole People. . . . We have forgotten the gracious hand which preserved us in peace, and multiplied and enriched and strengthened us; and we have vainly imagined, in the deceitfulness of our hearts, that all these blessings were produced by some superior wisdom and virtue of our own.

By the time of his Second Inaugural, he would come to doubt which side God was on, because both the Union and the Confederacy

read the same Bible, and pray to the same God; and each invokes His aid against the other. . . . The prayers of both could not be answered; that of neither has been answered fully. The Almighty has His own purposes.

Shortly thereafter, Lincoln doubted that this address had been "immediately popular," for, after all, "Men are not flattered by being shown that there has been a difference of purpose between the Almighty and them."

Lincoln's view of America was devotional and redemptive without being messianic. As he assumed and endured responsibility for hundreds of thousands of deaths in the course of steering the Union through the Civil War, his latent religiosity came to the surface. But he grew paradoxically less certain of the content of America's providential nature. Surely it had one, but it was not for him to know what it was. Yet, if the proceedings of God were opaque, by fits and starts Lincoln came to understand emancipation as a renewal of the national covenant, a collective atonement for the sin of slavery, and a ceremony of respect for the purposes of God.

In his depth and subtlety, Lincoln was at cross-purposes with most of his countrymen. The immensity of the Civil War brought to a boil the sense, shared in North and South alike, that America must have a providential role to play in God's design. Was the carnage not itself stupendous? Must there not be a corresponding stupendous purpose at work behind the scenes? It became common to suggest that God must have a purpose in this war. The question was, what purpose? In the North at large, especially among the more evangelical Protestant churches, religious understandings of the Union cause flourished as the war went on, and accordingly, Lincoln found it politic to ally himself with the militant clergy. Some Protestant clergymen in the North went so far as to say that the war was hastening the millennium. More common was the humbler belief that America's suffering marked it for a distinct mission.

Once the nation was purged of its original and besetting sin, what could stand in the way of that mission? The *Chicago Tribune* was not alone in expressing the judgment that the Civil War "is in its profoundest aspect, a religious contest . . . a war for Christian civilization, for God's pure truth," and in wondering what subsequently "shall prevent the American Union from being, henceforth the crowning national work of the Almighty, the wonder of the world?"

But the Union's ministers did not have God's mission all to themselves. In 1861, the influential Louisiana clergyman Benjamin M. Palmer delivered himself of a jeremiad declaring that the Confederacy's "historic mission" had been "unequivocally assigned by a higher power": "to ratify the covenant." The republic had been tainted by "the fatal error of our Fathers in not making a clear national recognition of God at the outset of the Nation's career," all because the Constitution's drafters had been infected by the "freethinking and infidel spirit which swept like a pestilence over Europe in the seventeenth and eighteenth centuries." But fortunately, the Confederacy could overcome "this perilous atheism," along with the spirit of disobedience that thrived when boys were no longer threatened with being "beaten with rods," and the people were corrupted "by a groveling devotion to merely material interests." "From the beginning," Palmer declared, identifying the Union with Jacob and the Confederacy with Esau, "two nations were in the American womb;

and through the whole period of gestation the supplanter has had his hand upon his brother's heel." No longer! "The separation of North and South was . . . surely decreed of God."

According to the religious historian Mark A. Noll, "For the theologians the end of the war only tightened the bond between God and his American chosen people." The sheer scale of the bloodshed—more than one in fifty Americans died as a direct result of the war—was taken to have reconfirmed that America had been uniquely called, that God's intentions had been rendered self-evident in the restored nation. At Yale's 1865 commencement, to honor graduates who had fallen in battle, the renowned theologian Horace Bushnell indulged in a one-man orgy of consecration on the theme that "without shedding of blood, there is almost nothing great in the world" and thus that "the blood of our dead has . . . begotten . . . the possibility of . . . a true public greatness." At the time of the Constitutional Convention, he said, "We had not bled enough, as yet, to merge our colonial distinctions and make us a proper nation."

Bushnell so effusively, so breathtakingly stirred together the themes of blood sacrifice, national destiny, and the Genesis and Christian frames as to warrant quotation at length. He declared that

> as when the flood of Noah receded . . . [s]o the unity now to be developed, after this war-deluge is over, is even like to be more cordial. It will be no more thought of as a mere human compact . . . but it will be that bond of common life which God has touched with blood; a sacredly heroic, Providentially tragic unity, where God's cherubim stand guard over grudges and hates and remembered jealousies, and the sense of nationality becomes even a kind of religion.

To Bushnell, no previous suffering had ever matched the scale or even the type—the popular, democratic nature—of the Civil War bloodshed:

107

So much worth and character were never sacrificed in a human war before. And by this mournful offering, we have bought a really stupendous chapter of history. . . . Nations can sufficiently live only as they find how to energetically die. In this view, some of us have felt, for a long time, the want of a more historic life, to make us a truly great people. This want is now supplied; for now, at last, we may be said to have gotten a history. . . . Henceforth our new world even heads the old, having in this single chapter risen clean above it. The wars of Caesar, and Frederic, and Napoleon, were grand enough in their leadership, but there is no grand people or popular greatness in them, consequently no true dignity. In this war of ours it is the people, moving by their own decisive motion, in the sense of their own great cause.

All the arts would thrive in America now that it had come into its nationhood. The very language would be reborn. "Henceforth we are not going to write English, but American. . . . We are now to have our own civilization, think our own thoughts, rhyme in our own measures, kindle our own fires, and make our own canons of criticism, even as we settle the proprieties of punishment for our own traitors." The martyred Lincoln would stand first in a new line of leaders: "In the place of politicians we are going to have, at least, some statesmen; for we have gotten the pitch of a grand, new, Abrahamic statesmanship, unsophisticated, honest and real; no cringing sycophancy, or cunning art of demagogy."

America, in sum, would become more than "a light unto the nations," a bringer of truth to the unenlightened world of Gentiles—in Bushnell's rhetoric, it looked more like a conflagration:

In these rivers of blood we have now bathed our institutions, and they are henceforth to be hallowed in our sight. Government is now become Providential,—no more a mere creature of our human will, but a grandly moral affair. . . . What then shall we look for but for a new era now to break forth, a day of new gifts and powers and holy endowments from on high, wherein great communities and friendly nations shall be girded in sacrifice, for the cause of Christ their Master?

By severest contrast, the war only intensified Lincoln's doubt that Americans were God's people. But by the time Bushnell orated in New Haven, Lincoln was dead.

Bushnell's address resounded in a nation desperate to assure itself that the war had been worth its human toll. "The war's staggering human cost," the historian Drew Gilpin Faust has written, "demanded a new sense of national destiny, one designed to ensure that lives had been sacrificed for appropriately lofty ends." But what "sense" was that to be?

There had long been an alternative notion of what it would mean to be chosen: that the true test for God's people was in their approximation to justice. During much of American history such a notion was, in a sense, recessive—buried just beneath the surface, eclipsed by the idea that America had been chosen by sheer grace of God, by some combination of geography, nature, race, and enshrined belief. During the war, the escaped slave and abolitionist leader Frederick Douglass declared that the war had a "manifest destiny," a "sacred significance," a "mission" of "national regeneration"—"to unify and reorganize the institutions of the country." But even more:

> The blow we strike is not merely to free a country or continent, but the whole world, from slavery; for when slavery falls here, it will fall everywhere. . . . We are writing the statutes of eternal justice and liberty in the blood of the worst of tyrants as a warning to all aftercomers.

Then, on the very day of Lincoln's assassination, Gilbert Haven, a white Methodist antislavery minister (later appointed bishop) in

Boston, preached that racial equality was integral to America's providential mission, and that *blacks* were "the chosen people of God who for three centuries have groaned in their prison-houses, and whose liberation and exaltation, not our Union nor our liberties, are the great, almost the sole cause, of the outstretching of His arm." This theme found a resonant spokesman in the great abolitionist agitator Wendell Phillips, who told an 1868 meeting of the American Anti-Slavery Society that "the lips of Providence" were telling the American people, "Only by being just shall you be strong," and "Wherever you go, wherever you touch American history, God has marked the relations of this [African American] race to ourselves as the test of American moral life—as the fulcrum and the lever of American political progress." According to the literary historian Christopher Z. Hobson, it was a "constant element" in the African American prophetic tradition "that the United States would be tested and judged by its turn toward or from God's justice, and that the race's trials begun on the shores of Africa were destined to end . . . in a redeemed, transfigured United States."

There was an even more focused way to construe divine election. If white Americans were "the new Israel," drawing sustenance from the book of Revelation and the New Testament, it was common for black Americans to see themselves as (in the historian Silke Lehmann's words) "members of the old and still suffering Israel." African Americans turned to the Old Testament for inspiration, referring to Exodus, Babylonian exile, and the "suffering servant" passage of Isaiah 53:

> To whom is the arm of the Lord revealed? . . . He [who] is despised and rejected of men; a man of sorrows, and acquainted with grief . . . wounded for our transgressions . . . bruised for our iniquities . . . cut off out of the land of the living.

In 1808, marking the abolition of the slave trade, Absalom Jones, a former slave himself and the first African American priest of the

Episcopal Church, declared that "Jehovah has as in the case of his ancient and chosen people the Jews, come down to deliver our suffering countrymen from the hands of their oppressors." Bondage was preparation, and would culminate, thanks to God, in deliverance—and not for the oppressed race alone.

Providence was dangerous medicine, of course. It could serve as balm for a wicked system or an alibi for inaction. During the Civil War, no less a figure than Frederick Douglass scorned the use of references to Providence "to make the black man of America the open book out of which the American people are to learn lessons of wisdom, power and goodness." He found it "cowardly to shuffle our responsibilities upon the shoulders of Providence." He condemned the deployment of providential references against emancipation and, weirdly, in favor of black colonization—for until emancipation, many whites, including Lincoln, viewed the "base passions" of racial prejudice as what Douglass called "inevitable ordinations of Divine Providence."

But the theme of redemption through suffering outlasted emancipation, as when, in 1877, the Pan-Africanist Episcopal priest Alexander Crummell, in a sermon on "The Destined Superiority of the Negro," heralded

> the great truth, that when God does not destroy a people, but, on the contrary, trains and disciplines it, it is an indication that He intends to make something of them, and to do something for them. . . . In a sense, not equal, indeed, to the case of the Jews, but parallel, in a lower degree, such a people are a "chosen people" of the Lord. There is, so to speak, a covenant relation which God has established between Himself and them; dim and partial, at first, in its manifestations; but which is sure to come to the sight of men and angels, clear, distinct, and luminous.

Evidently the grandest thing to be said about a people was that, in God's eyes, they ranked second to the Jews.

Few of any race were willing to discard altogether the entire drama of chosenness, as did the abolitionist William Lloyd Garrison when, in 1876, he complained about a proposal for inscribing a centennial monument with words from I Samuel 7:12: "Hitherto hath the Lord helped us." Wrote Garrison:

> I object to this phraseology because it seems to imply that the Lord has a deeper concern for American interests than he has for those of any other people outside of our territorial limits.

Garrison minced no words about Israel old or new:

> The ancient Jews had the egotism and self-complacency to consider themselves "the chosen people of God" and fancied that they were the special objects of his regard as against the rest of mankind; but, instead of having been the better for this boast, the final result was their utter overthrow, and miserable dispersion in various parts of the earth, which continues to this day.

Since pride in chosenness went before a fall, Garrison considered America forewarned to relinquish the idea of a special mission in favor of a radical universalism in which America would "present to the world the sublime spectacle of a nation in which there are none to molest or make afraid, equal and exact justice is meted out to every man, liberty and peace reign universally, and righteousness shines in its constellated crown a star of the first magnitude."

"Have Done with Childish Days"

But in an era when white superiority was in the air, America's "covenant relation" to God could be defined without recourse to the highly charged idea of emancipation. For in the Civil War's aftermath, not only did the states of the former Confederacy mobilize to roll back Reconstruction—by ejecting African Americans from power, establishing the lawless terror of the Ku Klux Klan, and installing Jim Crow—but by 1877 the North was willing to let the vanquished Confederacy get away with it. If the American nation had been promoted by Providence, the "sacred significance" of the Civil War could be detected elsewhere than in the racial justice that was paramount for Frederick Douglass and William Lloyd Garrison. Increasingly, white Americans came to believe—in Drew Gilpin Faust's words—that "the United States' new and elevated destiny became bound up with the nation itself: its growing power, its wealth, its extent, its influence." With the devaluing of individual life, amid all the carnage, came numbness, and after numbness came a surge of vigorous, aggressive, militaristic love for the nation that had suffered, and commanded, so much death.

One of the nonfiction best-sellers of the nineteenth century—it sold 130,000 copies during its first five years in print, and excerpts were widely reprinted in newspapers—was a millenarian tract by an Ohio missionary declaring: "Ours is the elect nation for the age to come. We are the chosen people. We cannot afford to wait. The plans of God will not wait." The Reverend Josiah Strong swathed his enthusiasm with demographic and economic statistics, and in support of his fervor for American destiny quoted Charles Darwin, Herbert Spencer, and Horace Bushnell. But unlike many of his ideological descendants to come, Strong warned against "political optimism, one of the vices of the American people . . . as senseless as pessimism is faithless." It was "foolish," Strong thought, to neglect the "perils" by which America was gravely beleaguered—immigration, Romanism, secular schools, Mormonism, intemperance, socialism, decadent cities, and the abuse of wealth in the form of "Mammonism," "materialism," and "luxuriousness." (As an instance of the latter, Strong cited "the material splendor" of Solomon's reign over Israel, which culminated in "the immediate dismemberment of the kingdom.") To live up to its mission in "one of the closing stages in the world's career," America would have to "struggle," to "become

God's right arm in his battle with the world's ignorance and oppression and sin." To use a favorite word of Theodore Roosevelt, one of his later readers, America needed to live *strenuously*.

Reverend Strong's dithyramb swept toward a crescendo of race-mindedness. "The Anglo-Saxon race" were the people best suited to work the will of God—even superior to the Jews, in fact, because the former were "highly mixed," more so than the English, and destined toward what Herbert Spencer called "the eventual mixture of the allied varieties of the Aryan race." Civilization could now "leav[e] behind the barbarism of war" thanks to the mental improvements that accompanied physical ones in America. The Anglo-Saxons had "an instinct or genius for colonizing," whence "it is chiefly to the English and American peoples that we must look for the evangelization of the world." God was "training the Anglo-Saxon race for an hour sure to come in the world's future," when "the world would enter upon . . . *the final competition of races, for which the Anglo-Saxon is being schooled.*"

Scarcely pausing to draw a breath, Strong piled on: "Does it not look as if God were not only preparing in our Anglo-Saxon civilization the die with which to stamp the peoples of the earth, but as if he were massing behind that die the mighty power with which to press it?" Simultaneously, God was also "preparing mankind to receive our impress," and thus, "no war of extermination is needful; the contest is not one of arms, but of vitality and of civilization." Missionary work was the key. In short, Strong asked,

> Is there room for reasonable doubt that this race, unless devitalized by alcohol and tobacco, is destined to dispossess many weaker races, assimilate others and mold the remainder, until, in a very true and important sense, it has Anglo-Saxonized mankind?

Even Africa would not long repel colonization, Strong explained, as the Dutch Boers, with their "aggressive vigor," had established by showing how to supplant races already enfeebled. Thus, in what Dr. Bushnell calls "the out-populating power of the Christian stock," may be found God's final and complete solution of the dark problem of heathenism among many inferior peoples.

Strong was one of the authorial lights to emerge from the complex mélange of the Third Great Awakening, which featured, throughout the latter third of the nineteenth century, renewed waves of revivalism and missionary work, the founding of denominational colleges, YMCAs, and religious youth groups, the campaign for Prohibition, as well as the progressive reform politics of the Social Gospel. Toward the end of the nineteenth century and the beginning of the twentieth, much of this work received a boost from Theodore Roosevelt, though he was not so breathlessly messianic.

Indeed, the younger TR was deeply suspicious of the "emotionally religious" who came to the fore during the Third Great Awakening. He preferred the allure of racial superiority, which filled the intellectual atmosphere in which he came of age. Such thinking, in the Social Darwinist vein, suffused the courses he took at Harvard (1876–80) and Columbia (1880–81). As he was drawn to grand strategy practiced by the naval advocate Alfred Thayer Mahan, he was also drawn to big biological theory—to Darwin, who had "fairly revolutionized thought," as well as much lesser lights who thought that race was destiny. For fully fifteen years, in the dominant tenor of his time, Roosevelt's historical writing was pervaded by talk of "Anglo-Saxonism" and "Aryan" as well as the then-fashionable "Teutonic" civilization. Later, he would say that if he were rewriting his early books, he would not have used the term "Anglo-Saxon," calling it "an absurd name unless applied to the dominant race in England between the Fifth and the Eleventh Centuries." "Aryan," he would eventually conclude, was a linguistic description, not a biological one. In later years, he gravitated toward the term "English-speaking race."

Still, according to the historian Thomas G. Dyer, a close student of what he calls Roosevelt's "racial rhapsodizing," while Roosevelt discarded the earlier labels, "he preserved the substance of [their] most central tenets." During his years in the presidency, he read devotedly—obsessively—on racial themes, and while quarreling at times with one or another author over particulars, he continued to embrace overall the notions of racial hierarchy and determinacy. In his letters, Dyer writes, "a crude idiom always lurk[ed] just beneath the surface of the more genteel, theoretical terms." In 1906, Roosevelt wrote to his friend Owen Wister, the novelist, that blacks are "altogether inferior to whites."

In one respect Roosevelt far outmuscled Josiah Strong, who viewed martial prowess as no more than a preliminary phase in the coming battle of civilizations. Writing in 1889, Roosevelt celebrated American settlers who gave no quarter in their 1776 war with the Cherokees: "Bible-readers" who "joined in prayer and thanksgiving for their successes; but this did not hinder them from scalping the men they killed. They were too well-read in the merciless wars of the Chosen People to feel the need of sparing the fallen; indeed they would have been most foolish had they done so; for they were battling with a heathen enemy more ruthless and terrible than ever was Canaanite or Philistine." Once they had been defeated definitively in battle, Roosevelt added, Indians would be absorbed into the superior race through miscegenation. Given the "breeding powers of the old-stock Americans," Roosevelt could affirm "the melting pot" without fear that the "new race" of "Americanized" Americans would cease to improve. Nevertheless, throughout his last quarter-century he was fixated on the declining fertility of the "old-stock" and, as a result, obsessed with the dire prospect of "race suicide." Worst of all, he was convinced that black soldiers were inferior fighters.

Roosevelt does not seem to have repeated direct references to the "Chosen People," but his martial insistence did not slacken, with chosenness quivering between the lines when he told the officers of the Naval War College, in June 1897, "All the great masterful races have been fighting races. . . . Cowardice in a race, as in an individual, is the unpardonable sin." As assistant secretary of the navy under President William McKinley, who required prodding to go to war with Spain, Roosevelt still found it necessary to add that while the point of a "great navy" was to guarantee peace, "no triumph of peace is quite so great as the supreme triumphs of war." The Spanish-American War vindicated his insistence that war was a necessary test for civilization: "It is only the warlike power of a civilized people that can give peace to the world. . . . [T]hat the barbarians recede or are conquered . . . is due solely to the power of the mighty civilized races which have not lost the fighting instinct, and which by their expansion are gradually bringing peace into the red wastes where the barbarian peoples of the world hold sway." Accepting the 1900 vice presidential nomination, he took pains—more than a little defensively—to link his views with those of American predecessors:

> There is nothing even remotely resembling "imperialism" or "militarism" involved in the present development of that policy of expansion which has been part of the history of America from the day she became a nation. . . . This policy is only imperialistic in the sense that Jefferson's policy in Louisiana was imperialistic; only military in the sense that Jackson's policy toward the Seminoles or Custer's toward the Sioux embodied militarism.

Though slower to war than TR liked, President McKinley came to consider it "a holy cause" to advance "the banner of liberty" across the Pacific. The Spanish-American War itself fueled popular—specifically religious—feeling that the cause of expansion was not only just but divine. "The Philippines, like Cuba and Puerto Rico, were entrusted to our hands by the providence of God," McKinley proclaimed in February 1899. Missionary work awaited. Expansionist Christians of both major parties agreed that national tutelage was a duty; for example, a college professor named Woodrow Wilson in 1901 celebrated the annexation of the Philippines and Puerto Rico on the ground that "they are children and we are men in these deep matters of government and justice." For all his attachment to "muscular Christianity," TR contemplating the Philippines was (at least publicly) stirred less by the divinity of the mission and more by his friend Rudyard Kipling's urgings in behalf of the self-sacrificial obligations of empire based on racial superiority. Kipling wrote "The White Man's Burden," after all, to urge Congress to support the takeover of the Philippines. "Go bind your sons to exile," Kipling urged—not in the name of self-interest but "to serve your captives' need" in the "thankless" duty "to seek another's profit." "Take up the White Man's burden—/ Have done with childish days—" Childishness, after all, was the *Filipinos'* sad condition (as Roosevelt's staunch ally, Senator Albert Jeremiah Beveridge of Indiana, also said); Americans were born to greater things. If eventually the likes of the Filipinos were to become capable of self-government, all the greater was the greatness of America.

Despite earlier flirtations with the idea of the Americans as a chosen people, TR, who read the Bible avidly throughout his life, for the most part did not consider them *innately* divine. The superiority of the English-speaking peoples was not a timeless fixture of divine manufacture; it was the product of their own struggle toward a higher civilization, and required unending virility and sacrifice to sustain. "Backward" peoples such as the Filipinos, if they accepted American tutelage, could rise, too.

In the spirit of forced uplift, TR also diverged from the divinity-inspired bombast of allies such as Senator Beveridge. Like Roosevelt, Beveridge believed that a core purpose of government was to "manufacture manhood"—ruling the Philippines, whose inhabitants were "children," would enable Americans to become the "master people of the world"—but he underscored (in a 1900 Senate speech thumping for annexation of the Philippines) that it was *God* who made Americans "the master organizers of the world to establish system where chaos reigns. . . . He has marked the American people as His chosen nation to finally lead in the regeneration of the world. This is the divine mission of America. . . . We will not renounce our part in the mission of the race, trustees under God of the civilization of the world. And we will move forward to our work, not howling out regrets like slaves whipped to their burdens, but with gratitude for a task worthy of our strength, and thanksgiving to Almighty God that He has marked us as His chosen people, henceforth to lead in the re-generation of the world." American principles constituted a "divine event." "The eternal movement of the American people toward the mastery of the world . . . is a destiny neither vague nor undesirable. It is definite, splendid and holy."

The counterview was stated by the anti-imperialists—among them William Jennings Bryan, William James, and Mark Twain—who in various ways imagined America as a veritable "city upon a hill" lighting the way for other nations by fashioning itself into a more just society. America had, in a sense, chosen itself as a moral exemplar—and could, Bryan insisted, "shake thrones and dissolve aristocracies" not through force of arms but through "its silent example," giving "light and inspiration to those who sit in darkness," becoming "the supreme moral factor in the world's progress and the accepted arbi-ter of the world's disputes, a republic whose history, like the path of the just, 'is as the shining light that shineth more and more unto the perfect day.'" Addressing the Democrats' 1900 convention, Bryan was quoting from Proverbs to promote a millenarian version of American universality—for the American message was as limitless as it was anti-imperialist. "I would not exchange the glory of this republic for the glory of all the empires that have risen and fallen since time began," he trumpeted. America hastened "the coming of an universal broth-erhood," because the republic "rested securely upon the mountain of eternal truth," because it stood "erect while empires all around are bowed beneath the weight of their own armaments—a republic whose flag is loved while other flags are only feared."

The anti-imperialists had their own idea of what conquest would do to the American flag. In a letter of 1898, the philosopher William James declared that the country had foregone its erstwhile claim to be "a better nation morally than the rest . . . exert[ing] great international influence by throwing in our 'moral weight.' Dreams!" In 1901, Mark Twain, at his most scathing, noted that the colonized Filipinos "have become suspicious of the Blessings of Civilization," and proposed "as for a flag for the Philippine Province . . . our usual flag, with the white stripes painted black and the stars replaced by the skull and cross-bones." In 1902, the prominent critic Charles Eliot Norton came close to saying that it was the anti-imperialists themselves who truly held title to the status of chosenness: "While all the congregation of the children of Israel are wandering in the wilderness of Sin . . . we, the little remnant of the house of Judah that has escaped, must comfort one another as best we may." In 1907, James still believed that America in the latter years of the nineteenth century had taken a drastically wrong turn—that "the manner in which the McKinley administration railroaded the country into its policy of conquest was abominable, and the way the country puked up its ancient soul at the first touch of temptation, and followed, was sickening," even if McKinley subsequently "did what he could to redeem things" through more benign administration.

"Against the Rulers of the Darkness of This World"

From Theodore Roosevelt's martial flamboyance to Woodrow Wilson's Christian sobriety was more than a stylistic shift—it marked an ideological rupture over the question of what made America chosen. In TR's view, the America exceptionally designated for a global mission was Christian and race-based; for Wilson, it was democratic. Not that Wilson's views on race were more advanced than TR's. By heritage as well as belief, he was arguably as much of a white supremacist as TR (whose mother was raised in a slave-owning plantation family; her two brothers were Confederate naval officers). Wilson, who as president tolerated segregation in government agencies, was a Virginian whose father owned slaves; in one of his prepresidential history books, he wrote that "in the heart of the South, . . . [d]omestic slaves were almost uniformly dealt with indulgently and even affectionately by their masters," and that "in the States where the negroes were most numerous, or their leaders most shrewd and unprincipled," Reconstruction produced "an extraordinary carnival of public crime."

But Wilson's faith in America's unique calling was rooted in political ideals and religious faith, not race. He was raised by a schismatic Confederate Presbyterian minister who was himself both the son and nephew of Presbyterian ministers; both father and son described themselves as "Covenanters"—descendants of the Scots who allied with the Puritans in seventeenth-century Britain and, like them, took inspiration from God's covenant with the Jews. Throughout his life, Wilson was outspoken in public about his idea of divine mission. In a 1911 lecture on "The Bible and Progress," he proclaimed: "Nothing makes America great except her thoughts, except her ideals, except her acceptance of those standards of these [biblical] pages of revelation."

During the 1912 presidential campaign, Wilson resorted to the language of divinity when he expressed confidence that America was "chosen, and prominently chosen, to show the way to the nations of the world how they shall walk in the paths of liberty," and in the same speech: "If I did not believe in Providence I would feel like a man going blindfolded through a haphazard world." It was during this same campaign that apocalyptic fervor swept away the Bull Moose candidate Theodore Roosevelt as well, with his famous declaration: "We stand at Armageddon, and we battle for the Lord."

Indeed, during the first two decades of the twentieth century, the spirit of Social Gospel rode high across party lines, proposing that millennial hopes were to be delivered by a holy *nation*. In 1909, Reverend Washington Gladden, a Social Gospel leader befriended by TR, articulated this view in full prophetic glow:

Has not the time come when we must learn to look for employment of the nations by the divine Power, in the evangelization of the world? . . . [T]he salvation of the world . . . is certainly the prophetic conception. It was through the nation that the kingdom of God was to be set up in the world. . . . All these glowing promises made by the old prophets, of the triumphs yet to be won for the kingdom of God in the world, are made to the nation and not to the church. . . . In truth, the evangel which the divine love is seeking to proclaim to all the peoples, is a truth so large that it can only be adequately uttered by a nation's voice.

For Wilson, too, religious fervor with a nationalist bent generated the moral imperative to actively take the part of good against evil. Early and late, he cited Ephesians 6:12 to defend the Manichaean proposition that "we wrestle, not against flesh and blood, but against principalities, against powers, against the rulers of the darkness of this world, against wickedness in high places." As president, he marked the fiftieth anniversary of the Battle of Gettysburg on July 4, 1913, by calling America "the nation that God has builded by our hands" and declaring that "war fitted us for action, and action never ceases." He felt this way when he launched armed interventions in Mexico, Cuba, the Dominican Republic, Haiti, Honduras, and Nicaragua, proclaiming, on July 4, 1914, "I am going to teach the South American republics to elect good men." And when his ventures in liberal imperialism did not work out as planned, he reconsidered America's tactics and shifted to multilateralism, while retaining his confidence that America was designated the carrier of a unique global mission—redefined as a matter of making the world "safe for democracy."

Wilson successfully spoke for the bulk of popular sentiment in his 1916 reelection campaign, when he harnessed his missionary ideals for national preeminence to the compelling slogan "He kept us out of war." He channeled America's exceptionalist fervor in January 1917, when he claimed to transcend politics-as-usual by playing peacemaker between the warring alliances, insisting that "Americans set up a new nation in the high and honorable hope . . . [to] show mankind the way to liberty," and that "[m]ankind is looking now for freedom of life, not for equipoises of power." (The political scientist Adam Gómez rightly calls Wilson's speech "messianic and millennial," possessed of "a strong element of the apocalyptic.") Wilson continued to feel this way when he brought America into World War I as a crusading universalist ("the wrongs against which we now array ourselves . . . cut to the very roots of human life"). He continued to feel this way during the war, when he stood for "Force, Force to the utmost, Force without stint or limit, the righteous and triumphant Force which shall make Right the law of the world, and cast every selfish dominion down in the dust. . . . We shall give all that we love and all that we have to redeem the world and make it fit for free men like ourselves to live in."

During and after America's engagement in World War I, Wilson often identified America with the Crusaders. This was no merely partisan view: ex-president TR, who continued to joust with President Wilson over war policy, declared in September 1917: "To my fellow Americans I preach the sword of the Lord and of Gideon." Wilson told the Senate in 1919 that the Versailles Treaty was "produced by the hand of God." Defending the League of Nations, he harked back to the religious declarations of his youth when he declared: "I am a Covenanter!" But for the most part, Wilson believed that God conducted His work by wielding the strong arms of the nation. Although his explicit references to God or Christianity dwindled after the war—perhaps because Wilson discerned that the Republican case against the League might be strengthened if he resorted to any more rhetorical overreach—he continued to speak of faith, crusades, and martyrdom, with American *political* ideals now justifying religious zeal. In Boston on February 24, 1919, Wilson exulted that Europeans, at the moment when they realized America's mission was selfless, "raised their eyes to heaven, when they saw men in khaki coming across the sea in the spirit of crusaders." On Memorial Day that year, he declared that American troops, whose "like has not been seen since the far days of the Crusades . . . had a touch of the high spirit of religion, that they knew they were exhibiting a spiritual as well as a physical might, and those of us who know and love America know that they were discovering to the whole world the true spirit and devotion of their motherland." Adam Gómez does not exaggerate when he characterizes Wilson's view this way: "The War would be the Armageddon to the League's Millennium, as the old world ended and a new one began."

Soon enough, of course, that new world arrived stillborn. Wilson's millennial utopia fell afoul of Republican realism. True to Wilson's vision, some shards of the shattered empires of Europe and the Levant made the most of self-determination, but the Great War also "made the world safe" for a punitive peace that shattered Germany and opened a door to the Nazi seizure of power. The onetime Allies stood by as Adolf Hitler tore up Versailles. Divinity seemed to retire from the scene. World War I turned out to be only the first act of another Thirty Years' War.

Public rhetoric after Wilson was more reticent—embarrassed, perhaps, or simply more businesslike—about referring to Americans as a chosen people. The theme of divine favoritism slid into the shadows to manifest itself in a more secular vernacular. The Republican presidents who succeeded Wilson had little use for his expansive rhetoric. Neither, most of the time, did Franklin Roosevelt, though he was more than willing to quote Scripture in public, to speak straightforwardly of "good" versus "evil," even to speak of "one of the great choices of history—religion against godlessness" in his 1940 acceptance speech, and otherwise to avail himself of quasi-religious terminology during his twelve years in the White House. "We are fighting to cleanse the world of ancient evils, ancient ills," he concluded his State of the Union Address, January 6, 1942.

We are inspired by a faith that goes back through all the years
to the first chapter of the Book of Genesis: "God created man

in His own image." . . . We on our side are striving to be true to that divine heritage. We are fighting, as our fathers have fought, to uphold the doctrine that all men are equal in the sight of God. Those on the other side are striving to destroy this deep belief and to create a world in their own image— a world of tyranny and cruelty and serfdom. . . . No compromise can end that conflict. There never has been—there never can be—successful compromise between good and evil. Only total victory can reward the champions of tolerance, and decency, and freedom, and faith.

But FDR's emphasis was hortatory rather than boastful. Americans needed to strive, to take nothing for granted. He appealed to God on behalf of universal values rather than resting on the assumption that America was the beneficiary of divine election. Still, if ever there was a time for presidential language to flirt with moral absolutism and biblical authority, this was the time. Even America's most hardheaded, anti-apocalyptic theologian, Reinhold Niebuhr, saw wartime tribulation as a measure of God's having "chosen us in this fateful period of world history," though he explicitly dissociated himself from the exclusivity of Amos's declaration in God's name that "You only have I chosen: therefore will I visit you with your iniquities."

Piety outlasted the war, as did much of World War II's millennial shading, now transposed into the key of the Cold War. Both Harry Truman and Dwight Eisenhower were more devout than FDR, and had been even before the general religious upwelling of the fifties. Truman, the Baptist, was comfortable with the notion that America was chosen by God. "Divine Providence has played a great part in our history," he declared in 1951. "I have the feeling that God has created us and brought us to our present position and strength for some great purpose." Truman's counsel, Clark Clifford, who was deeply involved in the president's decision to recognize the newly declared State of Israel in 1948 against fierce State Department opposition, wrote later, at a time when there could no longer be any political advantage to win points for himself, or Truman, with the Jews:

> From his reading of the Old Testament he felt the Jews derived a legitimate historical right to Palestine, and he sometimes cited such biblical lines as Deuteronomy 1:8: "Behold, I have given up the land before you; go in and take possession of the land which the Lord hath sworn unto your fathers, to Abraham, to Isaac and to Jacob."

Meanwhile, in 1948, Ike published *Crusade in Europe,* wherein he wrote: "Because only by the utter destruction of the Axis was a decent world possible, the war became for me a crusade in the traditional sense of that often misused word." Ike quoted the Bible at staff meetings and corrected misquotations. During his presidency, national prayer breakfasts began, the words "under God" were inserted into the Pledge of Allegiance, and "In God We Trust" became the national motto, to appear not only on coins but on paper money as well. During those years, the notion of a more or less cogent (though anodyne) "Judeo-Christian tradition"—a notion floated in the 1940s, partly in order to put a name on the anti-Nazi consensus—was on the upswing, and its theological credentials were burnished. But it was not only the religious establishment that Eisenhower encouraged. While in the White House, Ike regularly hosted Billy Graham, whose tent revival meetings had begun in 1949.

Like Graham, in the words of the religious historian Gary Scott Smith, Ike "frequently depicted" the Cold War "as a struggle between God and Satan or good and evil"—although he was opposed to overthrowing the Satanic adversary by force, believing that it would eventually collapse of its own weight. Unquestionably and unquestioningly, he believed in the moral superiority of the United States. He thought it "the greatest force that God" had "ever allowed to exist on His footstool." Nuclear weapons, not unrealistically, fueled his apocalyptic imagination. At the same time, he insisted that the United States was "truly trying to follow in the footsteps of the Prince of Peace, and to establish a just peace for the world," as he told a religious assemblage in 1956, having dispatched the CIA to overthrow democratically elected regimes in Iran and Guatemala. Like other presidents before him, all the way back to George Washington, Eisenhower saw "the hand of Providence" at work in American life.

Eisenhower's faith was both more and less than a credo. At the time he ran for president in 1952, he did not belong to a church, and was baptized (as a respectable Presbyterian, at Billy Graham's suggestion) only after his election. Ike's faith demanded little but symbolic affirmation, though it came surrounded by a haze of religiosity—a belief in belief. In this amorphousness, he was in tune with the religious tone of the postwar years, when (in a 1947 poll) religious leaders ranked highest for their contributions to national well-being, outranking politicians and businessmen, and (in 1957) *96 percent* of Americans professed membership in a church or synagogue. The important thing for America was a negative—not to be secular, not to be (like the USSR) atheist. From a political point of view, the vagueness of Ike's religiosity was also its strength, for it allowed all manner of the faithful to take shelter within its embrace. Ike was easily—and unfairly—mocked for declaring, "Our form of government has no sense unless it is founded in a deeply felt religious faith and I don't care what it is," but in this remark he was true to the circumambient piety of his moment. With his broad smile, Eisenhower had a particularly winning way of displaying his faith—a convention mocked in *Mad* magazine's Alfred E. Neuman's "What, me worry?" idiot grin.

Neither John F. Kennedy nor Lyndon Johnson offered new twists on the notion that America was chosen, nor did they veer in the direction of millennial expectations. The religious controversy that swirled around Kennedy took place during his campaign—it had to do with whether the Pope would have a private tunnel into the White House—but once in office, Kennedy was not given to religious, let alone millennial, language. Johnson had been raised in the Disciples of Christ, which had millennial origins in the Second Great Awakening but in the middle of the twentieth century demanded no belief other than "acceptance of Jesus Christ as Lord and Savior." Johnson was fond of quoting Isaiah 1:18: "Come now, and let us reason together"—he is said to have had the line inscribed on a plaque on his desk—but what he meant by these words was muscularly persuading opponents into agreement; he showed no interest in End Times thinking, and Isaiah had no particular bearing on his understanding of America's place in the world. In his inaugural address of 1965, Johnson said: "The American covenant called on us to help show the way for the liberation of man," and, in a momentary return to the old-time spirit of the jeremiad, proceeded to quote Solomon, who proclaimed that "the judgment of God is harshest on those who are most favored." But as with Kennedy, Johnson's religious sentiments were muted, his End Times rhetoric was nonexistent, and his sense of America's relation to God was far more like Eisenhower's than different from it.

By this time in American history, indeed, the leadership consensus had shifted from strenuousness to cheerfulness. Except in the eschatology of the hardcore Christians who anticipated a coming thousand-year reign of Jesus (the so-called "premillennial dispensationalists"), tribulation was no longer a mark of America's distinctive place in history. Rather, cheerfulness was required, coupled with relentless optimism. Some historians detect this shift as early as the late nineteenth century, but it is most visible after World War I, with the growth of the consumer economy. Commercial culture came to commend—or command—cheerfulness, as did Dale Carnegie's best-selling success manual of 1936, *How to Win Friends and Influence People*. The universally recognizable smiley face first cropped up in 1963, becoming well-nigh ubiquitous even (or especially) in the subsequent course of a decade of conspicuous violence. It was as if

the appropriate leadership style was now to show that a life strenuously lived included facing the future with unflagging cheer.

The most novel note in the sixties' approach to American chosenness was struck by the opposition. The heresy was musical. The decade's most brilliantly savage minstrel proposed sardonically that
the entire idea of God's choosing a people was fundamentally—absurdly—misconceived. The notion of a covenant relation with God
came from "history books," but history books were not the proper
authority. Interestingly, when he ticked off dubious wars in American history, Bob Dylan in 1963 found no fault with the notion that
the country had fought something like a holy war against the Axis
powers; rather, his lament about World War II was that having forgiven the Germans, we could subsequently decide that now they
"too / Have God on their side." Lincoln had found the mind of God
impenetrable and human pretensions to read it impertinent; Dylan
found them worse than impertinent—he found them cynical. But
like Jefferson, who wondered "if ever [God] had a chosen people,"
Dylan closed on a conditional note. He abandoned his sardonic tone
for a straightforward declaration that if there was really a covenant
with America, it bound *God:* "If God's on our side / He'll stop the
next war." The subversive note could not have been more stark.

For the most part, though, during the decade between the mid-
1950s and the mid-1960s, reform movements avoided the dynamite
of the chosenness theme. Chosenness was neither much affirmed
nor much deplored. Instead, the movements renewed the theme
that America's proper mission was a mission of justice. The Reverend Martin Luther King, Jr., like many another African American
cleric before and since, evoked the Exodus story, identifying African
Americans with the Israelites—and also with an all-around America
that was propitious for justice because it was constituted with the
right values, divinely inspired ones among them. At the beginning of
the Montgomery, Alabama, bus boycott in 1955, King told a prayer

meeting: "If we are wrong, then the Supreme Court of this nation is wrong. If we are wrong, the Constitution of the United States is wrong. If we are wrong, God Almighty is wrong." But when King heralded "the glory of America, with all of its faults," he was not exactly saying that America had been divinely chosen from the start, that it was predestined to stand first among nations, or that there was any prospect of End Times apocalypse.

On a scale of potentially world-saving projects, the civil rights movement and the early New Left regarded themselves in a modest light, as the salvation of an America that deserved to be saved, though not because Americans were divinely chosen to liberate the rest of the world. In all of Martin Luther King's papers thus far published, we find no explicit references to America as chosen. The closest he comes is this passage from a 1958 sermon in Detroit:

> The God of the universe stands there in all of His love and forgiving power saying, "Come home . . . America, I'm not going to give you up. If you will rise up out of the far country of segregation and discrimination, I will take you in, America. And I will bring you back to your true home."

King imagines that God will save America if America will save itself—from itself. But this is not to say that America is chosen. Rather, in 1960, King declared that "it may well be that the Negro is God's instrument to save the soul of America." On many occasions, including his luminous 1967 sermon against the Vietnam War at Riverside Church in New York, King spoke of the movement as "a fight to save the soul of America."

> In 1957 when a group of us formed the Southern Christian Leadership Conference, we chose as our motto: "To save the soul of America." We were convinced that we could not limit our vision to certain rights for black people, but instead affirmed the conviction that America would never be free or

saved from itself until the descendants of its slaves were loosed completely from the shackles they still wear.

America unsaved would be America "doomed," condemned to "lose her moral and political voice because she failed to live up to the great dream of America and to her great ideas." But still, there is no promise of absolute once-and-for-all salvation of the sort trumpeted in Revelation theology.

King's clarion voice proclaimed an American road not—or not yet—taken: the road of self-renewal. What if the mighty thing about America was that it had a mighty soul to be saved? That it could transcend itself? What if greatness lay in movement along the trajectory of what he liked to call "the arc of the moral universe," which, while long, "bends toward justice"—though never quite reaches it? What if the operative word in American history was the "almost" that Abraham Lincoln had deposited, like a time bomb, before the phrase "chosen people"?

King's prophetic call spoke for most of the civil rights movement, and its reverberations spilled into the political system. As the political bloc that had governed for three decades starting with FDR shattered, Senators Eugene McCarthy and Robert F. Kennedy tested American readiness for a refoundational moment. As Lyndon Johnson undermined his own reform ambitions with an increasingly insupportable war, the liberal voice came alive in varying keys—McCarthy's ironic, Kennedy's stirring. McCarthy spoke mainly to intellectuals, Kennedy to a wide swath of Democrats and independents. How far Kennedy might have taken his refashioning of liberalism is not, of course, to be known. During much of the brief time he spent on his own in public life, he assumed an American mission for good in the world. His speeches on Vietnam during the two years he sat in the Senate were undistinguished, standard-issue moderation. He was not given to any direct claim of chosenness, any millennial claims, or, indeed, any of the higher-flying forms of exceptionalism. For the most part, he adhered to the path of national self-redemption and, especially in his speeches abroad, struck a distinctly modest, internationalist chord. Yet in 1965, he cited John Winthrop and added: "As long as millions of Americans suffer indignity, and punishment, and deprivation because of their color, their poverty, and our inaction, we know that we are only halfway . . . to the city upon the hill." Addressing an audience in the small town of Scottsbluff, Nebraska, during his short-lived 1968 presidential campaign, he began by saying that "John Adams once said that he considered the founding of America part of 'a divine plan for the liberation of the slavish part of mankind all over the globe.'" Kennedy went on to say that Adams hadn't meant "grandiose schemes of empires abroad," but rather a faith that "grew instead from confidence that the example set by our nation—the example of individual liberty fused with common effort—would spark the spirit of liberty around the planet." The America he heralded would be a "light unto the nations," an inspiration to others more than a mighty crusade.

But during the annus horribilis of 1968, the light flickered and sputtered. King's murder, and Kennedy's, closed out the reform moment and accelerated the direction in which much of the New Left was already moving. America, to the later radical left, seemed chosen for wickedness, its barbarism preordained by a sort of negative Providence. In the rhetoric of the late New Left and Black Power, there was direct continuity from the America of seventeenth-century Indian clearance to the America of free fire zones, napalm, and the My Lai massacre. From this point of view, if America was so grotesquely committed to ongoing slaughter in Vietnam, then the prospects for national self-rectification seemed to dwindle toward the vanishing point. The American people, or most of them, appeared to be Richard Nixon's victorious "silent majority"—a people chosen for racism and imperialism. Perhaps, then, if there were any truly chosen peoples at all, they would have to be found elsewhere, even (or especially) in the camp of the enemy—Vietnam and Cuba, possibly China as well, and the aspiring National Liberation Fronts of the Third World, undergoing their own earthly tribulations. This mental schema preserved the idea of a special mission but transposed it into an international key, with "revolutionary vanguard" substituting for "chosen people" and history's God, dressed as "the Third World revolution," firmly enrolled on somebody else's side.

These were marginal views. The more modest version of a salvageable America had promised to redefine the field of practical possibilities. But that more modest version was enfeebled without inspiring leadership. Now, its most incandescent leaders murdered, the "almost chosen people" vanished from sight. The debacle of George McGovern's "Come home, America" campaign of 1972 extinguished the "light unto the nations."

"We Are the Country of Tomorrow"

The Nixon years shattered whatever general faith remained that America was chosen by God. Tribulation was more evident than the apocalyptic transit to the millennium. Amid the ruins of American virtue, the Democratic Party, and then the nation, chose as its standard-bearer a pious, self-declaredly "born-again" evangelical Baptist, Jimmy Carter, who spoke unabashedly, at the outset of his inaugural address, of "the inner and spiritual strength of our Nation" and proceeded to quote from one of the Hebrew prophets.

Carter was the most devout president since Wilson, though he surrounded his rhetoric with a formidable barrier between church and state (to the dismay of supporters who wanted him to legislate his personal opposition to abortion). "We are a purely idealistic Nation," he insisted, and mentioned America's "special obligation" to take on "moral duties," but in the spirit of Reinhold Niebuhr he stopped far short of claiming that the country had divine sanction. Although the United States was founded "on an awareness of the will of God," God having created the nation "to set an example for the rest of the world" by nurturing human rights, Carter, who read the Bible every night, denied that Americans had any "special claim to be God's chosen people." Perhaps fearing to incur the wrath of members of other Christian denominations and religions, as well as secularists, he accepted America's post-sixties chastening and maintained that "even our great Nation has its recognized limits." What he beheld upon a hill was more a village than a city, let alone a shining one. National self-renewal interested him more than a mission to transform the world.

The ringing counter to Carter's Baptist humility came from a Baptist televangelist who had supported racial segregation, considered the 1964 Civil Rights Act "civil wrongs" legislation, and founded a white Christian school to circumvent a desegregation order. Jerry Falwell had no doubt: "God loves America." "If the world is to have revival, I believe it must begin here." "America is the last logical launching pad for world evangelization." Following Falwell, the rhetoric of American chosenness was revived by Carter's church-averse successor, who found a way to mobilize a veritable Fourth Great Awakening of evangelical Christians who had been roused into politics in a recoil against "the sixties"—against the Warren Supreme Court's decision barring mandatory school prayer, against pornography and abortion, against a culture of disrespect for authority. Ronald Reagan was an apostle of optimism who was fascinated by the prospect of Armageddon (though was not sure whether it would come in "a thousand years . . . or the day after tomorrow"), who frequently professed belief in a "Divine Providence" that watched over the United States, who declared after a would-be assassin's bullet missed his heart by a single inch that "he was more convinced than ever that he was doing God's work," and who, profoundly uninterested in theological niceties, scheduled official events to conform to the judgment of his wife's astrological adviser. A speechwriter during his 1984 reelection campaign drafted a line that would have had him call the United States "the greatest nation God ever created," only to have it expunged at the suggestion of a punctilious White House lawyer who noted: "According to Genesis, God creates things like heavens and the earth and the birds and the fishes, but not nations." But just as Reagan believed that "God has a plan for everyone," he was sure that God had created the United States of America to do His work. God had "intended" and "called" the American people to play its role as an "exemplar of freedom and a beacon of hope" for the whole world. God was the "author" of America's "dream of freedom." "I have always believed," the then-governor of California told the first Conservative Political Action Conference in 1974, in the same speech where he cited John Winthrop trumpeting the "city upon a hill," "that there was some divine plan that placed this great continent between two oceans to be sought out by those who were possessed of an abiding love of freedom and a special kind of courage." Just as America had been kind to Ronald Reagan, God had been kind to America.

The mind of Ronald Reagan was not haunted by any hobgoblin of foolish consistency. Rather, it was tantalized by dreams of a utopia of unbridled free enterprise, of miracles and millennial redemption—though also haunted by nightmares of big government, moral decay, and personal failure. Reagan liked to cite Emerson, and to say things like "Americans live in the future" and "We are the country of tomorrow" (did he know he was echoing Emerson's remark of 1844, "America is the country of the Future. It is a country of beginning, of projects, of vast designs and expectations"?) and while this was a half-truth—Americans, including Reagan himself, care for a properly culled past, too—it was a penetrating one. The son of a working-class alcoholic feared and despised failure; the onetime lifeguard longed for a small town writ large of freestanding and upstanding citizens, an idealized version of his native Dixon, Illinois; the actor longed for a world commensurate with cinematic perfection; the libertarian revolutionary liked to cite the Deist ("filthy atheist," Theodore Roosevelt called him) Thomas Paine, who wrote, "We have it in our power to begin the world over again."

"The genius of Reagan," wrote the historian John Patrick Diggins, "was to keep God and get rid of guilt. . . . [H]e was a liberal romantic who opened up the American mind to the full blaze of Emersonian optimism." He believed the covenant people could be freed of the burden of tribulation. Who Ronald Reagan "really was" is one of the unanswerable questions; even his devoted wife, Nancy, once said, "There's a wall around him." Unlike the Berlin Wall that he famously told the Soviet leader Mikhail Gorbachev to tear down, this one, as Reagan aged, took the form of conspicuous cheerfulness. Unlike Richard Nixon, whose smiles were forced punctuation marks, and Jimmy Carter, whose flashing grin seemed to erupt out of a darkness before vanishing, Reagan's sunny persona seemed his natural state—at least during his years in the White House.

One of Reagan's personae, the one that excited most of his political base, sounded like Theodore Roosevelt on San Juan Hill. This was the Reagan of rollback, the Manichaean Reagan who hailed the Nicaraguan contras as "the moral equivalent of our Founding Fathers"; whose eponymous Doctrine enjoined aid of all kinds to anticommunist fighters no matter what their persuasion, including a Salvadoran government that deployed death squads against priests, left-wing activists, and plain peasants; whose 1985 State of the Union Address proclaimed: "We must not break faith with those who are risking their lives . . . on every continent, from Afghanistan to Nicaragua . . . to defy Soviet aggression and secure rights which have been ours from birth." This was the Reagan who spent more on the military in peacetime than any previous American president, driving the country into unprecedented debt.

But this Reagan did not always follow his rhetoric, or equipment, into the heat of battle; he spoke loudly but was willing to lay down his big stick. Directly after 241 American troops in Beirut were blown to pieces by Islamist suicide bombers, this Reagan covered the ignominy with a two-day war on the 133-square-mile island of Grenada—producing an unequivocal victory for a change—only to beat a full retreat from Lebanon a few months later. This Reagan, in the end, was compelled to own up to trading arms (to the Islamic Republic of Iran, an avowed enemy of the United States) for hostages, though with what degree of presidential awareness has never been established and probably cannot be.

His millenarian streak popped out rhetorically, but in hindsight turns out to have been more complex than his liberal adversaries understood at the time. His theology, such as it was, veered toward the Manichaean, but it disdained Puritanism and was blessedly imprecise. It was in character, and also good politics, that Reagan was not given to parse theological nuances. What he did harbor, on his utopian side, was a willingness to think radically. Liberals did not understand the degree to which, during his second term, especially after Mikhail Gorbachev took power in the USSR, Reagan turned his millennial sensibility toward freeing the world of nuclear weapons, just as he had advocated in his liberal phase, in the late forties, when he passed briefly through World Federalism. He had shelved those views when he turned to the right, as for example in 1964, when he campaigned for Barry Goldwater without objecting to his casual suggestion that "defoliation of the forests [in Vietnam] by low-yield atomic weapons could well be done." When Reagan denounced the Soviet Union as an "evil empire" and "the focus of evil in the modern world" in a March 1983 speech to the National Association of Evangelicals, he was attuned to his audience and no doubt sincere as well. So, too, when one year later, partly in (unacknowledged) reaction to the popular movement for a nuclear freeze, and the ABC television movie it spawned, *The Day After,* Reagan declared that it was his "highest priority to deter and prevent" a nuclear war. When Reagan stood four-square behind the utopian scheme of a Strategic Defense Initiative that would render nuclear weapons "impotent and obsolete," he was sincere. When he declared that mutual assured destruction was immoral, and when, at the 1986 Reykjavik summit, he came within a hair of agreeing to eliminate nuclear weapons, many of his advisers saw—to their horror—that Reagan meant it, he was also sincere.

If Reagan had ever been willing to admit that not everything in American history was graced, he might have tried to finesse the problem through a classic biblical recourse (with a Christian twist)—that tribulation is not only the price of progress but somehow a prerequisite for it. But that effort would have negated his own late-life spirit, which was more at ease contemplating deliverance than tribulation. Someday, in a hazy but luminous future, consternation would cease as free men and women dissolved their contradictions and the American romance would once and for all be requited. This line of thought compelled his followers only because Reagan himself seemed to embody it. In public, at least, he had the gift of making vast numbers of people believe that it was almost always "morning in America." His everyday sunniness, his knack for the anecdote, his smoothly sculpted voice created the impression that he, in his person, was the incarnation of God's gift.

History is indeed made by ideas, as Reagan believed, but most especially the history of nations is made by ideas with ragged edges, torn away from their origins, clutched in the hands of leaders. Until the last two years of his second term, when the Iran-Contra scandal punctured his image, the Americans who twice elected Reagan by runaway margins could behold their president and pride themselves on having chosen him. Surely—so the majority could commend themselves—only a chosen people could have made such a choice.

"A Calling from Beyond the Stars"

"God is near," President George W. Bush declared in his first State of the Union Address, on January 30, 2002. On their face, these words were meant to directly console the bereaved. But for Bush, at least in public, the Almighty's proximity was established long before the massacres of September 11, 2001. The millennialism of divine plans, and America's duty to serve them, already hovered over his First Inaugural on January 20, 2001, when he spoke of "our nation's grand story" in these terms: "We are not this story's author, who fills time and eternity with his purpose. . . . And an angel still rides in the whirlwind and directs this storm." "Whirlwind" and "storm": the apocalyptic register was redolent of Revelation.

In his 2000 campaign, Bush had directly stoked the evangelical base that had delivered votes not only for Ronald Reagan but for Richard Nixon before him. Bush excited both their zeal and their turnout when he sent a barrage of signals that evangelical Christians would find him congenial; not least, he declared straightforwardly that Jesus had "changed [his] heart" when he was "born again." Republicans ran away with the devout white evangelical vote in 2000 and 2004, in proportions significantly higher than in the 1960s, though they had dominated this population in the 1970s, 1980s, and 1990s, too. It was not therefore surprising that, when the September 11 attacks evoked apocalyptic scenarios, Bush's millenarian proclivities slipped the leash. Three days after the attacks, Bush declared that America was obliged to "rid the world of evil," and he then let drop, four days later, that America's "war on terrorism" was a "crusade." Normally careful to exempt Islam as a whole from his enemies list, and to distinguish between Islam, "a religion of peace," and the false, murderous prophets of al-Qaeda and its allies (including, he insisted, Saddam Hussein), Bush here gave voice to a Manichaean message that he reinforced many times with absolutist references to "evildoers," the "axis of evil," and so on. He renewed his providential sense of American destiny when he said, in his 2003 State of the Union message: "The liberty we prize is not America's gift to the world; it is God's gift to humanity." His messianic certainty amplified his messianic vision.

Pursuing that prize with unbridled fervor, Bush attacked Iraq. Displaying absolute certainty about his justifications as he ticked off a series of erroneous, tendentious, and ignorant claims— "fix[ing] . . . the intelligence and facts . . . around the policy," in the words of the famous "Downing Street Memo" of July 23, 2002— he permitted no contrary arguments to penetrate the shield he had erected in the face of logic and evidence. Overseas antagonism to American foreign policy soared as a consequence. Still, accepting his second presidential nomination, Bush not only declared that "America is called to lead the cause of freedom" because freedom "is the

Almighty God's gift to every man and woman in the world," but also insisted that America had "a calling from beyond the stars to stand for freedom." But he was at pains in his Second Inaugural (written chiefly by the evangelical Christian Michael Gerson) to backtrack and renounce the overt claim that America was "chosen":

> We go forward with complete confidence in the eventual triumph of freedom. . . . Not because we consider ourselves a chosen nation; God moves and chooses as He wills. We have confidence because freedom is the permanent hope of mankind, the hunger in dark places, the longing of the soul. . . . History has . . . a visible direction, set by liberty and the Author of Liberty.

More than any other recent American president, as the political scientist Rogers M. Smith pointed out, Bush implied that America possessed divine sanction not just in a general sense but on behalf of particular policies. Surpassing Ronald Reagan's invocations of America as a redeemer nation, Bush repeatedly evoked America's providential mission in both divine and semi-secular keys, as in: "We've been called to a unique role in human events." "Once again, we are called to defend the safety of our people, *and the hopes of all mankind*" (italics added). "Liberty is both the plan of Heaven for humanity, and the best hope for progress here on Earth. . . . [America has a] mission to promote liberty around the world." America was targeted by al-Qaeda, he insisted, "because we are freedom's home and defender, and the commitment of our Fathers is now the calling of our time." Later, attacking Iraq, Bush defended that war, too, as a mission undertaken on universally mandated grounds: "The advance of freedom is the calling of our time. . . . [I]t is the calling of our country." If the yearning for freedom lived in every human breast, Bush maintained, America was its authorized liberator, the divine author's translator and intermediary. God acted through the United States of America. In effect, the United States was a next-to-Supreme Being.

It is impossible to know exactly which sentiments inhabited his own human breast, and exactly when, but Bush was probably the American president who lived closest to a sense of messianic mission and an End Times mystique. Whatever his private feelings, this was politically advantageous. That he was chosen to lead a divinely sanctioned nation was, if not an article of faith, an article of political base-building. It was not lost on him or his advisers that his story of being born again resonated spectacularly well with his evangelical followers.

"To Choose Our Better History"

George W. Bush might have been original in the extravagance of his certitude, in the extremity of his doctrine, and in the clumsiness of his articulation of it—not to mention his execution—but he was not original in the general contours of his idea of America's divinely inspired passion. America was founded with a messianic mission it can neither free itself from nor comfortably settle into. Sometimes the mission has been construed as divinely granted; sometimes it has been framed as a secular myth; sometimes it has dangled in ideological space, without definite provenance. Sometimes it has emphasized freedom, sometimes prosperity. But the power of the idea throughout all its variants may be measured by its endurance—a tribute to its success in binding together a nation of disparate origins, unrepentant individualism, and clashing ideals. The mission's partisans and antagonists alike have agreed that only forward momentum in some common direction could keep the disparate elements from flying apart in centrifugal motion. For much of American history, that common direction has been outward—into the wilderness, against enemies.

The immense social movements and efforts at liberal reconstruction in the sixties were efforts to overhaul the national destiny, to shift from a messianic, world-saving identity to one that longs to deliver on the promise that what the world expects of America, when "the eyes of all people" open wide in this direction, is progress toward a justice in which "all men are created equal." That moment was thwarted by racial backlash and savage violence, though its embers continued to glow even as America turned toward conservative restoration. Now, with that restoration played out, Barack Obama opens another door.

Some of what Obama contributes to the long-running saga of American chosenness arrives in his very person—he is, after all, a self-described "mutt." Now, the idea that a melting-pot America is specially equipped to conduct the American mission is not brand new. President Woodrow Wilson, campaigning for the League of Nations, declared:

> This nation was created to be the mediator of people, because it draws its blood from every civilized stock in the world and is ready by sympathy and understanding to understand the peoples of the world. Every other nation in the world is set in the mold of a particular breeding. We are set in no mold at all. . . . We know what all peoples are thinking, and yet we, by a fine alchemy of our own, combine that thinking into an American plan and an American purpose.

Obviously, in 1919, Woodrow Wilson did not envision the nation someday electing the child of a white woman from Kansas and a visitor from Kenya. Wilson's idea of "civilized stock" did not extend to African Americans. Nor did Wilson focus his hope for the nation on the identity of its leader—he was speaking of American virtue as a national characteristic. Obama carried Wilson two huge steps further—from white peoples to all peoples, and from America as a melting pot writ large to America led by a biracial man.

Obama's ascendancy would not have been possible without the vast change in the nation's literal complexion made possible by Lyndon Johnson's immigration reform of 1965, clearing the way for a new demographic reality—that America's non-Hispanic white majority, still Republican, would shrink from 1980's 88 percent to 2008's 74 percent. Obama's multiracial identity gave particular bite to his inaugural preachment:

> We remain a young nation, but in the words of Scripture, the time has come to set aside childish things. The time has come to reaffirm our enduring spirit; to choose our better history; to carry forward that precious gift, that noble idea, passed on from generation to generation: the God-given promise that all are equal, all are free and all deserve a chance to pursue their full measure of happiness.

What was God-given, Obama said, was not an exalted moral position, or a land, but a "gift" and a "promise." The gift to be "passed on" was not a solid object, not the codified thing ordinarily referred to as a "legacy" or a "heritage," but a work in progress, perennially incomplete; becoming, not being; to be renewed, its meaning contested; a compound, in fact, of equality, freedom, and the pursuit of happiness, a mixture of ideals that in practice might well conflict with one another and therefore *require* choices. A "God-given promise" is one-half of a covenant, but the other half is the free choice of a people to define itself.

By inviting Americans to "choose our better history," by placing collective freedom at the heart of the matter, Obama turned from the original emphasis on America as a nation chosen by God to establish dominion, to the less predetermined and more modern notion of America as a choosing people. His goal fell short—realistically short—of Tom Paine's "begin the world over again," for it recognized that the present is founded on an unending past. As he bid us to "choose our better history," he acknowledged implicitly that there is also a worse. The George Washington who opposed torture also owned slaves. The worse history Obama didn't dwell on—that was not the place of an inaugural address. Rather, he invited a new beginning, though without amnesia or false innocence. In Obama's version, Americans get to choose—to choose perennially—from among multiple, intertangled strands. We were, from the beginning (in fact, from before the beginning), a people of more than one history—freedom *and* slavery, cooperation *and* savagery, republic *and* empire. Those histories were, and remain, intricately connected and not easily disentangled. That is why the choosing must be deliberate and ongoing.

In the spirit of the classical jeremiad, Obama acknowledged the fact of tribulation but located it in the transcendable and, indeed, transcended past: "Because we have tasted the bitter swill of civil war and segregation and emerged from that dark chapter stronger and more united, we cannot help but believe that the old hatreds shall someday pass; that the lines of tribe shall soon dissolve; that as the world grows smaller, our common humanity shall reveal itself; and that America must play its role in ushering in a new era of peace." The repeated "shall" evoked echoes of Lincoln's now-archaic discourse and its promise of overcoming. Here Obama displayed a tone somewhere between the conflict-averse and the prophetic-utopian.

There was a new note, too, one that went largely unmentioned in the punditry of subsequent days. Identifying the American ideal with the dissolution of the "lines of tribe" and the revelation of "common humanity"—this was a new angle on what it was America had been chosen for: not exclusivity, certainly not the exclusivity of self-determined European nation-states, but mixture. In Obama's interpretation, life, liberty, and the pursuit of happiness needed to overcome tribal boundaries. The American destiny was to be more than a nation, or at least not a nation like previous (European) nations, but the avant-garde of a new cosmopolitanism, as in the once-presumptuous song "We Are the World." In a world more tightly drawn together than ever before by migration, trade, and communication, America was to point the way toward an evolution of nationalism elsewhere as well—from exclusivity to inclusiveness. Obama offered no road map toward that ideal, but it was the direction in which his compass pointed.

In other words, Obama's "choose our better history" extended Lincoln's theme of the "almost chosen people" in the direction of still greater modesty. Repressed manifest destiny themes were not the only ones capable of bursting through the surface of American history, as in George W. Bush's recycling of Theodore Roosevelt. Obama's task would be to see that the humility ideal, long embattled, long repressed, had staying power.

3. The Unchosen

THE NOTION THAT God chose one particular set of human beings from among all the human beings on earth and singled them out to be His people is jarring to the chosen and the unchosen alike.

As we have seen, this idea delights, encourages, and—once they stop to think about it—weighs down those who regard themselves as chosen. But the announcement also spills beyond their limited circle; it reaches others to whom it is both an insult and an incitement. If true, it is somewhere between irritating and devastating. If false, it is the most extraordinary act of presumption in history. Whether true or not, it is bound to inspire disbelief, sarcasm, and accusations: *How dare those people have the gall to elevate themselves? What about us? If God is the one God before whom there are no other gods, how could He have been so unfair as to impose the ultimate double standard? But if He did not do that—and surely, if He is the God we think He is, He did not—then the people who claim to be chosen turn out to be not only mistaken but arrogant to the point of depravity.* Reactions of this sort tend to flare into holy wars, for the abstractions of nationhood and peoplehood nourish institutions such as states and churches that have a stake in preserving themselves and securing their power and boundaries.

Now, the nation-states of chosen peoples are not unique in being founded with acts of dispossession. When a people feel in their bones that God has promised them and only them a particular land that is already occupied, they naturally set up a zero-sum game against the natives. When the voice of God sets hearts on fire, conflagrations follow. The land's native inhabitants strive to make sense of the new arrivals and to struggle against a theology that declares them to be, in effect, the children of a lesser god. These unchosen resent, hate, avenge, and raise their children accordingly. When they resist becoming history's beautiful losers, they tend to construe their defeats as martyrdom, build identities around humiliation, and set out to regenerate themselves through acts of magic and will. They begin to rationalize the next war.

Yet when the two peoples meet, individual to individual, in one Promised Land or another, what they feel for each other may well be a confused and complicated tangle of emotions. Should the adversaries, the "others," conclude that the chosen intend to take over the land exclusively, they have no alternative but fight or flight—all the more so when some of the adversaries also claim to be, themselves, chosen. But a more complicated, wrenching, and mysterious form of relationship is possible. Suppose the two peoples violently disagree about what the land *means*. Suppose their dispute concerns more than boundaries, acreage, and security. Suppose the chosen see the land as a reward that redeems their suffering, an abstract proof of the holiness—the very identity—of the people. Suppose that the others see the land as nothing more—or less—than a specific territory, the sum of *these* groves, *these* hillsides, *these* cemeteries, *these* stones and streams. Then the peoples are living in different landscapes. They cannot even agree on what they are fighting about.

"Utterly Destroyed"

In the biblical texts addressing the chosen people, God's special relationship was exclusive. The Israelites were led to understand that insofar as they were chosen, others were not. Toward some of the unchosen people whom they encountered, they could afford to be indifferent, for there was no direct conflict of interest. But where the same land was at stake, ruthlessness was the way of the ancients. Forty years into the Exodus, according to Moses, God arranged that the undesignated occupiers of the Promised Land should be frightened, defeated, and crushed. The Bible drives the grim point home, and home, and home again. "This day," God told the Israelites, "will I begin to put the dread of thee and the fear of thee upon the nations that are under the whole heaven." God even intervened to "harden" the "spirit" of a resisting king—as he had earlier done to the Pharaoh who refused to free the enslaved Jews—whereupon He "delivered him over" to the Israelites, who "struck him down, together with his sons and his whole army" and "took all his towns and completely destroyed them—men, women, and children," leaving "no survivors," carrying away livestock and plunder. Then, in threescore more cities under the rule of a second king, the Israelites also "utterly destroyed . . . the men, women, and children." Having heard what the Israelites did to their enemies, another people, the Gibeonites, surrendered, whereupon Joshua "made them that day hewers of wood and drawers of water for the congregation, and for the altar of the Lord, even unto this day."

Overall, the Hebrew Bible offers the conquered no solace. This is not a book for those who have been "utterly destroyed," nor does it strive to persuade those bystander peoples who might fear the selfsame fate. The lesson is plain for those who later discover that the hill where they hope to build their city is already occupied, and cite scriptural precedent for their conquests.

Once Found, Then Lost

The idea of divine election lends itself to the Bible's either/or way of thinking. In time, the earliest chosen people, the Jews, gave rise to two great, imperial, monotheist and universalist rivals, Christians and Muslims. Each transposed the idea of chosenness into its own key. Each set out to grow by accretion—an expedient essentially denied the Jews, who originated in a time when other peoples held to their own national gods, whom they did not abandon. For both Christianity and Islam, the history of the Jews was no more than a prologue—a ladder to be tossed aside once it satisfied its purpose—

or even, in certain interpretations, a false start. Each claimed to have superseded the Jews as the favorites of a unique God: Christians, composed originally of onetime Jews and onetime Gentiles, as a church of the chosen, destined to complete the task begun by the Jews but unwisely abandoned; Muslims, subsequently, as a whole people, "the best nation ever brought forth for men," in the words of the Qur'an (Sura 3:110)—yet a nation recognizing that God had once granted the Jews a privileged position.

Both Christianity and Islam were rooted in the same, original covenant with the Almighty. Each honored Jewish priority in the eyes of God but proposed to substitute itself now that the Jews' work was, in effect, done. Each claimed lineage—spiritual in the case of Christians, biological in the case of Muslims—from the same ancestral stem. St. Paul told his followers: "They which are of faith . . . are the children of Abraham" (Galatians 3:7) and "If ye be Christ's, then are ye Abraham's seed, and heirs according to the promise" (Galatians 3:29). St. Peter was even more explicit about the possibility of growing into a distinctive people, and thus eligible to be "the people of God," in the course of time: "But ye are a chosen generation, a royal priesthood, an holy nation, a peculiar people . . . Which in time past were not a people, but are now the people of God: which had not obtained mercy, but now have obtained mercy" (1 Peter 2:9–10). (Presumably Peter, or whoever wrote as him, meant that the new people consisted of those, whether Jew or Gentile in origin, who were prepared to recognize the divinity of Jesus.) The God of the Qur'an reminded the Jews of His covenant with them: "I blessed you more than any other people" (Sura 2:122)—and cited Moses: "O my people . . . Enter the holy land which Allah has prescribed for you" (5:21). As for the Jews, they were chosen to "dwell securely in the promised land" (17:104).

In both cases, the Jews once were found but now they were lost. Having claimed to have inherited God's mantle, Christians and Muslims unleashed furies against their predecessors. The Jews were cast as obstacles, heretics, misleaders, persecutors. In the eyes of Christians, the Jews erred by overplaying law, underplaying love, and crucifying Jesus—never mind that he lived and died as a Jew. The Christians eventually established their own hierarchy and persecuted Jews for having killed the Jew of Nazareth. Thus St. Paul (I Thess. 2:14–15): "The Jews . . . both killed the Lord Jesus, and their own prophets, and have persecuted us; and they please not God, and are contrary to all men."

The Qur'an does not offer more forgiving sentiments. The Jews, it says, "distorted" the "word of God" (2:75, 4:46). Their "arrogance" led them to forfeit the covenant that God had made with them (2:83). They became "evildoers" (3:63), "confound[ers]" of "truth with falsehood" (3:71), "corrupters" (5:64), and mockers (4:46) whose "disbelief" justly subjected them to "humiliation" and "retribution" (2:84–86).

What was to be done with these retrograde ones who refused to "accept Jesus," or who, albeit "People of the Book" (29:46), failed to accept the Qur'an as the proper continuation of that Book? They might be invited to choose correctly—that is, convert. To accept Jesus or submit to Allah, all they needed to do was perform a minimal ritual. This was one way in which the chosen community could enlarge its ranks. But in the early centuries after the life and death of Christ, many Jews, still "stiff-necked," persisted in being Jews. In the time of Muhammad, the Jews of Medina refused to convert. The lot of such peoples was to be subordinated—by force if need be.

The logic of either/or chosenness still guides those who adhere to a strict reading of the Qur'an. The 1988 charter or covenant of Hamas, the Islamic Resistance Movement of the Palestinians, borrows its central theme from its hated adversaries when it begins with a quotation from the Qur'an (3:110–11) that addresses all Muslims as "the best nation" and proceeds immediately to point a finger at the Jews:

And if the People of the Scripture had believed, it had been better for them. Some of them are believers; but most of them are evil-doers. They will not harm you save a trifling hurt, and if they fight against you they will turn and flee. . . . Ignominy will be their portion wheresoever they are found save [where they grasp] a rope from Allah and a rope from man. . . . [T]hey used to disbelieve the revelations of Allah, and slew the Prophets wrongfully.

The charter continues: "Israel will rise and will remain erect until Islam eliminates it as it had eliminated its predecessors."

The either/or theme continues throughout the charter. The truly chosen are enjoined to make war on those who falsely claim to be chosen and occupy land in the name of this falsehood. Land is of the essence: "When our enemies usurp some Islamic lands, Jihad becomes a duty binding on all Muslims. In order to face the usurpation of Palestine by the Jews, we have no escape from raising the banner of Jihad" (article 15). Palestine is indivisible, "an Islamic Waqf [religious trust] throughout the generations and until the Day of Resurrection" (article 11). Article 7 quotes the Hadith to make it plain that this Jihad is to be violent: "The prophet, prayer and peace be upon him, said: The time [for the realization of Allah's promise] will not come until Muslims will fight the Jews (and kill them); until the Jews hide behind rocks and trees, which will cry: O Muslim! there is a Jew hiding behind me, come on and kill him!" Eventually, Islam may "coexist in safety and security" with Christians and Jews, but only "under the shadow of Islam" (article 31). The message is plain: the pretenders must be displaced by the truly chosen. God's will is not to deny the logic of divine election but to transpose its subject.

Fourteen centuries on, in a spasm of reaction against Zionism, Hamas resurrects Islam's original harshness against Jews across the board. Though for centuries Jews were granted a place—though a subordinate one—in Muslim societies, the twentieth-century Jewish settlement in Palestine ignited great hostilities, manifest in a vast and continuing production of lurid, often state-sponsored, propaganda. The grand mufti of Jerusalem, Mohammad Amin al-Husayni, vehemently defended Nazi views during Hitler's entire reign, recruited Muslim S.S. units, and broadcast on Nazi radio: "Kill the Jews wherever you find them. This pleases God, history, and religion. This saves your honor." During the Vichy and Nazi occupations of Morocco, Algeria, and Tunisia, most Arabs accepted the persecution of Jews largely with indifference, like Europe's Christians—though there were in North Africa, again as in Europe, both heroes of rescue and distinct villains. But with the declaration of the Israeli state in 1948, Jews in Arab lands were persecuted and dispossessed. Increasingly thereafter, down to the present day, in newspapers, on radio and television, and in textbooks, hostile anti-Semitic caricatures thrive across the Arab world. The immensely influential Egyptian Sayyid Qutb, ideologue of the Muslim Brotherhood and later inspiration to al-Qaeda and other terrorists, denounced the Jews for their "wicked opposition" to Islam, their "conspiracies," their damnable and unforgivable "scheming against Islam," perpetually at work trying to lure believers away from the true faith. What was to Arabs the unspeakable humiliation of their crushing defeat in 1967's Six-Day War led first to despondency, then to the rejection of nationalism and Pan-Arabism and to a religious revival that raised the sense of inflammation to an even higher power.

At the far end of a spectrum of paranoia emerged the apocalyptic flourishes of al-Qaeda, as forecast at the 1981 trial of its future leader, the Egyptian Ayman al-Zawahiri, when he and his codefendants chanted: "The army of Mohammed will return, and we will defeat the Jews!" The theme of revenge for Muslim humiliation at the hands of the United States—seen as a front for the Jews—looms large among the terrorist jihadis of al-Qaeda and other such networks. From its inception, al-Qaeda played on, and inflamed, Muslim wounds to pound home its Manichaean view that (as Osama bin Laden said in 1990) "we are very humiliated" by the "attack" on "our brothers in Palestine," among other places, and (as he added in a video broadcast on October 7, 2001) that "the whole world" is "divided . . . into two sides—the side of believers and the side of infidels."

History seems awfully dire—and familiar. The Hebrew Bible honors the elimination of those unfavored by God who wrongfully occupy the Promised Land. Its theological offspring, following Jesus and Muhammad, greatly enlarge the circle of the chosen—Christianity to the Church, Islam to the community of all Muslims—and in different degrees chastise those who choose to ignore the good word. Over the centuries, the chosen have frequently sought to be not only God's favorite sons but His only ones. The same was true of the early Americans. When Yale's Ezra Stiles called George Washington "the American Joshua" in 1783, he added that "never was the possession of arms used with more glory or for a better cause, since the days of Joshua." He went on to explain that for America to fulfill its godly promise, it not only had to expel the British but also had to defeat, contain, or wipe out the Indians.

As we saw, when Thomas Jefferson declared that "those who labour in the earth are the chosen people of God, if ever he had a chosen people," he did not include the Indians—most of them, at any rate—among those "who labour in the earth." Hunters and gatherers, however admirable as souls, failed to mix their sweat into the soil; they were therefore vulnerable to a "corruption of morals," and were incapable of generating a government that could constitute "the world's best hope." Jefferson, like earlier colonists, devoted a great deal of effort to converting the Indians into yeomen. A sincere missionary of hearts and minds, he failed. He also hoped the races would merge into the "one people" of which the Declaration of Independence spoke. These stratagems proving ineffectual, he determined on transfer. Typically, one of his supporters at the time of the Louisiana Purchase declared that it would be "god-like work" to transform Indian "tomahawks and scalping knives into ploughshares and pruning hooks." Neither he nor Jefferson was bloodthirsty. But the Indians, given their barely reconstructed way of life, remained inconvenient. If they were not to be "pacified," they would have to be moved; if they were not moved, they would have to be killed.

The drama of a single chosen people colliding with pretenders and unsalvageables haunts the story of bloody encounters from the Crusades to the Arab Revolt of 1936–39, from Little Big Horn to the Yom Kippur War, from Wounded Knee to Hebron. The history of the chosen people, in America and Israel alike, is at first glance a history of all-or-nothing massacre and war. But a closer look suggests otherwise. Threaded amid the history of battles, wrath, and treachery runs a more intricate history of human relations that can be traced in fiction, poetry, and testimonials—culture of all sorts taken to heart by the chosen and the unchosen alike. The chosen and the unchosen are entangled together by resentment and resignation, mercy and anger, humor and heartbreak, cacophony and harmony. The relationship between the chosen people and those whom they dispossess—the Palestinians in the case of Israel, the Native Americans in the case of the United States—is partly an extended war dance, but it is also a sequence of movements, sometimes slow, sometimes stormy, in which the vanquished, while never triumphant, nonetheless help determine the rhythm of history. To better understand this sequence, we must first look at the early encounters between the chosen and the others.

"Distracted Between Hope and Fear"

Native Americans did not, at first, know what to make of the European newcomers. Were they visitors? Conquerors? Gods? Divine messengers? Guests? Should the natives feel sheer curiosity? Fear? Hope? Awe? Should they embrace, or anyway accept, coexistence? All these reactions occurred. For example, the Delawares of the New Jersey–New York coast thought of the first Dutch ship they encountered as a sort of tabernacle, a mobile dwelling of God. Believing that the Supreme Being was coming to visit, they readied meat for a sacrifice, arranged their religious effigies, and produced a dance to welcome him, while the shamans tried to comprehend the point of his visit, and to placate their brethren, who were "distracted between hope and fear." The "Indians" were awed not only by the whites' weapons but by their other possessions, including printed books, silver chalices, and iron pots, all considered "spirits."

Why were the Indians frightened? The evidence suggests that neither primordial xenophobia nor race-based antagonism was a prime reason. Although the European visitors of the early seventeenth century did not know it, writes a prominent ethnohistorian of the colonial period, James Axtell, "many of the native peoples of the Atlantic seaboard had experienced fifty or a hundred years of contact with European ships, men, and erstwhile colonies. Predictably, many of those contacts ended in suspicion, fear, and conflict." The natives were often vengeful. Still, Axtell writes, "European encounters with the North American Indians at the very beginning were predominantly peaceful and the natives generally welcomed the newcomers." In New England, the Indians' generosity toward the Puritans was all the more impressive because "their only previous knowledge of the English was likely to have been of rapacious seamen and adventurers." When the settlers acted civilly and showed that they had come to stay, the Indians "extended the English every courtesy, advice, and endeavor to help them."

Still, the newcomers were suspicious, having brought with them "prefabricated images of the 'savage,' occasionally noble but mostly ignoble, from their experiences in Africa and Asia and from their reading of ancient, biblical, and Renaissance travel literature. They expected the worst and, in their ignorance or ham-handedness, often provoked the natives into fulfilling their expectations." For above all, the Europeans were inclined to believe that they were not only divinely favored but bearers of civilization itself. Christian missionary societies, whether Protestant or Catholic, believed it was their task (in the words of one Rhode Island record) to "civilize Savages before they can be converted to Christianity, and that in order to make them Christians, they must first be made men"—for they were regarded as (in Axtell's words) "deficient in Order, Industry, and Manners."

The Indians, for their part, did not feel deficient. Ethnocentric in their own ways, they were cheerfully content with themselves. Like the Europeans, they felt like higher beings. When the French landed in eastern Canada in 1610, they were astonished to find that the local Indians—Micmacs—felt "better, more valiant and more ingenious" than the French, and even "richer." When the French offered them red wine and stale biscuits, the horrified Micmacs, convinced that these barbarians drank blood and ate wood, chucked the biscuits into the St. Lawrence River. A full eighty years later, the Micmacs still felt superior. "There is no Indian," said a Micmac chief, "who does not consider himself infinitely more happy and more powerful than the French."

The same was evidently the case with the English. John Lawson, who traveled extensively among the Indians of North Carolina, noted in 1709: "There is one Vice very common every where, which I never found amongst them, which is Envying other Mens Happiness." Lawson thought their "natural Vertues and Gifts" insulated them from envy. Another eighteenth-century Englishman well acquainted with natives wrote that "they seem always to Look upon themselves as far Superiour to the rest of Mankind and accordingly Call themselves *Ongwehoenwe,* i. e. Men Surpassing all other men." Some, like the Frenchman-turned-American John Hector St. John de Crèvecœur, even found them so enviable as to have given their captives good reason to welcome captivity, since with the Indians they could enjoy "the most perfect freedom, the ease of living, the absence of those cares and corroding solicitudes which so often prevail with us."

Accordingly, missionaries felt the need to humble the natives, to "reduce" them and place them "in the yoke of Christ." At this, they had some success. But, in Axtell's summary, "at the end of two centuries of effort both the French and the English were forced to admit that they had largely failed to convert the native Americans to European religion and culture." Meanwhile, as the natives were depleted by disease (to which the whites were mysteriously immune) and overcome by European weaponry, their generosity decayed. In

Indian eyes, the strangers degenerated from benevolent deities to dangerous "spirits" or shamans and finally to possibly subhuman "enemies" who had better be killed before they did terrible damage. As the Indians defended themselves, many *became* the "savages" whom the Europeans had expected in the first place. The strongest among them fought. They massacred whites. They scalped them. They captured them. But sometimes they married them. They emulated some of their ways. Sometimes they relocated.

As the whites pushed further and the Indians died, the invaders appeared even more powerful. As game grew scarcer, natives began attaching themselves to the colonial economy—to hunt and trap for the whites, to scout, interpret, and carry messages for them, even to track runaway slaves for them. Land was, as always, the heart of the matter. When the Indians went into debt, they agreed to sell land, or indentured themselves as servants—an undignified restriction on their freedom, in their eyes. Since agriculture was "women's work," they experienced farm labor as loathsome and undignified.

To the whites, buying land was self-evidently legitimate. Contracts certified that exchanges were—by definition—equitable; after all, if either party believed that it was getting short shrift, it could freely refuse to sign. But the more land was purchased, the more crowded the Indians became, and the less sustainable their way of life. They turned to alcohol. By the late eighteenth century, they were devising messianic cults. Their curiosity about the mysterious whites curdled. Their willingness to accord them the benefit of the doubt dwindled. Fear and belligerence grew. This was not just abstract feeling. It led to an emotionally satisfying, endlessly deadly, ever-defensible cycle of revenge.

The Meaning of Land

Samoset, the first Native American to encounter the Puritans (in 1621), was also the first to grant them a land deed (in 1625). Within the four-year interval, so many trees were felled in New England that the colonial settlements were encroaching upon one another, whereupon the Puritans asked Samoset for twelve thousand more acres. In Samoset's eyes, the land belonged to the Great Spirit. But the white men were insistent, so Samoset humored them by attending a ceremony and making his mark on a document of transferral.

An equivalent clash of experience and perception stood between the early Zionist settlers and their Arab neighbors. For the Arabs, the land was specific and at the same time primordial. It consisted of particular hillsides, ravines, wadis, groves, orchards, stone walls, and twisted olive trees, their leaves turning silver as the wind moved them in the light—places where they practiced subsistence agriculture and raised children. Moreover, tradition lived there. The land was soaked in immediate family history, carrying the memory of parents and grandparents, who were also buried there. For the Zionists, the land was abstract in two senses. It was a commodity that could be divided into lots, bought and sold. Moreover, most of the land that they could acquire was a stand-in for the actual territory that the Jews of antiquity had inhabited hundreds of generations before. The center of biblical Israel had been the hills of Judea, Samaria, and the Galilee, but already in the nineteenth century these areas were heavily settled by Palestinian Arabs. Accordingly, many of the new settlements took place in inland valleys and on the coastal plain, where, in biblical times, not Jews but Philistines had lived. In brief, as the sociologist Gershon Shafir reminds us, "Zionism saw a remarkable territorial shift of the Jewish homeland."

Most of the land the Jews bought was sold to them by owners who did not work it. According to Shafir's research, between 1878 and 1936 more than three-quarters of the land was purchased from big landowners, many of them absentee landlords (Ottoman nobles living in Beirut, for example) who had purchased their land as an investment not long before they sold it. At times, Arab peasants, fellahin, discovered only when the absentee owners sold the land that they had forfeited their rights. Less than one-tenth of the land the

Zionists purchased was sold to them directly by fellahin taking advantage of rising land prices.

Like the Native Americans faced with incoming Europeans, the Arab farmers at first reacted to their new neighbors with a combination of awe, trepidation, neighborliness, and hostility. As Shafir notes, "without the cooperation of Palestinian Arab villagers the earliest Jewish settlers would have been in dire straits." The pre-1914 Jewish immigrants received some of their agricultural training from their Arab neighbors, with whom they also traded produce and whom they sometimes hired to assist in farmwork. They adapted techniques and crops from the Arabs. Jointly they planted watermelons; for fertilizer they purchased heaps of manure from Palestinian villagers. Even more telling, perhaps, the Zionists hired Arabs to guard their land. Such collaboration led one coexistence-minded immigrant to write that "in general, the relations between Jews and Arabs in the old moshavot [agricultural communities] were good."

But this was not the whole picture. Arab laborers were often directly hostile to the Jewish settlers, who not only arrived with mercantile assumptions about land ownership but flouted local customs, took advantage of a backward Ottoman land registration system, oftentimes inadvertently, and sometimes committed acts of flagrant dispossession. Arab wrath grew stronger as the men and women of the Second Aliyah—the 1904–14 wave of immigration that included many refugees from Russia's anti-Semitic pogroms—espoused the stringently nationalistic principle of "conquest of labor." The phrase had two meanings. One was that Jews, traditionally unskilled in manual labor, should transcend their shortcomings and redeem their ancestral homeland by cultivating its fields, erecting its homes, and paving its roads. The other was more blunt: Jews should be the sole and exclusive laborers on Jewish property.

"A necessary condition for the realization of Zionism is the conquest of all branches of work in Eretz Israel by Jews"—this was the slogan of Hapoel Hatzair, a small but influential group founded in

1905 and regarded as the conscience of the labor movement in the *yishuv,* the pre-state Jewish settlement in Palestine. Hapoel Hatzair—and especially its founder, A. D. Gordon—viewed labor in mystical terms. They spoke of "the religion of work." Gordon wrote that "Hebrew laborers are for the *yishuv* what blood is to a healthy body." But while most of the *yishuv* embraced the idea of Hebrew labor in principle, they had to acknowledge that Arab workers were both less costly and more skilled. First, the *yishuv* reserved most of the skilled work for fellow Jews; later, most of the less-skilled work as well.

Jewish settlers continued to endorse "conquest of the soil." In defense of their newly acquired lands, they were inclined to take up arms against Arab tenant farmers. We may easily understand them. They felt beset. They had come to Palestine to implement a radical ideology of cooperative settlement, but also to take refuge from the anti-Semitic waves that swept Europe—the Russian pogroms and the czarist propaganda including the *Protocols of the Elders of Zion;* the French persecution triggered by the prosecution of Captain Alfred Dreyfus; the German cry "The Jews are our misfortune!" Breathing room was scarce. They were on edge. The *yishuv* became both more exclusive and more forceful. The settler-laborers became soldiers; from their ranks came a disproportionate share of the later *yishuv's* commanders and fighters. As the historian Tom Segev notes, the concepts of land, labor, and armed struggle were intertwined, all using the same masculine language:

> Zionism made frequent use of military terminology. There was the "labor army," the "labor battalion," "the battalion in defense of the language," the "conquest of the language," the "conquest of the land," the "conquest of the sea," the "conquest of labor," and so on. David Ben-Gurion spoke of "conquering pioneers."

Like other left-wing nationalist movements, Zionism was trapped between two loyalties, socialism and nationalism. The socialist spirit faded; defending and building the nation felt more urgent. The labor movement armed itself and prepared for conflict. The kibbutz, promoted by collective land purchases, socialist in ideology, mutated, in a sense, into the armed yeomen of the *yishuv*. Embattled, the Zionists organized self-defense groups, replacing the Arab guards with a new paramilitary organization of their own. But the settlers of the *yishuv* were not those of the Old Testament, who smote the natives with absolute, even genocidal, ruthlessness. The modern newcomers admired the Arab natives. They did not cultivate cultural purity. Rather, they dressed in traditional Arab garb, learned Arabic, and adopted local customs—for example, establishing Palestinian-style hospitality rooms to entertain passersby. This was more than practical tactics or "knowing one's enemy"—it was cultural emulation. "Not only did [the militant socialist-Zionist movement] imitate the Bedouin outwardly," Shafir writes, but it "also derived its idea of heroism from the Bedouin and the Circassian. In the Second Aliyah, to be an upright Jew meant to be like a mounted Bedouin!" Other Jews accused these militant young Zionists of "going native."

Yet while they sometimes romanticized the "other," the settlers believed that the land needed *them,* and that their attachment to it would grow into something more solid than an abstraction of biblical provenance. In *Altneuland,* his utopian novel of 1902, Theodor Herzl charged one of his characters with explaining why young Jewish settlers, inexperienced farmers all, would succeed where generations of Arab peasants had failed to make the desert bloom: "The sacred soil . . . was unproductive for others, but for us it was a good soil. Because we fertilized it with our love." In the Second Aliyah movement that followed, the young Jewish emigrants from eastern Europe arrived with a stronger interest in redeeming their ancient homeland than in the particular contours of the actual land itself.

In the eyes of many Zionists, they were, after all, "a people without a land" come to occupy "a land without a people." (The phrase was first published in 1901 by the English Zionist Israel Zangwill, curiously enough the same writer who coined "melting pot" for the

United States.) The immigrants were sometimes ignorant, but more: what they meant was that the Arabs of Palestine were not *a* people— not a nationality. The Jews had acquired the land by means that were, in their eyes, scrupulously legal, whereas the Arabs mainly rested their case on a continuous—though at times undocumented—history of inalienable rights. This collision of cultures preexisted Britain's 1917 Balfour Declaration, which envisioned "a national home for the Jewish people," albeit stipulating that "nothing shall be done which may prejudice the civil and religious rights of existing non-Jewish communities in Palestine." If the Jews encountered Arab hostility, they were acutely mindful that the alternative for them was the violence that came their way in the Diaspora. At least in the *yishuv* they were standing up for their nation. Yet most Zionists hoped to avoid the either/or, zero-sum logic of European colonialists. Their agricultural successes would, they believed, redound to the benefit of the Arabs, too. Eventually, coexistence ought to be possible. This was the logic of mixture or partition, not ethnic cleansing.

Increasingly, Arabs saw Jews as aliens who meant to displace them— strangers backed, moreover, by colonial powers, first the Ottoman Empire, then the British Mandate. Not only were they losing ownership of the land, but the "conquest of labor" policy also excluded them from paid farmwork, the next best thing. Ottoman security was weak, and Arabs launched armed attacks on Jews. Such violence amounted to more than simple "marauding" and "banditry," to use the Zionists' terms. What was taking place was a radical collision of land tenure systems.

In the eyes of the Palestinians, the fact that their fields were legally, formally sold to the Zionist settlers counted for little. Neither written contracts nor occasional compensation outweighed traditional attachments to the land. "Sometimes, the fellahin accepted compensation from Jewish settlement bodies," the historian Rashid Khalidi writes. "But at other times, they resisted their dispossession, on occasion with violence." Then the Zionists relied on the state—first the Ottoman Empire, later the British Mandate—to permit them to take over the land. Resentments festered, along with violence against the new settlements.

Ambivalent Intertwinings

America's settlers, too, as we have seen earlier, saw the land not only as a wondrously fertile terrain but also as a divine reward, God's promised gift to His chosen people. But the same land was already inhabited, awkwardly enough, by exotic others. What to do? The newcomers proselytized the others, fought them, but at the same time—contradictory as it might seem—admired them, befriended them, even entertained fantasies of romancing them.

Ambivalence toward the natives showed up as early as Columbus's letter to the king and queen of Spain shortly after his landing in the New World, wherein he called them

> a loving people, and without greed, and docile in everything.
> I assure Your Highnesses that I believe that in the world there
> are not a better people or a better land. They love their neigh-
> bors as themselves, and they have the sweetest speech in the
> world, and [they are] gentle and always laughing.

But respect was not recognition on equal terms. Columbus also wrote that the natives were "good for ordering about and for forcing to work, to plant, and to do all that may be necessary, and to make them build towns, and to teach them to go about clothed and according to our customs." With no sign of bad conscience, he proceeded to abduct ten of his tractable and peaceable hosts back to the Old World. Further pursuing the logic of what would later be called "the clash of civilizations," the early English colonists in their imaginative works gravitated toward tales of combat, featuring white hunter-heroes resorting to arms to defend civilization (especially imperiled womanhood) against savage depredations.

But while sagas of white heroes up against wily Indians poured out over the subsequent centuries, the colonists' culture left room for romance, not least the pathos of doomed romance. Narratives of romantic relationships between whites and Indians were common throughout the eighteenth and nineteenth centuries. In this scenario of what the literary historian Werner Sollors calls "red-white fusion," the newcomers "becom[e] one with the continent," "gain legitimacy through love and in defiance of the greed for gold and the ruthless politics which were sometimes logically associated with white fathers." "Omnipresent in American folklore," in short, "is residual evidence of a covered-up love story."

With romance comes elegy. The story of Pocahontas's romantic union with the settler John Rolfe gives way to "tales of lovers' leaps," which "fill many volumes of folklore" from 1728 on—tales of Indian maidens jumping to their deaths when denied the chance to marry their true loves, who are either whites or members of rival tribes. Not only as individuals but as peoples, the noble savages remain connected with doomed romance. "In the cult of the vanishing Indian," Sollors writes, "the children of nature were forever imagined on the brink of the abyss; they were, as Cotton Mather had already put it [in 1702], the 'veriest Ruines of Mankind.'" This is one of America's longest-lasting literary and artistic traditions—the heartbroken white man contemplating the doleful consequences of incontrovertible progress through civilizational displacement, a theme running through Jefferson's writings (as we have already seen) and flourishing in James Fenimore Cooper's best-selling tributes to the vanishing Indian aristocracy, notably *The Last of the Mohicans*, which described the Indians as "fearless," "dignified," "noble," "proud," "determined," and "brave" precisely at the pinnacle of President Andrew Jackson's policy of Indian removal. This tradition of poignant farewell continued in the early-twentieth-century photos of Edward S. Curtis, the dioramas of New York's Museum of Natural History, sidekick characters such as the Lone Ranger's Tonto (1933–) and Hollywood movies such as *Broken Arrow* (1950), and through popular accounts such as *Ishi in Two Worlds* (1961) and *Black Elk Speaks* (originally published in 1932 and resuscitated in 1961). In its fascination with the virtues (sometimes exaggerated) of the defeated Native Americans, the American counterculture that popularized the noble savage tales was not really a counterculture at all—it was the mainstream.

The unchosen, too, struggled with the implications of their neighbors' odd theological conceits. They raged and robbed and killed, but the theme of dark love never entirely vanished. Jefferson, in his *Notes on the State of Virginia,* honored the Iroquois Chief Logan of Ohio, quoting at length his admission of defeat, which, authentic or not, explicitly spoke of love:

> I appeal to any white man to say, if ever he entered Logan's cabin hungry, and he gave him not meat; if ever he came cold and naked, and he clothed him not. During the course of the last long and bloody war, Logan remained idle in his cabin, an advocate for peace. Such was my love for the whites that my countrymen pointed as they passed, and said, Logan is the friend of the white men. I have even thought to live with you but for the injuries of one man . . . [who] the last spring, in cold blood, and unprovoked, murdered all the relations of Logan, not sparing even my women and children. There runs not a drop of my blood in the veins of any living creature. This has called on me for revenge. I have sought it: I have killed many: I have fully glutted my vengeance. . . . Who is there to mourn for Logan? Not one.

This is more the speech of a jilted lover than of a vanquished warlord. It is drastically different from the bloodthirsty speeches by other chiefs, particularly Tecumseh's later, bloodcurdling cry: "Let the white race perish! . . . War now! War always! War on the living! War on the dead!" But Logan's speech was also popular and resonant, perhaps because it fulfilled the benign wishes of early Americans. His elegiac tone must have struck them as genuine.

The case of Israelis and Palestinians is more complicated. Among neither is there a literary tradition of romantic unions such as that of Pocahontas and John Rolfe, nor is there tenderness like Logan's. Love stories are not nearly so common on either side of the Israeli-Palestinian divide. Palestinian hatred for Israelis—sometimes for all Jews—is easy to find. And yet, even as we write, at an inauspicious time for Israeli-Palestinian relations, the majority of Palestinians still reject the ferocious theology of Hamas. According to a survey conducted by the Palestinian Jerusalem Media and Communications Centre in June 2009 on the West Bank and Gaza, for example, only 19 percent of Palestinians supported the militant Islamist organization, compared with 27 percent five months earlier, when Israel's military campaign on Hamas-governed Gaza was at its peak. It seems likely that most Palestinians view Hamas in an instrumental fashion. They offer moderate support when they perceive the organization as capable of effective resistance to Israeli occupation, but do not necessarily share its vision of Muslims as the true chosen people destined to inherit the earth and punish the infidel Jews.

Judging from their most celebrated literature, Palestinians speak in more nuanced voices. They denounce the Zionists for dispossessing them, of course. What Jewish Israelis commemorate as their founding day, they mark as "al Naqba," the Catastrophe. Sometimes they embrace fury, bitterness, and vengeance; sometimes they yearn for normality. Like most refugee literature, that of the Palestinians evokes an idyllic past. It romanticizes the writer's childhood, which usually predates Israel. (Most major Palestinian poets were born before the establishment of the state.) Their responses mix rage, resignation, and hope.

The archetypal statement of this bittersweet combination is a 1974 novel, *The Secret Life of Saeed the Pessoptimist,* a recasting of *Can-*

dide written by Emile Habiby, an Israeli Arab who served for two decades in the Knesset (as a Communist) and was the only man ever awarded the highest civilian honors from both the Israeli government and the Palestine Liberation Organization. Its protagonist, like Habiby himself, finds himself, after Israel's founding, a citizen of the Jewish state. A simpleminded and kindhearted man, Saeed collaborates with the authorities only to be whisked away to outer space. Transformed from a stupid and petty collaborator to an independent man, he is determined to live a happy life in oppressive circumstances. The sole way to do that, Habiby claims, is by embracing pessoptimism—the principle of making the most of an absurd situation by "distinguishing between bad and worse." "It could have been worse" is Saeed's formula for living the best possible life in what is very far from the best of all possible worlds.

Poetry is the Palestinians' most popular literary form, and not surprisingly, much of it burns with incendiary rhetoric. Another Communist poet, Tawfiq Zayyad, onetime mayor of Nazareth and also a member of the Knesset, wrote, for example, these much-quoted lines:

> *we remain like a wall on your chests,*
> *in your throats,*
> *like a piece of glass, like a cactus thorn,*
> *and in your eyes,*
> *a storm of fire.*

Taha Muhammad Ali, whose family fled his native village near Nazareth when it was bombed by an Israeli warplane in 1948, wrote "Thrombosis in the Veins of Petroleum" in 1973:

> *I fell into a pit*
> *but didn't die;*
> *I sank in a pond*
> *When I was young,*

THE UNCHOSEN

But did not die . . .
I won't die! I will not die!
I'll linger on—a piece of shrapnel
The size of a penknife
Lodged in the neck;
I'll remain—
A blood stain
The size of a cloud
On the shirt of this world!

But Taha said later: "The poem is angry. It is too direct." Over the years, his writing evolved. In 1988, he declared, "bitterness follows me"—and this was not a blessing. By 1990, he was writing:

After we die,
hate will be
the first thing
to putrefy
within us . . .

and in another poem tracked through a complete emotional cycle from innocence—

I was a fool!
I was naïve . . .
and wanted to fly

—to fury:

I wanted to burn down the world!
Wanted to stab it
in its soft belly,
and see it dismembered
after I'd drowned it.

He confessed to "dreaming of bombers." But then he committed his "great apostasy":

> *I'm stunned*
> *and abandoned by everything,*
> *and nothing of me remains*
> *except . . . the fool! . . .*
> *He shakes hands with creatures of various sorts,*
> *embraces the righteous and wicked alike,*
> *greets the victim and hangman as one.*
> *The fool!*
> *He hugs the world like a pillow*
> *. . . without there appearing on his face*
> *any indication at all*
> *that he's bothered*
> *by the sobbing*
> *or the tears*
> *pouring from the sockets of his eyes!*

The vengeful poet may not forgive, but he has found a way to go on—and yet without being released from the Palestinian predicament. Like other pessoptimists, he has learned to distinguish between bad and worse and to embrace the simple delights of the world.

Mahmoud Darwish, the most celebrated of Palestinian poets, began his career writing taunts. But already in 1964, even before the Israeli occupation of the West Bank and Gaza, Darwish saw that the poetry of resentment had limits: "I do not hate people," reads "Identity Card," one of his most famous poems, "nor do I encroach / but if I become hungry / the usurper's flesh will be my food / beware . . . / beware . . . / of my hunger / and my anger!" Three years later, witnessing the messianic zeal common among Israel's Jews in the aftermath of the Six-Day War, Darwish wrote a poem in the voice of an Israeli soldier. "I want a good heart," says his narrator, "not the weight of a gun's magazine. / I refuse to die / turning my gun my love / on women and children."

The soldier dreams not of triumphs and conquests—as his brothers-in-arms so often did in the Hebrew poetry of Israel's first two decades—but "of a bird, of lemon blossom," of ordinary things. He is not attached to the land: "I don't know it," he says, "& I don't feel it as skin & heartbeat." Asked if he would die for it, he replies: "Let me tell you what keeps me in this place: / the speeches stirred me up / they taught me to love the idea of love / but I didn't share the land's heart. / The smell of grass / putting down roots / branches . . . / that part's a dream it's not real." The soldier seems to understand that his peaceable yearnings are doomed to be crushed by the steely wills of generals and politicians, and he departs, a foolish figure, to look for white lilies. The Israeli soldier has turned into a pessoptimist of sorts, a wretched figure who, crushed by history, finds solace and regains his humanity by refusing to succumb to grand historical and theological designs.

To suggest that Jews might dare to reject their divinely scripted calling and partake of simple pleasures—alongside Palestinians—was a subversive act of imagination on two fronts. Darwish's Palestinian readers were shocked by his attempt to humanize the Israeli occupiers, while his Israeli readers resented his speaking in the voice of a Jewish soldier. Just as his Palestinians are not the vitriolic warriors of Hamas trumpeting the Muslim version of chosenness, his Israeli is not the truculent settler crusading to retrieve biblical purity. The soldier understands "only the things / he could smell / the things beneath his hands / understanding . . . / that home / is sipping his mother's coffee / & coming back safely at evening."

This vision of simple joys rhymes with the most elemental modern value: the pursuit of individual happiness. It comports with the idea of Israel as a state founded so that Jews could finally live normal and satisfying lives. This vision is quiet. There is no call to martyrdom. There is no "Alpha and Omega," no Great Tribulation, no Second Coming, no rebellion of Satan, no Judgment Day, no New

Heaven or New Earth, no "finishing end" at hand. There is neither the thunder of messianic promise nor the hatred that inflicts righteous punishment upon infidels and shakes the foundations of the earth. There can be conflict between people of "good heart," ordinary women and men who "hug the world like a pillow." What there cannot be is Armageddon.

The Rise of the Counter-Chosen

Then why, again and again, do some (by no means all, but recurrently some) of those who presume to speak in the name of the dispossessed yearn for "the final conflict," the absolute confrontation between pure good and pure evil? Why see history as melodrama? Why demonize the adversary? Why not defend righteous interests and fight for the good without the aim of annihilating an enemy? Why yield to the siren song of Armageddon?

Chosenness gives rise to an unanticipated tragedy. This idea that accomplishes so much for the people who embrace it—that not only keeps them intact but also encourages them in the conviction that, whatever their suffering, they remain deserving—such a comforting idea is infectious. Chosenness begets chosenness—and rage against those who held themselves chosen before. It erupted in the Roman Empire when Christians castigated the Jews for killing their Lord. It erupts again in our own time when children of the Enlightenment lazily converge with religious absolutists in talking as though most of what troubles the world is the United States and Israel.

When Jews and Americans founded themselves on the idea of divine election, they triggered an ongoing tragedy of replication. When a people believe themselves to be God's representative on earth, their presumption is so immensely powerful, so world-shaking, that it stirs others as well, their neighbors and rivals, who may not, at first, have thought of themselves so grandly but come to appreciate what such thinking can accomplish—the morale it can build, the discipline it can instill, the stamina it can encourage. It stirs them to envy, resentment, and bitterness, to an all-or-nothing mood, even to the fervent use of world-scourging violence.

In other words, the idea of chosenness, once it came into the world, hardened into a portable ensemble, an ideological package, ready at hand but also adaptable, one that could be turned to use by other peoples, or at least by the would-be leaders of other peoples as they go about the process of acquiring credentials to justify their ascendancy. And so, in sum, a cascade began. The idea of chosenness by a single God, having shaken a polytheistic world millennia ago, set off aftershocks that continue to shake the ground well into our own day. And there is, in principle, no limit to the violence that can be justified against a people who were, after all, stamped long ago with the mark of Cain.

The Old Testament prophets were among the first to discover that the temptation of demonology acts as balm to the wounded, as does the promise of infinite reward. The prophets are remembered not despite but because of their extremity. No grand upheaval was ever drummed into being by becalmed pragmatists making modest promises. Those who quiver with the radical impulse can easily be tempted to hear Wagnerian cadenzas and behold the invisible visions of future utopias. Visions of the invisible have an eerie power, for the visionary, like the shaman, cannot be refuted. The vision erases the past: "Every valley shall be exalted, and every mountain and hill shall be made low: and the crooked shall be made straight, and the rough places plain" (Isaiah 40:4). Has anyone seen such a future come to pass? No. Does anyone live there? No. But neither has anyone seen it fail to come to pass. Surely it is so magnificent that the righteous are obliged to invoke "the wrath of the Lord" (Jeremiah 6:11) to bring it on, so that "the nation and kingdom that will not serve thee shall perish; yea, those nations shall be utterly wasted" (Isaiah 60:12).

The good versus the wicked, the blessed versus the doomed: the Manichaean scenario stands at an odd angle to ordinary life, so it tends to be the preoccupation of unusual people—prophets. Most people at most times are reconciled to lives of adjustment and increment. They live modest lives—content, more or less, with their discontent. They eke out a portion of happiness. There is enough life to live. Uneasily, with grumbles and shrugs, with pathologies and periodic revolts, and—not least—by carving out small, private satisfactions, most people get by with a modicum of salvation. Few require an unqualified remaking of the world.

But from time to time, the voices of prophets shatter the quietude, announcing that history trembles on a knife-edge. For them, suffering is proof of anointment. The whirlwind is nigh. The trumpet sounds. The new prophets decant old prophecies. The sacred book—written, interpreted, taught, studied, rewritten, reinterpreted—decrees that a radical turnover will cleanse the earth and bring forth new men and women. The call of Armageddon booms forth—sometimes from churches, sometimes from synagogues, sometimes from mosques, sometimes from Little Red Books. Spines shiver. After Year Zero will come Year One. The usurpers, those who falsely claimed to have been chosen by God, are singled out for opprobrium and doom. Destroy them and all will be well! Heralds of the apocalypse arise, calling upon the *truly* chosen to cleanse themselves of the impurities of everyday life, to scourge and depose corrupt and tyrannical princes, to follow headlong into the cauldrons of confrontation where once and for all the last are to be made first and the first, last.

If the scenario sounds familiar, it is because the Jews do not stand alone in the shadow of the Old Testament. The prophets' one-two combination—condemning those who fail the Lord while in the next breath promising an eternity incomprehensibly great—marks more than a few scripts for redemption. The prophecies and battle cries resound across the millennia, and they have not ceased to erupt during the past half century. Christians, down through the seventeenth-century Puritans and eighteenth-century American revolutionaries, took heart from Exodus, the Gospels, and the book of Revelation. Marx resorted to the prophetic template when he heralded the proletariat as the class to end all classes. So did Lenin; so did Mao, who stretched the ranks of the saved to encompass the peasantry; and so, in the 1960s, did Che Guevara and Frantz Fanon, heralding a global uprising by the "Third World" poor that Fanon called the "wretched of the earth." In another key, so did the most influential prophet of all, Muhammad of Mecca, and so do today's jihadis. Secular revolutionaries, prophets of Armageddon, messengers of the Ultimate, moderns who proclaim a new start to history—all sound like the ancients when they thunder that darkness is the prologue to absolute light.

Around the world, the year 1968, plus or minus, constituted a hinge moment in historical time. The reasons were by no means the same everywhere, nor were the means—although the language of revolution came easily to the lips whether the tactics involved civil disobedience, mob brutality, or automatic weapons; or, for that matter, psychedelics and electric guitars, or mystical disciplines, or the many varieties of tuning in, turning on, and dropping out. Insurgencies were colored by local emotions and ambitions, and they emerged primarily from below, though at times appearances were deceiving and they came from above, as in Mao's Cultural Revolution. It is not a moral judgment but an empirical one that from Mexico to the Middle East, from Cuba to China, from Prague to Paris, Berkeley to Berlin, intimations of a sharp break in history were loosed in the streets—and even, weirdly, in the recording studios, clubs, and dance halls, for inklings of a new world emerged not just, or not even mainly, in the form of ideas, but also in the longing for "new souls" via music, drugs, and style.

Intellectuals sometimes herald such moments in advance and are lionized, cursed, and feared for it. In his famous 1961 preface to Frantz Fanon's *Wretched of the Earth,* Jean-Paul Sartre sharpened

Fanon's own already razor-sharp Manichaeism with a paean to anticolonial violence. "The settler," Sartre wrote, "has only one recourse: force, when he can command it; the native has only one choice, between servitude or sovereignty. . . . [H]atred . . . is [the natives'] only wealth. . . . [A] fighter's weapon is his humanity. . . . [T]o shoot down a European is to kill two birds with one stone, to destroy an oppressor and the man he oppresses at the same time: there remain a dead man, and a free man. . . . [V]iolence, like Achilles' lance, can heal the wounds that it has inflicted." The giddy and mechanical absolutism of Sartre's either/or cast of mind—servitude vs. supremacy, oppressed vs. oppressor, native vs. settler, West vs. East, being vs. nothingness—had never sounded more urgent, more thrilling.

Fanon was an heir to Europe's universalist passions—a citizen of France who as a teenager had fought and been wounded in the war against the Nazis, and also a black man from Martinique confronted, face-to-face, with Europe's race hatred. He discovered for himself the horrors of French torture in Algeria and immersed himself in the Algerian revolt. He did not need Sartre to convince him that the violence of the colonized has "a positive, formative character," that it "unifies the people" and undermines "regionalism and tribalism"; that on the individual level, it "disinfects."

Fanon, age thirty-six, was dying of leukemia as he finished *The Wretched of the Earth*, attuned to the rhetoric of the precipice, the apocalypse, the sharpest of breaks—a striking parallel to the language of absolute rupture with which God had cried out to Abraham in the desert. Indeed, as Fanon invoked the need for an absolute new beginning, he turned to a form of chosenness. *The Wretched of the Earth* opens and closes with a clarion call to resistance, thundering with intimations of abrupt departures and last things:

> Now, comrades, now is the time to decide to change
> sides . . . shake off the great mantle of night . . . and reach
> for the light. . . . We must abandon our dreams, abandon our

old beliefs and former friendship. We must not lose time in sterile litanies or nauseating mimicry. Let us leave this Europe that never stops talking of man yet massacres him wherever it finds him, on all its own street corners and all over the world. . . .

As his life ran out, Fanon burst out in full prophetic voice about what was at stake—far more than Algerian independence, but an all-around anti-Europe, a "Third World" (itself a French coinage from the 1950s): "The Third World today faces Europe like a colossal mass whose aim should be to try to resolve the problems that Europe has not been able to solve." As for Europe's earlier rebel, America, it had become "a monster, in which the taints, the sickness, and the inhumanity of Europe have grown to appalling dimensions." Salvation was left to the great swath of the world that would constitute a newly promised land: "It is a question of the Third World starting a new history of Man. . . . We must invent, we must discover. . . . For Europe, for ourselves and for humanity, comrades, we must put on a new skin, develop new thinking, try to set afoot a new man." The revolution had to give birth to itself.

The Wretched of the Earth was released into a France confronting the indefatigable reality of the Algerian revolution. In the New World, too, the imagery of anti-imperial revolution was in the air. Revolutionaries were called upon to choose. In 1962, Fidel Castro declared to an adoring throng in Havana:

The duty of every revolutionary is to make revolution. We know that in [Latin] America and throughout the world the revolution will be victorious. But revolutionaries cannot sit in the doorways of their homes to watch the corpse of imperialism pass by. The role of Job does not behoove a revolutionary. Each year by which [Latin] America's liberation may be hastened will mean millions of children rescued from death, millions of minds, freed for learning, infinitudes of sorrow spared the peoples. Even though the Yankee imperialists are preparing a bloodbath for [Latin] America they will not succeed in drowning the people's struggle. They will evoke universal hatred against themselves.

The revolution. The corpse of imperialism. Universal hatred. Not Job but Jeremiah.

An English translation of *The Wretched of the Earth* appeared in 1963—the year Buddhist monks immolated themselves in Saigon, and the Vietnam War crashed into American consciousness. The next year and the one after that, the war escalated markedly—the Tonkin Gulf incident and congressional resolution in 1964, the bombing campaign over North Vietnam and the marines landing in 1965. In the United States and elsewhere, civil rights militants and black nationalists were casting about for a theory to unify their experience of the world. In this setting, Fanon's reputation flourished. He was a man of the Third World—the island of Martinique—but a cosmopolitan, a psychiatrist, educated on the French mainland, tempted by the grandeur of continental theory. He had been a witness to the misery of both the tortured and the torturers. Intellectuals who identified with the Third World found, in Fanon, both the aura of concreteness and the breathtaking abstraction of high-flying French rhetoric. Tributes to Fanon erupted on every continent. The third leaflet published by the Palestinian Fatah group, called "Revolution and Violence, the Path to Victory," has been described as "little more than a collection of quotations from" Fanon's *Wretched of the Earth.*

The Palestinian-American critic Edward Said, who in polemical moments indulged in a Manichaeanism inflamed by the Palestinian cause, was one of those who found in Fanon a link between Marxist totality and Third World anticolonialism. In *Culture and Imperialism,* Said later wrote admiringly of Fanon's insight into how a culture of black and white reproduces itself: "On the logical plane, the Manicheanism of the settler produces the Manicheanism of the native."

All in all, throughout the various New Lefts of the United States and Europe, in Latin America and North Africa, the late sixties were ripe for exaltation of "the other." It was the season of revolutionary guerrillas, their iconography as vivid as their leaders were picturesque. Che Guevara, martyred in 1967, represented Cuba's new revolutionary international, known as the Tri-Continental. In Vietnam, avuncular Ho Chi Minh and the rubber-sandaled Vietcong were courageous and, astoundingly, triumphant underdogs. In the midst of such a melodramatic landscape, what was to be made of events in the Promised Land?

Israel, victorious in the Six-Day War, now occupied the West Bank and Gaza. Israel was allied with the napalm-equipped carpet bombers of Vietnam. Israel was now cast as the deputy in the Middle East of an imperialist apparatus that was also allied with the settler regime in South Africa, Portuguese colonialists in Africa, and the Shah's torture state in Iran. Israel's joyous 1967 amounted to one immense humiliation for an Arab world where Marxism and then Pan-Arabism had failed—a region of absolutisms lacking any practical idea how to dig out from beneath the residue of Ottoman, French, and British colonialism or, indeed, its own tyranny.

The Manichaean imagination of Third Worldists knew where to look. The pattern of the world craved simplification into one single, ongoing, momentous collision of the north against the south, the First World against the Third, the falsely chosen against the truly chosen. To organize its world into a simple geometry, the Third Worldist left signed up with the Palestinians—not so much actual landlocked Palestinians in their harsh and intricate relationship with the Jews of Israel, but stylized Palestinian leaders who embodied "the resistance," a luminous abstraction that prophecy seemed to exculpate in advance as it pursued its armed struggle. Hapless when Israel crushed the Arab armies in 1967, these "victims of the victims," as Said called the Palestinians, were now ready-made to be cast as the wretched whose destiny—*manifest* destiny, one might have said—under Yasir Arafat was to inherit the occupied earth.

Faith in the ultimate triumph of prophecy now had a protagonist. The unchosen were cast as the newly chosen, the counter-chosen.

So it has come to pass that to this day, under prophetic banners, political movements continue to recruit the young and the passionate, advertising their fights as not so much for the Kingdom of Man but for the Kingdom of Heaven. Their ideological preoccupations vary. Many affirm justice, rationality, and other Enlightenment virtues, traditionally the gospel of the left. But following Fanon, too many critics of the established order demonize the irredeemable, hydra-headed enemies they find at the root of all evils—chosen for wickedness.

Let us be plain: for those who subscribe to the Manichaean worldview, the black-and-white absolutism of chosenness knows no political or religious bounds. We hear it in the ravings of Baruch Goldstein, the slaughterer of Muslims at the Cave of the Patriarchs in 1994. We hear it from the assassin of Yitzhak Rabin in 1995. We hear it in the vicious sermons of Osama bin Laden. We note how easily those who oppose America's wars slide into the assumption that the United States is everywhere and always the enemy of the Muslim world, as if the United States had not supported the Afghan mujahedin and their Arab allies, including Osama bin Laden, between 1978 and 1989; as if supporting the independence of Kuwait against Saddam Hussein's 1990 invasion was an assault upon Islam; as if the United States had not sided with Bosnian Muslims (1995) and Kosovar Muslims (1999) against Christian Serbia. We note the fact-free vitriol of Iranian president Mahmoud Ahmadinejad, denying that the Holocaust took place. We note that for Hugo Chávez of Venezuela, it is not enough to excoriate Israel (as we do) for the brutality of its attack on Gaza in December 2008, he must declare Israel "genocidal" and refer casually to "the descendants of those who crucified Christ" as being among those who "took possession of the riches of the world." But in a way somehow more shocking, we note echoes of the same all-or-nothing strain from many intellectuals and activists on the international left ostensibly committed to the rational and the factual. We observe the best-selling writer on the worldwide left, Noam Chomsky, who has for decades been so exercised by American and American-sponsored power and violence as to overlook or minimize or explain away the depredations committed by others, or (as he and Edward S. Herman did vis-à-vis the Khmer Rouge) to pin the blame for them on *American* crimes. We note how often, from a world of injustice and woe, Israel is singled out for malice by would-be partisans of universal rights who avert their eyes, most of the time, from slavery and slaughter in Sudan and the abuse of women throughout the Arab world. In a world of dispossession and monstrous injustice, why the rancor and disproportion?

It is hard to miss the counter-prophetic rage, the all-consuming execration of those whom the counter-chosen bid to replace— the chosen peoples of old. In these obsessive hatreds we hear not so much love for justice, or the dispossessed, as the curses cast by Paul and Mohammad at their most unforgiving, the faith and fury that herald the passing of the mantle of chosenness from some of God's children to others.

4. A Special Friendship

ASK AMERICAN POLITICIANS about the United States' relationship with Israel, ask their Israeli counterparts about the Jewish state's feelings toward America, and phrases like "special friendship" repeatedly crop up. It is as if they have chosen each other.

"Special friendship" is a platitude, of course, but it is a sincere and popular one, and evidently deeply held. A 2007 Gallup survey, for example, found that the majority of Americans not only hold a strongly favorable opinion of Israel but also view it as America's "vital friend"—the only foreign country regarded as both estimable and important. For their part, Israelis are more than eager to return the love. A recent study, conducted by the Pew Global Attitudes Project and surveying forty-seven nations, found that while "anti-Americanism is extensive," the citizens of Israel—more than their counterparts in any other developed nation in the world—hold overwhelmingly positive views of everything American, from its business conduct to its culture. As statements about how people experience the world, platitudes deserve stiff questioning, but they should also be explored, taken seriously. People live them.

Our journey through the two national histories points us toward the conclusion that there must be more to their alliance than meets the eye. The American-Israeli bond carries a host of benefits for both parties, true, but it *feels* like more than a marriage of convenience, more than a convergence of interests, more even than an alliance of democracies whose political systems resemble each other. The sense of underlying affinity carries deep emotions on both sides—deep enough for Washington and Jerusalem to override many sour moments and conflicts of interest. We can date it from Israel's birth on

May 15, 1948, when President Harry Truman was the first statesman to recognize the new nation, phoning David Ben-Gurion a mere eleven minutes after the latter announced the birth of the first Jewish state in two millennia.

Truman's support was far from a foregone conclusion. The State and Defense Departments were dead set against it. His defense secretary, James Forrestal, had told Truman's counsel, Clark Clifford: "There are thirty million Arabs on one side and about 600,000 Jews on the other. Why don't you face up to the realities?" On May 12, Truman had summoned his top aides, Clifford and Secretary of State George C. Marshall chief among them, to the Oval Office. He was scrambling to formulate a response to the expected events of the coming days: the end of the British Mandate in Palestine, the likely declaration of independence, and the armed conflict with neighboring Arab nations that would inevitably follow. Clifford favored recognizing the new state immediately. Ben-Gurion, he warned, was already relying on Czech armaments and could easily find himself increasingly beholden to the Soviets if Moscow decided to embrace Israel. America, Clifford said, would do well to send a strong message of friendship to the Palestinian Jews and, at the same time, bolster its security interests in the region by standing behind a newborn democracy.

Secretary of State Marshall was livid. The only way to avoid bloodshed in Palestine, he thought, was to replace the expiring British Mandate with a U.N. trusteeship over the disputed territory—an expedient meant to last until a reasonable solution could be designed. Marshall thought Clifford's position foolish and doubted aloud that the president's counsel even deserved to be in on such an important decision. "He is a domestic adviser," huffed the retired wartime commander, "and this is a foreign policy matter."

Truman replied drily that he himself had invited Clifford to present the case for immediate recognition. Marshall was not appeased. His face reddened, Clifford later recalled, and he seemed on the verge of combustion. Finally, Marshall could no longer contain his anger. By his own account: "I stated bluntly that if the president were to follow Mr. Clifford's advice, and if I were to vote in the next election, I would vote against the president."

These were extraordinarily harsh words coming from the man who was probably America's most popular public figure, the author of its postwar diplomatic doctrine, seen by many as the nexus between the seasoned FDR, whom he had served as wartime commander, and Truman, the inexperienced successor. Truman knew that Marshall was speaking not only for himself but for most of the foreign-policy elite as a whole, which was exceedingly attentive to Arab views and the oil that accompanied them. Sensing that Marshall's intense dissent could well be the prelude to a very public resignation, Truman adjourned the meeting, suggested that everyone "sleep on it," and hinted to his still incensed secretary of state that he was leaning his way.

This White House meeting brought to the surface a host of considerations that remain common today. First among them: the political weight of American Jews and the intensity of their attachment to Israel, as measured in campaign contributions as well as votes. Truman himself had no doubt that Jewish clout counted. Meeting in 1946 with American diplomats concerned about what they perceived as his undue sympathy for the struggling Zionist movement in Palestine, Truman spoke straightforwardly about his political calculus. "I am sorry, gentlemen," he said, "but I have to answer to hundreds of thousands who are anxious for the success of Zionism; I do not have hundreds of thousands of Arabs among my constituents." Fifteen years later, the newly elected John F. Kennedy, meeting with David Ben-Gurion at New York's Waldorf Astoria hotel, sounded the same theme. "You know I was elected by Jews," he told the Israeli leader. "I was elected by the Jews of New York. I have to do something for them. I will do something for you." And James Baker, President George H. W. Bush's secretary of state, expressed the darker side of the same sentiment when he allegedly muttered in 1992: "Fuck the Jews, they don't vote for us." Baker denied speaking those words, but the second part was incontrovertibly true.

Votes and campaign funds are never negligible considerations, but independently, Israel's supporters already viewed the Jewish state as an asset in the geopolitical gamesmanship of the Cold War. As Clark Clifford argued, Israel's dealings with Czechoslovakia, and the socialist beliefs of the Zionist founding fathers, made it look as much like a potential Soviet client as like an American ally. Washington's support for the Jewish state during the four decades that followed Ben-Gurion's declaration—from Kennedy's decision to supply Israel with an advanced missile defense system to Ronald Reagan's designation of Israel as a "major non-NATO ally," giving it access to advanced armaments as well as the right to bid on U.S. defense contracts—was often couched as a riposte to Moscow. Cold War considerations arguably guided Johnson to supply Israel with Phantom fighter jets in 1968. During his historic 1972 meeting with Zhou Enlai, Richard Nixon assured the Chinese premier that neither he nor national security adviser Henry Kissinger had any interest in Israel apart from its importance as a pawn in the geopolitical struggle against the Soviets. "My concern in the Middle East—and, incidentally, it is Dr. Kissinger's too, because while he is Jewish he is an American first—our concern is much bigger than Israel," Nixon told Zhou, as he recounted in his memoir. "We believe the Soviet Union is moving to reach its hands out in that area. It must be resisted." (Of course, Nixon might have simply been addressing Zhou in language he knew the Chinese would grasp.) It would be naive to think that geostrategic concerns were absent when, in 1973, Nixon and Kissinger airlifted 22,305 tons of tanks, artillery, and ammunition to resupply the Israel Defense Forces, which had been badly hurt after the Syrian-Egyptian surprise attack on Yom Kippur.

But electoral and geopolitical considerations alone, however significant in the thinking of American officials, fall short in explanatory power. They do not account for the emotional force of the bond. The special affinity that Americans feel for Israel and that Israelis feel for America enjoys an enduring visceral temperature hard to account for by calculations of mutual interest or by political parallels. The realist arguments in behalf of this friendship have ebbed and flowed with the vicissitudes of circumstance, but since 1967, at any rate—when Israel, having sought America's good graces for two decades, finally found geopolitical conditions favorable for strengthening the bond—its consistency has been remarkable.

On the American side, the affinity for the Jewish state overrides a myriad of severe political and financial costs. Even at times when its price in dollars and cents shoots upward—whenever the West Bank occupation and Israel's wartime conduct incur the wrath of Arabs and other Muslims and lead to spikes in the price of the world's most indispensable commodity, spikes that tear into American prosperity, not to mention the rest of the world's—the Israeli-American friendship mainly glows warmly. When, in 1973, OPEC reacted to the American resupply of Israel during the Yom Kippur War by launching an oil embargo that quadrupled the price of oil and sent the American economy into a tailspin, America did not reconsider its bond to the Jewish state. Nor did that bond weaken during the 1990s, when the collapse of the Soviet Union rendered obsolete the Cold War logic of client states. Nor has it loosened as millions of Arab-American voters have emerged to counterbalance, at least, some of the electoral benefits of cultivating American Jews. Rather, as the strategic rationale for America's alliance with Israel has become more tenuous, the special friendship has flourished, taking on more of the qualities of a resonance of identity, a unity of the soul, a deep and self-evident sympathy.

How to explain its intensity? Israeli and American elites repeatedly declare that it stems from shared values. Politicians of both nations invoke a "common heritage" and never tire of repeating that Israel is the only democracy in the Middle East. Representative government, a free press and speech, robust politics, capitalism: the similarities are indeed many. To American eyes, this political affinity counts for something. But how much? Neither the United States nor Israel parades any particular affinity with democratic India, say, or South Korea. These nations are friends, but not *special* friends.

Americans and Israelis do not look at Indians or South Koreans and feel that the same spirit flows through them, that they stand on the same ground of virtue. Even the United Kingdom, formerly the colonial sovereign of both Israel and America, falls short of this exalted status. Diplomats, journalists, and politicians may feel strong affinities for that other English-speaking democracy across the sea, but England fails to stir deep-set passions the way America does for Israelis and Israel for Americans.

It must matter that, between the United States and Israel, calculations of politics and affirmations of values are warmed by flames of religious conviction. The sense of mutual recognition has surely been bolstered by the political commitments of dispensationalism—the evangelical tendency that sees history as a series of preordained phases that culminate in the flourishing of a Jewish state and the subsequent return of Christ to Jerusalem. Dispensationalism prompted many American Protestants—Jerry Falwell and Pat Robertson the most prominent among them—to adopt a vigorous Zionism. In his spectacular best-seller of 1970, *The Late Great Planet Earth,* Hal Lindsey called Israel "the fuse of Armageddon"—a good thing, for the rebuilding of the Temple would lead to the Second Coming. Writing in 1981, Falwell was blander, but still blunt: "To stand against Israel is to stand against God. We believe that history and scripture prove that God deals with nations in relation to how they deal with Israel."

Such sentiments, resounding in an apocalyptic with-us-or-against-us vein, have not been limited to the pulpit. Since 1995, they have emanated from the *Left Behind* novels—which sold tens of millions of copies—coauthored by the evangelical Reverend Tim LaHaye, a prominent figure in the founding of the Moral Majority and other right-wing Christian associations. The Moral Majority is no more, but successor organizations continue to crop up. In 2006, the Reverend John Hagee, the spiritual shepherd of an 18,000-member-strong megachurch based in San Antonio, Texas, founded Christians United for Israel (CUFI), an organization dedicated to harnessing dispensationalist enthusiasm for the cause of militant Zionism. One year later, CUFI's national conference drew more than 4,500 people for a tribute to besieged Israel. There, and at subsequent annual rallies, Hagee unleashed one furious speech after the other, starting from the premise that the Palestinians had no right to any land, since Zion had been explicitly promised to Abraham and his Jewish descendants. American politicians joined ambassadors and other officials of the Israeli right in a parade of encomia. Senator Joseph Lieberman, for one, called Hagee a man of God and likened him to Moses, declaring that Hagee has "become the leader of a mighty multitude, even greater than the multitude that Moses led from Egypt to the promised land." President George W. Bush, unable to attend, sent his warm greeting, thanking Hagee and his flock for their "shining example," their "passion and dedication to enhancing the relationship between the United States and Israel." In the religious right wing of the Republican Party, unequivocal support for Israel's most uncompromising tendencies—a position that has come to be labeled "pro-Israel," as if encouraging a friend's most reckless behavior were an act of generosity—has been gospel for more than a quarter-century.

More heatedly debated is the role of the so-called Israel Lobby clustered around the American Israel Public Affairs Committee (AIPAC). Those who cherish its influence and those who deplore it actually share a consensus: that AIPAC weighs heavily on American public opinion and policy toward the Jewish state. That this nexus of influence plays a significant part in securing American aid to Israel is beyond dispute. That it weighs in on the rightward side of Israeli politics, and exercises a considerable pull on Congress, is equally incontrovertible. AIPAC and its allies certainly influence American *policies.* But even AIPAC's lobbying prowess and an often friendly news media cannot by themselves account for Israel's popularity even among the large majority of Americans who are neither Jewish nor Christian Zionists. AIPAC and other groups in its orbit surely capitalize on American feeling for Israel, activate, focus, apply, and amplify it, but they do not initiate it or keep it alive. Sentiments of mutual recognition are not the products of lobbies.

Two nations, two histories, two cultures, two sets of assumptions march to the same drummer. At the heart of the special friendship between Israel and America lies an extraordinary spiritual-cum-ideological bond: their unshakable attachment to the wild idea of divine election, which, however dampened, however sublimated, continues to ripple beneath the surface of everyday events. The sense of commonality even overrides what might be seen as a built-in conflict between two peoples who *each* believe they are chosen—presumably, if God proceeds by ordinary logic, exclusively so. Can *two* nations each be uniquely chosen? But in matters of divine judgment, if theologians can parse it, the rules of exclusivity must break down. Two nations that exist in time both cry out for eternity.

There is, of course, a blatant distinction that sets America and Israel apart. Israel's laws and symbols reflect an absolute national identification with one particular religious and ethnic population, while America, from its inception, has been a haven for different creeds and cultures. America's population has always been predominantly Christian, but its political system floats free of demography. Israel makes its religious origin clear with its flag, its holidays, its use of the Hebrew language, but the United States never seriously considered incorporating specific theological or ethnic components into its emblems or public life. At least outwardly, it remained committed to the universal values captured in that resonant phrase of the Declaration of Independence: life, liberty, and the pursuit of happiness.

Observe the two countries' histories side by side and the parallels are striking. In both cases, a small band of men and women set sail to unknown shores, moved not strictly by the privations of their homelands or the desire for richer, more prosperous futures but by a single, searing idea of consecrated mission. The names they gave themselves connoted the religious nature of their undertaking: the first residents of New England were *Pilgrims;* the European Jews who settled in Palestine early in the twentieth century *Olim,* or those who ascend. Both terms betrayed a deeper interest in the next world than in this one. Having set up camp, both groups made much of the importance of labor on the land. From Jefferson's yeomen to Zionist founding father A. D. Gordon's sanctified workers, early Americans and early Zionists imagined models for humanity among toiling farmers capable of both self-sustenance and self-governance. Both spoke of accommodating the native sons they encountered in their Promised Lands; the last words of the dying president in Herzl's Zionist novel, *Altneuland,* are: "The stranger must be made to feel at home in our midst." In each case, the same sterner logic set in. The stranger threatened the purity of the project, or so it appeared. He was too alien, too wild, too retrograde and unyielding to be granted a significant place in the grand work ahead. Wars flared up, from which the chosen people emerged triumphant. With time, this culture of victory shaped the settlers' sense of their missions. An aura of chosenness hovered around them, a heavenly mandate. It was interpreted as a license to expand in time and in space, godly proof that they were, indeed, most deserving. In the real world, on the earth that human beings share, these beliefs were often translated into marching orders and military commands. The beliefs became the ghosts in the machines of statehood. While seldom articulated anymore in so many words, these beliefs never evaporated. They sank into the nations' collective unconscious. As metaphysical as this may sound, we see no better interpretation of the known facts than to conclude that the foundation of chosenness remains eternally present.

When a people declare themselves chosen, or act as if they are, or were, there is no rolling back the history that ensues. The clock cannot be reset to zero. We cannot choose to be unchosen. We cannot end the ordeal. The cycles of race hatred, revenge, and war cannot be rescinded, erased from memory. History is unsparing.

The concept of chosenness leaves many Israelis and Americans baffled and ill at ease. For educated, largely secular Westerners to credit a biblical notion for the birth of nations seems a tall—even archaic—order. In classrooms and legislative chambers, on op-ed pages and in electronic shoutfests, we feel more comfortable in disputes about who did what to whom, or with policy debates choked with figures, than with inchoate stirrings emanating from the soul and thence heavenward. The subject of chosenness would seem best left to the true believers, the zealous minority who, in both countries, have fashioned theologies of divine election into agendas of narrowness and aggression.

But it would be naive to think that either Americans or Israelis can walk away from the extraordinary, entrancing, ancient, deep, and—in so many ways—odd idea that we are, or began as, God's chosen people.

Whether or not we approach the matter by taking the premise on faith, we must, like Israelites of old, willingly bear the immense burden of membership in a tribe many of whom feel, and have long felt, chosen by God. If we are to overcome the most reckless interpretations of chosenness, it is no use trying to bludgeon the notion into nonexistence. We must stare at it long and hard—must wrestle with it—must reject the crudest, most violent reflexes—must search for subtler, deeper, more constructive uses of the past.

In this arduous journey, we are not without guides. If we consult our national stories, we will see that the path was revealed before. It was marked by Moses, who rejected the surveyor's logic, the rigid dictates of materialism and conquest, for the vision of a kingdom of priests, a holy nation that governs itself with a keen eye to justice and mercy. It was marked again by Lincoln, who spoke of an "almost chosen people" as he pursued the difficult path to emancipation. In every generation, on either side of the ocean, there have been men and women who took the hard road and understood chosenness to be not a prize but a calling.

That calling sounds still. It is not shouted, but whispered softly, like a prayer. It is easy to miss amid all the sound and fury. Sometimes we strain to hear it. To heed it requires effort.

The chosen people must choose.

Acknowledgments

Authors are students—all the more so we two, neither of us a specialist in American or Jewish history. We owe an immense amount to the scholars on whose shoulders we perched, especially those whose work we cite in our Note on Sources. We also benefited from the generosity and sagacity of friends and colleagues who read, queried, objected to, argued with, and otherwise scrutinized our drafts: Allan Silver, Marshall Berman, Eric Alterman, Emmanuel Sivan, Nissim Calderon, Gadi Taub, Michael Kazin, Jackson Lears, and Richard R. John, all of whom understood, like Blake, that opposition was the true measure of friendship. They are not, of course, responsible for any and all weaknesses that remain after we overruled their advice.

Neither is Columbia University, which gave Todd Gitlin the opportunity to teach several sections of Contemporary Civilization, one of the college's core courses, and thereby revivified his taste for fundamentals, and set Liel Leibovitz off on his quest.

At Simon & Schuster, we are indebted to Dedi Felman, for taking this project on, and to Roger Labrie, for skillfully shepherding us through the editorial process.

As always, we remain endlessly thankful to our indefatigable agents, Ellen Levine and Anne Edelstein, bless them.

Finally, to our family and friends in Israel and in America, and to all those on either side of the ocean who work to repair what has been broken, we offer this book as a sober Hallelujah.

Note on Sources

Much like the subjects of our book, we began our inquiry into divine election and its ordeals by turning to the Bible—or rather, several of its English-language translations and, in dicey moments, the original Hebrew. In most cases, we preferred the unsurpassably beautiful King James Version, though occasionally we opted for the clarity of the New International Version, a collaborative effort compiled by dozens of biblical scholars and published in 1978. (Many renditions are conveniently available at www.biblegateway.com.) The reader will have no trouble discerning which translation is which. When drawing on other foreign-language sources, we frequently offer our own translations or modifications, acknowledged as such in the endnotes.

We found stimulus in several comparative studies, including Anthony D. Smith, *Chosen Peoples: Sacred Sources of National Identity;* William R. Hutchison and Hartmut Lehmann, eds., *Many Are Chosen: Divine Election and Western Nationalism;* and Donald H. Akenson, *God's Peoples: Covenant and Land in South Africa, Israel, and Ulster.*

Tracking the Jews' tortuous relationship with the Almighty—from the loins of Abraham to the settlements of modern-day Israel—we were instructed by Michael Walzer's *Exodus and Revolution,* which poses valuable questions about the nature of chosenness and coaxes otherworldly ideas down to the realm of political life, as does *The Jewish Political Tradition* (volume 2: *Membership*), which Walzer coedited with Menachem Lorberbaum, Noam J. Zohar, and Ari Ackerman. Hannah Arendt's essay "The Jews and Society," reprinted in *The Portable Hannah Arendt,* offers extraordinary insight into the traumas occasioned by Emancipation for Europe's Jews. Aviezer Ravitzky's *Messianism, Zionism, and Jewish Religious Radicalism* is an invaluable primer on Jewish eschatology, exploring the convictions of Zionism's precursors, founders, and early opponents. Arthur Hertzberg's *The Zionist Idea: A Historical Analysis and Reader* is a fine collection of works by the movement's guiding lights, and Walter Laqueur's *A History of Zionism* a well-organized guide. On the subject of the birth and growth of Israel's settlements movement, we walk in the paths of Gershom Gorenberg's *The Accidental Empire: Israel and the Birth of the Settlements, 1967–1977* and Akiva Eldar and Idith Zertal's *Lords of the Land: The War for Israel's Settlements in the Occupied Territories, 1967–2007.*

Imposing general surveys of American history useful for tracking the theme of the chosenness motif include Walter McDougall, *Promised Land, Crusader State: The American Encounter with the World Since 1776;* Sean Wilentz, *The Rise of American Democracy: Jefferson to Lincoln;* Daniel Walker Howe, *What Hath God Wrought: The Transformation of America, 1815–1848;* and Albert Weinberg, *Manifest Destiny: A Study of Nationalist Expansionism in American History.*

Among impressive surveys that focus on religious components of American history are Ernest Lee Tuveson, *Redeemer Nation: The Idea of America's Millennial Role;* Conrad Cherry, ed., *God's New Israel: Religious Interpretations of American Destiny;* Nicholas Guyatt, *Providence and the Invention of the United States, 1607–1876;* Mark A. Noll, *America's God: From Jonathan Edwards to Abraham Lincoln;* Garry Wills, *Head and Heart: American Christianities;* and John B. Judis, *The Folly of Empire: What George W. Bush Could Learn from Theodore Roosevelt and Woodrow Wilson.* On the colonial period, we made ample use of Perry Miller, *Errand into the Wilderness;* Andrew Delbanco, *The Puritan Ordeal;* Sacvan Bercovitch, *The American Jeremiad;* Ruth H. Bloch, *Visionary Republic: Millennial Themes in American Thought, 1756–1800;* and Patricia U. Bonomi, *Under the Cope of Heaven: Religion, Society, and Politics in Colonial America.* Necessary correctives to historians' overemphasis on New England are David Hackett Fischer, *Albion's Seed: Four British Folkways in America;* and Jack P. Greene, *Pursuits of Happiness: The Social Development of Early Modern British Colonies and the Formation of American Culture.*

Indispensible and well-written studies of specific presidents, bearing on how they navigated through the rapids of chosenness, include Joseph J. Ellis, *American Sphinx: The Character of Thomas Jefferson*; Anthony F. C. Wallace, *Jefferson and the Indians: The Tragic Fate of the First Americans*; Jon Kukla, *A Wilderness So Immense: The Louisiana Purchase and the Destiny of America*; H. W. Brands, *Andrew Jackson: His Life and Times*; Richard Carwardine, *Lincoln: A Life of Purpose and Power*; H. W. Brands, *T.R.: The Last Romantic*; Clark Clifford, *Counsel to the President*; John Patrick Diggins, *Ronald Reagan: Fate, Freedom, and the Making of History*; and James Mann, *The Rebellion of Ronald Reagan: A History of the End of the Cold War.* Gary Scott Smith, *Faith and the Presidency: From George Washington to George W. Bush,* is useful for its compendious sources.

Blessedly for concordance users and other searchers, many primary sources in American history, including all the presidents' inaugural addresses and the *Collected Works of Abraham Lincoln,* are now available online.

On relationships between the European settlers and Native Americans, we made abundant use of the historical work of James Axtell, particularly *After Columbus: Essays in the Ethnohistory of Colonial North America* and *Beyond 1942: Encounters in Colonial North America* as well as Werner Sollors's study of the literary nuances of those relationships, *Beyond Ethnicity: Consent and Descent in American Culture.*

On the Palestinians, we are indebted to Gershon Shafir's meticulous prehistory of the Arab-Israeli conflict, *Land, Labor and the Origins of the Israeli-Palestinian Conflict, 1882–1914;* as well as to Rashid Khalidi's informative *Palestinian Identity: The Construction of Modern National Consciousness.* The writings of Taha Muhammad Ali, Mahmoud Darwish, and Emile Habibi took us into Palestinian experience. For the Qur'an, we consulted a number of English-language versions, especially that by Arthur John Arberry.

Finally, in portraying the special friendship between the United States and Israel, we are indebted to Warren Bass's *Support Any Friend: Kennedy, Nasser, and the Origins of the U.S.-Israel Alliance,* which combines the scholar's depth with the storyteller's sweep.

Notes

INTRODUCTION

xiii   *"a people that have had a stamp upon them from God"*: Quoted in Conor Cruise O'Brien, *God Land: Reflections on Religion and Nationalism* (Cambridge, MA: Harvard University Press, 1999), p. 26.

xiii   *"Children of Israel once in Egypt"*: ibid., p. 27.

xiii   *"When we think of the former emigrants"*: Quoted in Donald H. Akenson, *God's Peoples: Covenant and Land in South Africa, Israel, and Ulster* (Ithaca, NY: Cornell University Press, 1992), p. 69.

xiii   *"the only god-bearing people on earth"*: Quoted in W. R. Ward, "Response," in William R. Hutchison and Hartmut Lehmann, eds., *Many Are Chosen: Divine Election and Western Nationalism* (Minneapolis: Fortress Press, 1994), Harvard Theological Studies 38, p. 51.

1. "A STIFF-NECKED PEOPLE"

3   *"between me and all flesh"*: Genesis 9:17.

4   *"Leave your country"*: Genesis 12:1.

4   *"great nation"*: Genesis 12:2.

4   *"Abram does as he's told"*: This, incidentally, is the etymology of the word *Hebrew,* or *Ivri,* meaning one who arrived from the other bank (or *Ever* in Hebrew) of the river, a foreigner.

4   *"Lift up your eyes"*: Genesis 13:14–17.

4   *"O sovereign Lord"*: Genesis 15:2.

4   *"Know for certain"*: Genesis 15:11–16.

5   *"In return, He promises a specific prize"*: Genesis 17.

5   *"I swear by myself"*: Genesis 22:16–18.

6   *"Although the whole earth is mine"*: Exodus 19:5–6.

6   *"stiff-necked people"*: Exodus 32:9.

7   *"perfect in his generations"*: Genesis 6:9.

8   *"For I know him"*: Genesis 18:19.

13   *"Will you sweep away the righteous"*: Genesis 18:23–24.

13 *"Abraham has now crossed a threshold"*: Susan Neiman, *Moral Clarity: A Guide for Grown-Up Idealists* (Princeton, NJ: Princeton University Press, 2009), p. 10.

14 *"Kierkegaard was neither the first nor the last"*: See Søren Kierkegaard, *Fear and Trembling* (Cambridge, UK: Cambridge University Press, 2006).

15 *"'The Lord'"*: Deuteronomy 7:7.

15 *"'Not for thy righteousness'"*: Deuteronomy 9:5.

16 *"'Now, therefore'"*: Exodus 19:5–6.

16 *"All that the Lord hath spoken'"*: Exodus 19:8.

16 *"'corrupt'"*: Exodus 32:7.

16 *"'utterly corrupt'"*: Deuteronomy 31:29.

16 *"'warped and crooked'"*: Deuteronomy 32:5.

16 *"'foolish and unwise'"*: Deuteronomy 32:6.

16 *"'a perverse generation'"*: Deuteronomy 32:20.

16 *"'a nation without sense'"*: Deuteronomy 32:28.

17 *"'Whatever you have commanded us'"*: Joshua 1:16–17.

17 *"'prostitute themselves'"*: Deuteronomy 31:16.

17 *"'You rebelled against the command'"*: Deuteronomy 1:26–27.

18 *"'Neither with you only'"*: Deuteronomy 29:14–15.

18 *"Most instructive"*: Since there is no definitive version of the Haggadah, we refrain from citing any partial edition. Readers interested in the range of texts adopted by divergent Jewish communities may wish to consult the open-source Haggadah at www.opensource-haggadah .com.

19 *"But this interpretation is problematic"*: See Michael Walzer, *Exodus and Revolution* (New York: Basic, 1986).

20 *"'holiness lies ahead in time'"*: ibid., p. 103.

22 *"'such as all the other nations'"*: 1 Samuel 8:5.

23 *"'He concedes'"*: 1 Samuel 8:7–9.

23 *"'the land would never be all that'"*: Walzer, *Exodus and Revolution*, p. 101.

23 *"'send the messiah'"*: ibid., p. 125.

25 *"'It is our duty'"*: Nosson Scherman, *The Complete Artscroll Siddur* (New York: Artscroll, 1989), p. 159.

26 *"'catastrophic character'"*: Gershom Scholem, *The Messianic Idea in Judaism* (New York: Schocken, 1971), p. 12.

26 *"They would regulate"*: ibid., p. 19.

26 *"'Let him [the Messiah] come'"*: BT Sanhedrin 98a.

27 *"The sons of Judah have to choose"*: George Eliot, *Daniel Deronda* (New York: Modern Library, 2002), p. 488.

27 *"He who sets oneself apart"*: Maimonides, Mishneh Torah, *Hilkhot Shemita v'Yovel* 13:13. Quoted in Isadore Twersky, ed., *A Maimonides Reader* (Springfield, NJ: Behrman House, 1972), p. 139.

28 *"My heart is in the east"*: Translated from the Hebrew by T. Carmi, as modified by the authors. Quoted in Ilan Stavans, *The Scroll and the Cross: 1,000 Years of Jewish-Hispanic Literature* (New York: Routledge, 2002), p. 46.

28 *"In the mid-seventeenth century"*: See Scholem, *The Messianic Idea,* pp. 58–141, and Scholem, *Sabbatai Ṣevi: The Mystical Messiah: 1626–1676,* trans. R. J. Zwi Werblowsky (Princeton, NJ: Princeton University Press, 1973).

29 *"Every Jew is a limb"*: Quoted in Paul Johnson, *A History of the Jews* (New York: Harper Perennial, 1988), p. 296.

29 *"separated"*: Leviticus 20:24–26.

29 *"living under the shadow"*: Princess Leonora Halm-Eberstein, in Eliot, *Daniel Deronda*, p. 572.

30 *"The messiah, for whom we prayed"*: Gabriel Riesser, quoted in Glenn R. Sharfman, "Jewish Emancipation," www.ohio.edu/chastain/ip/jewemanc.htm (accessed December 5, 2009).

30 *"We consider ourselves no longer a nation"*: Quoted in Nathan Glazer, *American Judaism* (Chicago: University of Chicago, 1988), p. 188.

30 *"the hoped-for return to Palestine"*: Moses Mendelssohn, "Remarks Concerning Michaelis' Response to Dohm," in Paul R. Mendes-Flohr and Jehuda Reinharz, *The Jew in the Modern World: A Documentary History* (New York: Oxford University Press, 1995), p. 48.

31 *"proclaiming that the civil law"*: Arthur Hertzberg, *The Zionist Idea: A Historical Analysis and Reader* (Philadelphia: Jewish Publication Society of America, 1997), p. 22.

31 *"a pious dream"*: ibid., p. 23.

31 *"The Jewish intelligentsia"*: Hannah Arendt, "The Jews and Society," in *The Portable Hannah Arendt* (New York: Penguin Classics, 2003), p. 94.

32 *"gave the Jews the first impetus"*: David Ben-Gurion, "The Kingdom of the Spirit," *The Atlantic,* November 1961, www.theatlantic.com/doc/196111/ben-gurion (accessed March 31, 2009).

34 *"In their most famous postulate"*: See Aviezer Ravitzky, *Messianism, Zion-*

ism, and Jewish Religious Radicalism (Chicago: University of Chicago Press, 1996), pp. 10–40.

35 *"We must not heed them"*: ibid., p. 15.

35 *"Nothing in our faith"*: ibid., p. 87.

35 *"the Messiah is not to be understood"*: ibid., p. 88.

35 *"Holiness will return"*: Cited in the World Mizrachi Religious Zionism e-History Series, available at www.mizrachi.org/elearning/View_history.asp?id=128 (accessed December 5, 2009).

36 *"Zionism has nothing to do with theology"*: Quoted in Ravitzky, *Messianism,* p. 93.

36 *"do not draw near"*: ibid., p. 96.

36 *"He identified Herzl"*: Shalom Goldman, *Zeal for Zion: Christians, Jews, and the Idea of the Promised Land* (Chapel Hill: University of North Carolina Press, 2009), p. 272.

36 *"There are times"*: Ravitzky, *Messianism,* p. 105.

37 *"It is established"*: ibid., p. 112.

37 *"the light of holiness"*: Quoted in Goldman, *Zeal for Zion,* p. 277.

37 *"influenced by the very air"*: Cited in the World Mizrachi Religious Zionism e-History Series.

37 *"Anyone who thinks"*: ibid., p. 34.

39 *"When I had the Balfour Declaration in my hand"*: Weizmann, "Reminiscences," in Hertzberg, *The Zionist Idea,* p. 580.

39 *"[The Messiah] took me in his arms"*: Quoted in Amos Elon, *Herzl* (New York: Holt, Rinehart and Winston, 1975), p. 16.

40 *"What Israel gave the world"*: Quoted in Hertzberg, *The Zionist Idea,* p. 616.

40 *"a mixed multitude of human dust"*: Quoted in Oz Almog, *The Sabra: The Creation of the New Jew* (Berkeley: University of California Press, 2000), p. 87.

41 *"Eventually, Israel's Chief Rabbinate"*: For more on this, see Amiram Barkat, "Rabbinate No Longer Recognizes Overseas Conversions," *Ha'aretz,* May 23, 2006.

41 *"the novelist A. B. Yehoshua"*: For more on this, see Shmuel Rosner, "How A. B. Yehoshua Lost His Crowd," on Rosner's Domain, a blog available at www.haaretz.com/hasen/pages/rosnerMain.jhtml (accessed December 5, 2009).

41 *"a type of heavenly surgery"*: Quoted in Goldman, *Zeal for Zion,* p. 280.

41   "*'among Zvi Yehuda Kook and his followers'*": In Ravitzky, *Messianism*, p. 124.

42   "*The State of Israel is divine*": ibid., p. 132.

43   "*In this interpretation*": See Gershom Gorenberg, "Israel's Tragedy Foretold," *New York Times*, March 10, 2006; and more extensively, Gershom Gorenberg, *The Accidental Empire: Israel and the Birth of the Settlements, 1967–1977* (New York: Holt, 2007).

43   "*not a religion but a tragedy*": Quoted in Jerold S. Auerbach, *Are We One?: Jewish Identity in the United States and Israel* (Piscataway, NJ: Rutgers University Press, 2001), p. 116.

44   "*The Wicked Son*": Ber Borochov, quoted in Eliezer Don-Yehiya and Charles S. Liebman, "The Symbol System of Zionist-Socialism: An Aspect of Israeli Civil Religion," in *Modern Judaism* 1, no. 2 (September 1981): 121–48.

44   "*No miracle happened to us*": ibid.

46   "*The Jewish people erred*": David Ben-Gurion, *In the Conflict*, vol. 4 (Tel Aviv: Hotza'at Mapai, 1949), p. 12 [Hebrew], quoted in Allan Silver, "Is Normal Politics Possible for Jews?" unpublished paper, 1997, pp. 4–5.

46   "*The State is the divine Idea*": G. W. F. Hegel, *Introduction to the Philosophy of History*, trans. Leo Rauch (Indianapolis: Hackett, 1988), p. 42.

47   "*'confronted Israel's political leadership'*": Akiva Eldar and Idith Zertal, *Lords of the Land: The War Over Israel's Settlements in the Occupied Territories, 1967–2007* (New York: Nation Books, 2009), p. 6.

48   "*We repeatedly emphasize*'": The entire document is reproduced in the Hebrew edition of the book *Adonei Ha'aretz: Ha'mitnachalim ve'medinat Yisrael, 1967–2004* (Tel Aviv: Kinneret, Zmora-Bitan, Dvir, 2004), pp. 574–77.

49   "*as a transitional phase*'": ibid., p. 16.

49   "*I haven't yet visited there for certain reasons*'": ibid., p. 19.

50   "*the government in its present composition*'": Quoted in Michael Oren, *Six Days of War: June 1967 and the Making of the Modern Middle East* (New York: Presidio Press, 2003), p. 134.

51   "*By putting on phylacteries*'": Quoted in Anita Shapira, *Yigal Allon, Native Son: A Biography* (Philadelphia: University of Pennsylvania Press, 2007), p. 1.

51   "*I followed all the instructions*'": ibid., p. 1.

52 *"'were raised to believe'"*: Quoted in the Hebrew edition of the book *Yigal Allon: Aviv Heldo* (Tel Aviv: Ha'sifriya Ha'hadasha, 2004), pp. 42–43.

53 *"'Here I am'"*: Yosef Shavit, "Hanan Porat, politikay al teken mashiach," in *Yediot Aharonot*, November 2, 1979; quoted in Eldar and Zertal, *Adonei Ha'aretz*, p. 18.

53 *"'I didn't want to approve'"*: ibid., p. 23.

54 *"'in a fit of absence of mind'"*: Sir John Robert Seeley, *The Expansion of England* (New York: Cosimo Classics, 2005), p. 8.

56 *"'anywhere war will allow us'"*: Quoted in Tom Segev, *1967: Israel, the War, and the Year that Transformed the Middle East* (New York: Metropolitan Books, 2007), p. 180.

56 *"'We must never come to terms'"*: The Knesset Protocols for March 25, 1970, vol. 57, pp. 1341–42. Quoted in Eldar and Zertal, *Adonei Ha'aretz*, p. 41.

59 *"'Perhaps we bit off too much'"*: Amos Oz, *In the Land of Israel* (New York: Harvest Books, 1993), p. 239.

60 *"'In Israel, we were always experts'"*: Quoted in the Third Protocol of the 18th Knesset's Committee to Investigate the Problem of Foreign Workers, June 3, 2009. Available at www.knesset.gov.il/protocols/data/rtf/zarim/2009-06-03.rtf (accessed December 7, 2009).

60 *"'a light unto the nations'"*: Quoted in Hizki Ezra, "Etzba ma'ashima hufneta klapei machaneh politi shalem," in *Arutz Sheva*, November 7, 2009. Available at www.inn.co.il/News/News.aspx/196253 (accessed December 7, 2009).

60 "The death of young people": The entire speech is available at www.haaretz.com/hasen/spages/784034.html (accessed December 7, 2009).

62 *"Prime Minister, Benjamin Netanyahu"*: Isabel Kershner, "Israel's Plans for 2 Sites Stir Unrest in West Bank," *New York Times*, February 23, 2010, accessed February 26, 2010, at www.nytimes.com/2010/02/23/world/middleeast/23mideast.html.

63 *"'there shall be one'"*: We follow the translation offered by Avishai Margalit and Michael Walzer in a letter published in the *New York Review of Books*, October 8, 2009, p. 46.

2. "THIS ALMOST CHOSEN PEOPLE"

65 *"a nation with the soul"*: G. K. Chesterton, *What I Saw in America* (1922), in *The Collected Works of G.K. Chesterton,* vol. 21 (San Francisco: Ignatius, 1990), pp. 41–45, quoted by the American Chesterton Society, chesterton.org/qmeister2/25.htm (accessed April 24, 2009). Chesterton also called the United States "the only nation in the world founded on a creed." This was technically true when he wrote it, given that the USSR was not formally established until the end of 1922, and is now true again.

65 *"Like Israel of old"*: Reinhold Niebuhr and Alan Heimert, *A Nation So Conceived: Reflections on the History of America from Its Early Visions to Its Present Power* (New York: Scribner, 1963), p. 123.

65 *"Columbus wrote"*: Cecil Jane, ed. and trans., *The Four Voyages of Columbus: A Documentary History,* vol. 2 (New York: Dover, 1988), p. 48. Columbus was alluding to Revelations 21:1, and also referred to God "having spoken of [the new heaven and new earth] through the mouth of Isaiah."

65 *"covenant of grace"*: Andrew Delbanco, *The Puritan Ordeal* (Cambridge, MA: Harvard University Press, 1989), pp. 95–97.

65 *"vastly more commercial"*: On differences between Virginia and New England cultures, see Jack P. Greene, *Pursuits of Happiness: The Social Development of Early Modern British Colonies and the Formation of American Culture* (Chapel Hill: University of North Carolina Press, 1988), pp. 11–12, 21.

65 *"God hath opened"*: Alexander Whitaker, "Good News from Virginia" (1613), smith2.sewanee.edu/courses/391/DocsEarlySouth/1613=Alex Whitaker.html (accessed April 23, 2009).

65 *"Genesis 1:28"*: Delbanco, *Puritan Ordeal,* pp. 90–91.

65 *"John Cotton"*: In "God's Promise to His Plantation" (London, 1630), digitalcommons.unl.edu/etas/22 (accessed April 23, 2009). Cotton added a Christian citation from Paul (Acts 17:26: "God hath determined . . . the bounds of our habitation"), but almost all his other citations were from the Old Testament. Even if his sermon contained no specific geographical referent, as Andrew Delbanco points out (*Puritan Ordeal,* pp. 71–72), he knew where the *Arbella* was destined.

66 *"we shall be as a city upon a hill"*: John Winthrop, "A Model of Chris-

tian Charity" (1630), Collections of the Massachusetts Historical Society (Boston, 1838), 3rd series, 7:31–48, as scanned by the Hanover Historical Texts Project, history.hanover.edu/texts/winthmod.html (accessed April 23, 2009). Reagan got the name wrong when he said the sermon was delivered on the *"Arabella,"* and there is no particular reason to think that the ship lay "off the Massachusetts coast."

66 *"Ronald Reagan":* Ronald Reagan, "Farewell Address to the Nation," January 11, 1989, www.ronaldreagan.com/sp_21.html (accessed April 23, 2009). (The site is called "The Shining Site on the Web.") "I've spoken of the shining city all my political life," Reagan noted. He used the image in declaring his candidacy in 1979, in accepting the nomination in 1984, and on many other occasions.

66 *"'carr[ied] a colony of chosen people'":* Cotton Mather, "Nehemias Americanus: The Life of John Winthrop, Esq., Governor of the Massachusetts Colony," www.moonstar.com/~acpjr/Blackboard/Common/Stories/JohnWinthrop.html (accessed April 24, 2009).

67 *"England's Puritans":* H. Richard Niebuhr, *The Kingdom of God in America* (New York: Harper, 1959), p. 27.

67 *"the Continental Congress":* www.greatseal.com/committees/firstcomm/index.html (accessed April 24, 2009).

68 *"'with ourselves'":* Herman Melville, *White-Jacket* (New York: Oxford University Press, 2000), p. 153.

68 *"'this country, the last found'":* Ralph Waldo Emerson, "Fortune of the Republic," delivered at the Old South Church, Boston, March 30, 1878 (Boston: Houghton, Osgood and Company, 1879), www.archive.org/stream/fortuneofrepubli00emerrich/fortuneofrepubli00emerrich_djvu.txt (accessed April 24, 2009).

68 *"'We stand at Armageddon and we battle for the Lord'":* "Address by Theodore Roosevelt Before the Convention of the National Progressive Party in Chicago, August, 1912," www.ssa.gov/history/trspeech.html (accessed April 25, 2009).

68 *"'purpose is achieved in our duty'":* George W. Bush, First Inaugural Address, January 20, 2001, en.wikisource.org/wiki/George_W._Bush%27s_First_Inaugural_Address (accessed April 25, 2009).

69 *"America's history":* John B. Judis, *The Folly of Empire: What George W. Bush Could Learn from Theodore Roosevelt and Woodrow Wilson* (New York: Simon & Schuster, 2004), p. 16.

69   *"Two original biblical"*: James H. Moorhead, "The American Israel: Protestant Tribalism and Universal Mission," in William R. Hutchison and Hartmut Lehmann, eds., *Many Are Chosen: Divine Election and Western Nationalism* (Minneapolis: Fortress Press, 1994), Harvard Theological Studies 38, p. 146.

69   *"Finley Peter Dunne"*: Finley Peter Dunne, *Mr. Dooley in Peace and in War* (Boston: Small, Maynard & Company, 1898, first published in the *Chicago Journal*), www.gutenberg.org/files/22537/22537-h/22537-h.htm#MR_DOOLEY_IN_WAR (accessed April 25, 2009).

69   *"'The children of Abraham'"*: Peter Bulkeley, *The Gospel-Covenant; or The Covenant of Grace Opened . . . Preached in Concord in New-England* (London: Printed by M.S. for Benjamin Allen, 1646), books.google.com/books?id=qpvpfzL0Eu8C&dq=gospel-covenant+bulkeley&printsec=frontcover&source=bl&ots=DJybcL3=tQ&sig=2Zh3AMLk2gHXkhn5mt_tlnZcuzQ&hl=en&ei=uy3zSaj7FKGxtgeLweGyDw&sa=X&oi=book_result &ct=result&resnum=2#PPA133.M1 (accessed April 25, 2009). Bulkeley cited Galatians 3:14 for Christian authority.

70   *"hidden, unknowable, unpredictable"*: Perry Miller, *Errand into the Wilderness* (Cambridge, MA: Harvard University Press, 1996 [1956]), p. 51.

70   *"the meanness of the place"*: quoted in Delbanco, *Puritan Ordeal*, pp. 95–96.

71   *"The Quaker leader William Penn"*: David Hackett Fischer, *Albion's Seed: Four British Folkways in America* (New York: Oxford University Press, 1989), p. 459.

71   *"But New England's Puritan clergy"*: Delbanco, *Puritan Ordeal*, pp. 86ff.

71   *"After twenty years of being American'"*: ibid., p. 116.

71   *"many migrated back"*: Andrew Delbanco, "The Puritan Errand Re-Viewed," *Journal of American Studies* 18, no. 3 (1984): 353, citing Harry Stout, "University Men in New England, 1620–1660: A Demographic Analysis," *Journal of Interdisciplinary History* 4 (1974): 375–400.

72   *"'His vengeance was a sign of love'"*: Sacvan Bercovitch, *The American Jeremiad* (Madison: University of Wisconsin Press, 1978), p. 8.

72   *"Johnson, typical of Puritan historians"*: Peter J. Conn, *Literature in America: An Illustrated History* (Cambridge, UK: Cambridge University Press, 1989), pp. 28–30.

72 *"forerunners of Christ's army'"*: Quoted in Nicholas Guyatt, *Providence and the Invention of the United States, 1607–1876* (Cambridge, UK: Cambridge University Press, 2007), p. 46.

72 *"'record of the providential Dispensations of God'"*: ibid., p. 48; quoting Increase Mather, *A Brief History of the Warr with the Indians in New-England* (Boston: John Foster, 1676), p. iii.

72 *"his son Cotton"*: ibid., p. 50.

73 *"'the beginning of this great work'"*: Jonathan Edwards, *Some Thoughts Concerning the Present Revival of Religion in New England* (1742), quoted in Conrad Cherry, ed., *God's New Israel: Religious Interpretations of American Destiny* (Englewood Cliffs, NJ: Prentice-Hall, 1971), p. 55.

73 *"'the absolute and despotic power'"*: Quoted in Ruth H. Bloch, *Visionary Republic: Millennial Themes in American Thought, 1756–1800* (Cambridge, UK: Cambridge University Press, 1985), p. 13.

73 *"'When God is about to turn'"*: Edwards, *Some Thoughts,* quoted in Cherry, *God's New Israel,* pp. 57–58. On Edwards and the Antichrist, see Patricia U. Bonomi, *Under the Cope of Heaven: Religion, Society and Politics in Colonial America,* rev. ed. (Oxford: Oxford University Press, 2003), p. 17.

74 *"'Come poor, lost, undone sinner'"*: George Whitefield, "The Kingdom of God," in *The Great Sermons of the Great Preachers* (London: Ward and Lock, 1857), p. 265.

74 *"religious fervor migrated"*: Mark A. Noll, *America's God: From Jonathan Edwards to Abraham Lincoln* (New York: Oxford University Press, 2002), p. 13.

74 *"evangelical church attendance ebbed"*: John M. Murrin, "No Awakening, No Revolution? More Counterfactual Speculations," *Reviews in American History* 11, no. 2 (June 1983): 161–71, www.jstor.org/stable/2702135 (accessed May 12, 2008).

74 *"first mass movement"*: Bloch, *Visionary Republic,* p. 14.

74 *"'hysterical agonies'"*: Miller, *Errand into the Wilderness,* p. 166.

74 *"'More colonists were prepared for armed resistance'"*: Cherry, *God's New Israel,* p. 62.

75 *"Sermons, devotional tracts"*: Bonomi, *Under the Cope of Heaven,* p. 4.

75 *"'the desert blossoming like a rose'"*: Bloch, *Visionary Republic,* p. 47.

75 *"French and Indian War"*: ibid., p. 17.

75 *"Contention became all the rage"*: Bonomi, *Under the Cope of Heaven,* p. 132.

75 *"American writers":* Guyatt, *Providence,* pp. 93–94. Jack P. Greene, who argues that the Chesapeake settlements were in many ways more influential than New England, also maintains that the Awakening spread providential sentiment throughout the colonies, even to areas that had early been largely indifferent to religious passions (*Pursuits of Happiness,* p. 203).

75 *"Moderate ministers":* Bloch, *Visionary Republic,* p. 47.

75 *"the Time, in which Christ's Kingdom":* Samuel Williams, *Discourse on the Love of Our Country* (Salem, 1755), p. 64; and Ebenezer Baldwin, *The Duty of Rejoicing Under Calamities and Afflictions . . .* (New York, 1776), p. 31, both quoted in Gordon S. Wood, *The Creation of the American Republic, 1776–1787* (Chapel Hill: University of North Carolina Press, 1969), p. 117.

75 *"'we have a right'":* John Adams, "Dissertation on the Feudal & Canon Law (1765), www.ashbrook.org/library/18/adams/canonlaw.html#2 (accessed May 2, 2009). Adams's original draft, recorded in his diary on February 21, 1765, contained a still more incandescent tribute to divine election and its global import: "I always consider the settlement of America with reverence and wonder, as the opening of a grand scene and design in Providence for the illumination of the ignorant, and the emancipation of the slavish part of mankind all over the earth." (Diary of John Adams, February 21, 1765, available at www.beliefnet.com /resourcelib/docs/80/Diary_of_John_Adams_February_21_1765_1.html (accessed May 2, 2009.) Whether Adams declined, in the end, to publish these words for fear of putting the providential theme too strongly, or because of an aversion to premature grandiosity, is hard to tell.

76 *"Deists and rationalists":* Bonomi, *Under the Cope of Heaven,* p. 9. Even the skeptical historian John M. Murrin concedes ("No Awakening," p. 169) that while "[t]he Awakening did not create the Revolution, it surely contributed to its success" to some degree, while in turn "the Revolution liberated the spirit of the Awakening," which had lately been flagging.

76 *"sincerely believed":* Nathan R. Perl-Rosenthal, "The 'Divine Right of Republics': The Debate over Kingless Government in Revolutionary America," *William and Mary Quarterly* 66, no. 3 (July 2009): 535.

76 *"'a form of government'":* Thomas Paine, *Common Sense,* www.ushistory .org/Paine/commonsense/singlehtml.htm (accessed May 20, 2009).

76   *"Christian-republican alliance":* Noll, *America's God,* p. 64.

76   *"contagion of liberty":* Bernard Bailyn, *The Ideological Origins of the American Revolution* (Cambridge, MA: Harvard University Press, 1967), p. 230.

76   *"divine punishment":* Bloch, *Visionary Republic,* p. 74; Wood, *Creation,* p. 116.

76   *"'The day of the American Israel's trouble'":* Enoch Huntington, *Sermon Delivered at Middleton, July 20th, AD 1775* (Hartford, [1775]), pp. 14–15; and Aaron Hutchinson, *A Well Tempered Self-Love* (Dresden, VT, [1779]), p. 17, quoted in Wood, *Creation,* p. 115.

76   *"'were grown up to our present strength'":* Quoted in Guyatt, *Providence,* p. 95.

77   *"clergymen not only sermonized":* Bonomi, *Under the Cope of Heaven,* p. 209.

77   *"John Witherspoon":* Jeffry H. Morrison, *John Witherspoon and the Founding of the American Republic* (Notre Dame, IN: University of Notre Dame Press, 2005), pp. 4, 35. Witherspoon's biographer may be overreaching when he claims that "Madison caught his theological bug from Witherspoon" (p. 36), but there is documentary evidence that Madison thought highly of Witherspoon.

77   *"'an animated Son of Liberty'":* Quoted in Morrison, *John Witherspoon,* pp. 1, 10.

77   *"'multitude of opposing hosts'":* Witherspoon, "The Dominion of Providence over the Passions of Men," May 17, 1776, quoted in Guyatt, *Providence,* pp. 97, 98.

77   *"other ministers were inhibited":* Ruth Bloch, personal communication, May 1, 2009.

77   *"Concord, Massachusetts":* Robert A. Gross, *The Minutemen and Their World* (New York: Hill and Wang, 1976), chap. 3. In 1741, George Whitefield had preached in Concord's open air to thousands of revivalists (p. 20). Preaching to Concord's Minuteman militia on March 13, 1775, the Rev. William Emerson took as his text a citation from Chronicles—"Behold, God himself is with us for our Captain"—and reminded his mobilized audience that the army of Judah had defeated an army twice its size thanks to "a firm and unshaken Reliance upon the God of Israel." William Emerson's grandson was Ralph Waldo, who commemorated the "embattled farmers." Gross, *Minutemen,* p. 72.

77   *"'Especially in New England'":* Bloch, *Visionary Republic,* p. 57. If this

argument seems somewhat contorted, there is at least an absence of negative evidence—that is, that the populations who had been more taken up in the Awakening were more likely to stay with the Tories.

78 *"Liberty, traced to her true source"*: Jacob Duché, quoted in Derek H. Davis, *Religion and the Continental Congress, 1774–1789* (New York: Oxford University Press, 2000), p. 59. Interestingly, Duché came to despair of the independence movement, going so far (perhaps because he found himself in British custody after surrendering in 1777) as to urge General Washington to abandon the fight and support the "glorious work" of reinstating British rule. (Once Duché's appeal to Washington was leaked to the press, he discreetly chose British exile for the next fifteen years.) Guyatt, *Providence,* p. 110.

78 *"Liberty is the cause"*: Nathaniel Whitaker, "An Antidote to Toryism" (Newburyport, MA, 1777), quoted in Bonomi, *Under the Cope of Heaven,* p. 212.

78 *"Christian soldiers"*: Bloch, *Visionary Republic,* pp. 76, 79.

78 *"the rankest deist"*: Robert Smith, *The Obligations of the Confederate States of North America to Praise God* (Philadelphia: Francis Bailey, 1782), p. 28, quoted in Guyatt, *Providence,* p. 105.

78 *"Newspapers transmitted"*: Guyatt, *Providence,* pp. 89–91.

78 *"The states organized fast days"*: ibid., pp. 115–16.

78 *"The Almighty . . . has made choice"*: Quoted in Richard W. Van Alstyne, *The Rising American Empire* (New York: Oxford University Press, 1960), p. 1.

79 *"Nicholas Street"*: Street cited specifically Isaiah 10:5–7. Quoted in Cherry, *God's New Israel,* pp. 69, 79.

79 *"David Ramsay"*: David Ramsay, *An Oration on the Advantages of American Independence* (Charleston: John Wells, 1778), quoted in Guyatt, *Providence,* p. 100.

79 *"victory sermons"*: Bloch, *Visionary Republic,* p. 94.

79 *"faith in Providence"*: Guyatt, *Providence,* p. 107.

79 *"Ezra Stiles"*: Quoted in Cherry, *God's New Israel,* pp. 83, 85, 90, and in Noll, *America's God,* p. 64. See also Ellis Sandoz, *A Government of Laws: Political Theory, Religion, and the American Founding* (Baton Rouge: Louisiana State University Press, 1990), pp. 103, 109.

80 *"the Divine Arm visibly outstretched"*: Address of December 26, 1783, in John C. Fitzpatrick, ed., *The Writings of George Washington,* vol. 27

(Washington, DC: Government Printing Office, 1938), pp. 259–89, as quoted in Guyatt, *Providence*, p. 129.

80 *"'this chosen race'"*: "Good Advice in Bad Verse," quoted in Cherry, *God's New Israel*, pp. 200, 201, 203.

80 *"'an angelic auxiliary'"*: Conor Cruise O'Brien, *The Long Affair: Thomas Jefferson and the French Revolution, 1785–1800* (Chicago: University of Chicago Press, 1996), p. 118.

81 *"'the revolution seems to have succeeded'"*: Quoted in Jack N. Rakove, *James Madison and the Creation of the American Republic*, 3rd ed. (New York: Longman, 2007), pp. 125–26.

81 *"'What principle in the political ethics'"*: *Niles' Register*, April 7, 1832. Quoted in Merrill D. Peterson, "The Jefferson Image, 1829," *American Quarterly* 3, no. 3 (Autumn 1951): 217–28.

81 *"'unassisted by the wealth'"*: *A Summary View of the Rights of British America*, quoted in Joseph J. Ellis, *American Sphinx: The Character of Thomas Jefferson* (New York: Knopf, 1997), pp. 32, 33.

81 *"'Those who labour in the earth'"*: Thomas Jefferson, *Notes on the State of Virginia* (1781), etext.virginia.edu/etcbin/toccer-new2?id=JefVirg .sgm&images=images/modeng&data=/texts/english/modeng/ parsed&tag=public&part=all (accessed May 20, 2009).

82 *"In his First Inaugural"*: Thomas Jefferson, "First Inaugural Address," www.bartleby.com/124/pres16.html. (accessed May 20, 2009).

82 *"Jefferson himself"*: Anthony F. C. Wallace, *Jefferson and the Indians: The Tragic Fate of the First Americans* (Cambridge, MA: The Belknap Press of Harvard University Press, 1999), p. 9.

83 *"'the late defection of France'"*: Quoted in Rakove, *James Madison*, p. 160.

83 *"Jefferson, once president"*: Jefferson to Pierre Samuel du Pont de Nemours, February 1, 1803, quoted in Reginald Horseman, "The Dimensions of an 'Empire for Liberty': Expansion and Republicanism, 1775–1825," *Journal of the Early Republic* 9, no. 1 (Spring 1989): 6.

83 *"'there is on the globe'"*: Quoted in Ellis, *American Sphinx*, pp. 205–206.

83 *"Jefferson warned in 1803"*: Jefferson to Lord Buchan, July 10, 1803; quoted in Sean Wilentz, *The Rise of American Democracy: Jefferson to Lincoln* (New York: Norton, 2005), p. 108.

83 *"Alexander Hamilton"*: Hamilton, July 5, 1803, quoted in Jon Kukla, *A Wilderness So Immense: The Louisiana Purchase and the Destiny of America* (New York: Knopf, 2004), p. 291.

84 *"Nicholas Guyatt"*: Guyatt, *Providence*, p. 159.

84 *"February 27, 1803"*: Jefferson to Harrison, in Francis Paul Prucha, ed., *Documents of United States Indian Policy*, 3rd ed. (Lincoln: University of Nebraska Press, 2000), pp. 21–22. Harrison, for his part, got with the system. He addressed the Indiana legislature in 1809 with a Jeffersonian rhetorical question: "Is one of the fairest portions of the globe to remain in a state of nature, the haunt of a few wretched savages, when it seems destined, by the Creator, to give support to a large population, and to be the sea of civilization, of science, and true religion?" Quoted in Albert Weinberg, *Manifest Destiny: A Study of Nationalist Expansionism in American History* (Baltimore: The Johns Hopkins University Press, 1935), p. 79.

85 *"Looking back after his presidency"*: Letter from Thomas Jefferson to Alexander von Humboldt, December 6, 1813, www.let.rug.nl/usa/P/tj3/writings/brf/jef1224.htm (accessed May 21, 2009).

85 *"the main line"*: Guyatt, *Providence*, p. 177.

85 *"'propagating of Christian religion'"*: Quoted in Miller, *Errand into the Wilderness*, p. 105.

85 *"The Virginians sustained"*: ibid., p. 101.

85 *"John Cotton"*: Quoted in Delbanco, "Puritan Errand," p. 356.

86 *"John Locke"*: David Armitage, "John Locke, Carolina, and the Two Treatises of Government," *Political Theory* 32, no. 5 (2004): 607–608 and 615–19, quoting Locke, *Second Treatise*, para. 34.

86 *"Both advocates and opponents"*: Guyatt, *Providence*, pp. 194–203.

86 *"in the same letter"*: Jefferson to Humboldt, December 6, 1813. Speeding within the confines of a single letter from romantic nostalgia to brutal eliminationism to radical regret, Jefferson went on: "The confirmed brutalization, if not the extermination of this race in our America, is therefore to form an additional chapter in the English history of the same colored man in Asia, and of the brethren of their own color in Ireland, and wherever else Anglo-mercantile cupidity can find a two-penny interest in deluging the earth with human blood. But let us turn from the loathsome contemplation of the degrading effects of commercial avarice." Humboldt, fresh from five years exploring Spanish America, had exulted in 1804 about the Louisiana Purchase: "This country that stretches to the west of the mountains presents a vast area to conquer for science!" Letter to William Thorn-

ton, June 20, 1804, from Ulrike Moheit, ed., *Alexander von Humboldt: Briefe aus Amerika. 1799–1804* (Berlin: Academia Verlag, 1993), quoted in translation at www2.ku.edu/~maxkade/humboldt/main .htm (accessed May 21, 2009).

87   *"A land whose otters"*: Rep. Fisher Ames to Thomas Dwight, October 31, 1803, quoted in Kukla, *Wilderness,* p. 293.

87   *"'the means of tempting'"*: ibid., p. 301.

87   *"Jon Kukla"*: ibid., pp. 302, 303.

88   *"Sphinx-like character"*: This is of course the metaphor governing Ellis's impressive study of Jefferson, *American Sphinx.*

88   *"convinced him that words"*: See, for example, his letter to William Short of April 13, 1820, expressing his fear "that the inquisition of the public might get hold of" the "syllabus" on his religious views that he had writen for his confidants in 1803. In Dickinson W. Adams, ed., *Jefferson's Extracts from the Gospels: The Papers of Thomas Jefferson,* second series (Princeton, NJ: Princeton University Press, 1983), p. 391. For an authoritative discussion of this "syllabus," see Adams, ed., *Jefferson's Extracts,* pp. 23–25.

88   *"Unitarian view of God"*: See Adams, *Jefferson's Extracts,* pp. 36, 39.

88   *"'rational Christianity'"*: Jefferson to Timothy Pickering, February 27, 1821, in Adams, ed., *Jefferson's Extracts,* p. 402.

88   *"it is in our lives"*: Jefferson to Mrs. Samuel H. Smith, August 6, 1816, www.let.rug.nl/~usa/P/tj3/writings/brf/jef1247.htm (accessed December 5, 2009).

88   *"he wrote James Madison"*: Jefferson to Madison, December 16, 1786, in James Morton Smith, ed., *The Republic of Letters: The Correspondence between Thomas Jefferson and James Madison, 1776–1826,* vol. 1 (New York: Norton, 1995), p. 458.

88   *"insulting the clergy"*: Jefferson to Mrs. Samuel H. Smith, August 6, 1816.

88   *"fastest-growing churches"*: Noll, *America's God,* pp. 166–82.

89   *"On March 4, 1805"*: Jefferson's Second Inaugural, March 4, 1805, www.bartleby.com/124/pres17.html (accessed May 26, 2009).

89   *"Four years later to the day"*: Jefferson's address of March 4, 1809, etext .virginia.edu/jefferson/biog/lj33.htm (accessed December 5, 2009).

90   *"In 1808"*: Leonard W. Levy, *Jefferson and Civil Liberties: The Darker Side* (Cambridge, MA: The Belknap Press of Harvard University Press, 1963), pp. 119, 137.

90 *"he went so far":* Jefferson to Albert Gallatin, September 9, 1808, quoted in Garry Wills, *James Madison* (New York: Times Books, 2002), p. 54.

91 *"In 1824":* Quoted in David S. Reynolds, *Waking Giant: America in the Age of Jackson* (New York: Harper, 2008), p. 40.

91 *"Jackson left behind":* The apparent exception, his 1832 Bank Veto message, was actually written by a committee.

91 *"The aged Jefferson":* Notes recorded by George Ticknor, who visited Monticello with Daniel Webster. "Notes of Mr. Jefferson's Conversation 1824 at Monticello," in Charles M. Wilts, ed., *The Papers of Daniel Webster: Correspondence,* vol. 1 (Hanover, NH, 1974–86), pp. 375–76, as cited in Wilentz, *Rise of American Democracy,* p. 851, note 59. Wilentz believes the "veracity [of these notes] is dubious."

91 *"Adams captured":* Quoted in Wilentz, *Rise of American Democracy,* p. 391.

91 *"rough-hewn Jackson":* H. W. Brands, *Andrew Jackson, His Life and Times* (New York: Doubleday, 2005), p. 17.

92 *"'Every man with a gun'":* Jackson to James Monroe, March 18, 1817, quoted in ibid., p. 321.

92 *"In 1780":* ibid., p. 26.

92 *"I have long believed":* Quoted in Merrill D. Peterson, *The Jefferson Image in the American Mind* (Charlottesville, VA: University of Virginia Press, 1998), p. 72.

92 *"farewell address":* Jackson, Farewell Address, March 4, 1837, www.presidency.ucsb.edu/ws/index.php?pid=67087 (accessed December 5, 2009).

93 *"hero of New Orleans":* Wilentz, *Rise of American Democracy,* pp. 323, 325.

93 *"President James Monroe":* ibid., p. 322.

93 *"A dire 'fate'":* Jackson, First Annual Message to Congress, December 8, 1829, www.presidency.ucsb.edu/ws/index.php?pid=29471 (accessed May 24, 2009).

93 *"they insisted on their own sovereignty":* Wilentz, *Rise of American Democracy,* p. 325.

94 *"gold was discovered":* ibid., p. 322.

94 *"'to preserve this much-injured race'":* ibid., p. 325.

94 *"'the remnant of that ill-fated race'":* Jackson, Farewell Address, March 4, 1837, xroads.virginia.edu/~cap/jackson/jack~1.htm. (accessed May 24, 2009).

94 *"Indian Removal Bill"*: Wilentz, *Rise of American Democracy*, p. 425.

94 *"Jackson told Congress"*: Jackson, Special Message to Congress, January 16, 1833; quoted in Brands, *Andrew Jackson*, p. 478.

94 *"'I will die with the Union'"*: Jackson, proclamation of December 10, 1832, quoted in Brands, *Andrew Jackson*, p. 478.

94 "democracy": It was actually Jackson's adversary John Quincy Adams who first spoke heartily of democracy in a major address. See Richard R. John, "John Quincy Adams," in Alan Brinkley and Davis Dyer, eds., *Reader's Companion to the American Presidency* (New York: Houghton Mifflin, 2000), p. 90.

95 *"fierce man on horseback"*: On Jackson as both plebeian and "nature's nobleman," in the words of his supporters, see Wilentz, *Rise of American Democracy*, pp. 7–10.

95 *"Later, Emerson wrote"*: *The Later Lectures of Ralph Waldo Emerson, 1843–1871*, Ronald A. Bosco and Joel Myerson, eds. (Athens: University of Georgia Press, 2001), p. 107. These lines were possibly first delivered as early as 1839, but in any event no later than 1848 (p. 101).

95 *"'Tis a wild democracy'"*: Emerson quoted in Reynolds, *Waking Giant*, p. 250.

95 *"Second Great Awakening"*: Daniel Walker Howe, *What Hath God Wrought: The Transformation of America, 1815–1848* (New York: Oxford University Press, 2007), pp. 172ff.

95 *"Emerson captured the spirit"*: Reynolds, *Waking Giant*, p. 125.

95 *"joined Protestant churches"*: ibid., p. 124.

96 *"'immaculate manliness'"*: Herman Melville, *Moby-Dick* (New York: Oxford University Press, 1998), pp. 102–103.

96 *"his 1837 farewell address"*: Jackson, Farewell Address, March 4, 1837, xroads.virginia.edu/~cap/jackson/jack~1.htm (accessed May 24, 2009).

97 *"wrote Perry Miller"*: Miller, *Errand into the Wilderness*, p. 209.

97 *"typical and widely reprinted"*: James Brooks in *The Knickerbocker* of 1835, quoted in ibid., p. 210.

97 *"'with more of milk and more of honey'"*: Quoted in Robert Pogue Harrison, "The Ecstasy of John Muir," *New York Review of Books*, March 12, 2009, p. 21.

97 *"John O'Sullivan"*: John O'Sullivan, "The Great Nation of Futurity," *United States Democratic Review* 6, no. 23 (November 1839): 426–30,

cdl.library.cornell.edu/cgi-bin/moa/moa-cgi?notisid=AGD1642-0006-46 (accessed May 27, 2009).

98   *"The term distinguished":* Cherry, *God's New Israel,* p. 114. See also Richard T. Hughes, *Myths America Lives By* (Urbana: University of Illinois Press, 2003), p. 109.

98   *"Thomas Hart Benton":* Quoted in Weinberg, *Manifest Destiny,* p. 73.

98   *"Benton called American settlers":* Quoted in Judis, *Folly of Empire,* p. 23.

98   *"When, in 1836":* Jesús Velasco-Márquez, "A Mexican Viewpoint on the War with the United States," www.pbs.org/kera/usmexicanwar/prelude/md_a_mexican_viewpoint.html (accessed May 29, 2009).

99   *"An editorial in the* Brooklyn Daily Eagle *asked":* [Walt Whitman], "Our Territory on the Pacific," *Brooklyn Daily Eagle,* July 7, 1846, in Walt Whitman, *The Gathering of the Forces,* ed. Cleveland Rodgers and John Black, vol. 1 (New York: G. P. Putnam's Sons, 1920), p. 247.

99   *"Another clinching proof":* [Walt Whitman], "The Victory," *Brooklyn Daily Eagle,* October 13, 1846, in Whitman, *Gathering,* vol. 1, p. 248.

99   *"lofty views":* [Walt Whitman], "Mr. Gallatin's Plan of Settling Our Dispute with Mexico," *Brooklyn Daily Eagle,* December 2, 1847, in Whitman, *Gathering,* vol. 1, p. 266.

99   *"An ignorant, prejudiced":* [Walt Whitman], "When Will the War Be Ended?" *Brooklyn Daily Eagle,* September 23, 1847, in Whitman, *Gathering,* vol. 1, p. 261.

99   *"Ultimately, Whitman":* [Walt Whitman], "Mr. Gallatin's Plan," in Whitman, *Gathering,* vol. 1, p. 266.

100   *"John Quincy Adams":* Guyatt, *Providence,* p. 220.

100   *"the same argument":* Weinberg, *Manifest Destiny,* p. 149.

100   *"he had resolutely declared":* Adams speech of July 4, 1821, www.presidentialrhetoric.com/historicspeeches/adams_jq/foreignpolicy.html (accessed May 28, 2009).

100   *"As he asked rhetorically":* Adams, "An Oration Delivered Before the Inhabitants of the Town of Newburyport" (Newburyport, MA: Charles Whipple, 1837), p. 5.

100   *"estimated at 40 percent":* Richard Carwardine, *Evangelicals and Politics in Antebellum America* (New Haven: Yale University Press, 1993), p. 44.

100   *"the Puritan idea":* Hughes, *Myths,* p. 110.

101   *"James Buchanan of Pennsylvania":* Buchanan, March 12, 1844, in *The Congressional Globe . . . of the First Session of the Twenty-Eighth Congress,*

vol. 13, ed. Francis Preston Blair and John Cook Rives (Washington, DC: Congressional Globe, 1844), p. 380.

101 *"Senator Sam Houston"*: *New York Herald,* January 30, 1848, quoted in ibid., p. 178.

101 "New York Herald": *New York Herald,* May 15, 1847, quoted in ibid., p. 171.

101 "New York Sun": *New York Sun,* October 22, 1847, quoted in ibid., p. 173.

101 *"'to be the Model Republic'"*: Albert Gallatin, *Peace with Mexico* (1847), quoted in ibid., p. 224.

101 *"Robert C. Winthrop"*: Winthrop, "The Oregon Question and the Treaty of Washington," March 18, 1844, quoted in Guyatt, *Providence,* pp. 221–22. Winthrop was merciless toward Polk's line of argument, declaring on January 3, 1846, that in the light of "that new revelation of right which has been designated as *the right of our manifest destiny to spread over this whole continent* [his italics], I suppose the right of a manifest destiny to spread will not be admitted to exist in any nation except the universal Yankee nation!" (Quoted in Weinberg, *Manifest Destiny,* p. 143.) Winthrop got the joke of a nation professing itself universalist. Calling for negotiation and diplomacy instead of war in a subsequent debate about Oregon (June 25, 1846), Winthrop mockingly speculated that "in *Adam's Will* . . . a clause giving us the whole of Oregon, can be somewhere hunted up. Perhaps it may be found in that same Illinois cave in which the Mormon Testament has been discovered." Robert C. Winthrop, *Addresses and Speeches on Various Occasions* (Boston: Little, Brown, 1852), p. 490.

101 *"Abraham Lincoln"*: Abraham Lincoln, speech of January 12, 1848, in *Collected Works of Abraham Lincoln,* vol. 1 (New Brunswick, NJ: Rutgers University Press, 1953), p. 433.

102 *"Lincoln thought Polk"*: ibid., p. 439.

103 *"On February 21, 1861"*: Lincoln, *Collected Works,* vol. 4, pp. 235–36.

103 *"'an humble instrument in the hands of the Almighty'"*: ibid., pp. 235–36.

104 *"As he speechified"*: Richard Carwardine, *Lincoln: A Life of Purpose and Power* (New York: Knopf, 2006), p. 146.

104 *"urging them not to 'insult'"*: Lincoln, *Collected Works,* vol. 4, p. 274.

104 *"National Fast Day"*: Lincoln, *Collected Works,* vol. 6, p. 156.

105 *"Second Inaugural"*: Lincoln, *Collected Works,* vol. 8, p. 333.

105 *"Shortly thereafter"*: Lincoln to Thurlow Weed, March 15, 1865, in ibid., p. 356.

105 *"immensity of the Civil War"*: Guyatt, *Providence,* p. 259.

106 *"Lincoln found it politic"*: Carwardine, *Lincoln,* p. 277. In *Evangelicals and Politics in Antebellum America.* As mentioned on p. 100, above, Carwardine estimated that by the mid-1850s, some 40 percent of Americans north and south were adherents of evangelical Protestant churches.

106 *"Some Protestant clergymen"*: See James H. Moorhead, *American Apocalypse: Yankee Protestants and the Civil War, 1860–1869* (New Haven: Yale University Press, 1978), pp. 96ff.

106 "Chicago Tribune": *Chicago Tribune,* August 4, 1864, and September 28, 1864, quoted in Carwardine, *Lincoln,* p. 302.

106 *"Benjamin M. Palmer"*: Benjamin M. Palmer, June 13, 1861, quoted in Cherry, *God's New Israel,* pp. 182–93. In *This Republic of Suffering: Death and the American Civil War* (New York: Knopf, 2008), pp. 188–90, Drew Gilpin Faust offers evidence that some Unionists and Confederates disagreed.

107 *"Mark A. Noll"*: Noll, *America's God,* p. 435.

107 *"The sheer scale"*: Faust, *Republic of Suffering,* p. 268.

107 *"Horace Bushnell"*: Horace Bushnell, "Our Obligations to the Dead," in *Selected Works,* vol. 7 (New York: Charles Scribner's Sons, 1881), pp. 319–55, www.archive.org/stream/selectworks07bush/selectworks07bush_djvu.txt (accessed May 30, 2009).

109 *"Lincoln's doubt"*: Noll, *America's God,* p. 435.

109 *"The war's staggering human cost"*: Faust, *Republic of Suffering,* p. 268.

109 *"Frederick Douglass"*: Frederick Douglass, "The Mission of the War," January 13, 1864, www.blackpast.org/?q=1864-frederick-douglass-mission-war (accessed June 11, 2009).

109 *"Gilbert Haven"*: Gilbert Haven, "Jefferson Davis and Pharaoh," April 12, 1865, in *Sermons, Speeches and Letters on Slavery and Its War* (Boston: Lee and Shepard, 1869), p. 531.

110 *"Wendell Phillips"*: Quoted in Guyatt, *Providence,* p. 314.

110 *"Christopher Z. Hobson"*: Christopher Z. Hobson, "Ralph Ellison, Juneteenth, and African American Prophecy," *Modern Fiction Studies* 51, no. 3 (Fall 2005): 619.

110 *"members of the old and still suffering Israel"*: Silke Lehmann, "Response,"

in William R. Hutchison and Hartmut Lehmann, eds., *Many Are Chosen: Divine Election and Western Nationalism* (Minneapolis: Fortress Press, 1994), p. 198. See also Steven Waldman, *Founding Faith: Providence, Politics, and the Birth of Religious Freedom in America* (New York: Random House, 2008), p. 21.

110 *"suffering servant"*: On the "suffering servant" motif in black Christian thought, see Albert Raboteau, "Exodus, Ethiopia, and Racial Messianism: Texts and Contexts of African American Chosenness," in Hutchison and Lehmann, eds., *Many Are Chosen*, p. 154.

111 *"to make the black man of America"*: Quoted in Guyatt, *Providence*, p. 316.

111 *"He condemned"*: Frederick Douglass, speech at Cooper Institute, February 1862, quoted in ibid., p. 316.

111 *"Alexander Crummell"*: Alexander Crummell, "The Destined Superiority of the Negro," in Philip Sheldon Foner and Robert J. Branham, eds., *Lift Every Voice: African American Oratory, 1787–1900*, rev. ed. (Tuscaloosa: University of Alabama Press, 1998), p. 598. It is interesting that Crummell, a black nationalist, gave priority to the Jews as a chosen people.

112 *"William Lloyd Garrison"*: William Lloyd Garrison, letter of December 2, 1876, quoted in Guyatt, *Providence*, p. 325.

113 *"Drew Gilpin Faust's"*: Faust, *Republic of Suffering*, p. 268.

113 *"devaluing of individual life"*: See Faust, *Republic of Suffering*, pp. 59–60. The militarism theme is developed at length in Jackson Lears, *Rebirth of a Nation: The Making of Modern America, 1877–1920* (New York: Harper, 2009), esp. introduction and chap. 1.

113 *"millenarian tract"*: Josiah Strong, *Our Country: Its Possible Future and Its Present Crisis*, ed. Jurgen Herbst (Cambridge, MA: The Belknap Press of Harvard University Press, 1963 [1891, 1886]), pp. 3, 216.

113 *"Josiah Strong"*: ibid., p. 214, citing Bushnell's *Christian Nurture* (1861) in behalf of the view that "there is a tremendous overbearing surge of power in the Christian nations, which, if the other [nations] are not speedily raised to some vastly higher capacity, will inevitably submerge and bury them forever." Still, Bushnell thought that "[w]hether the feebler and more abject races are going to be regenerated and raised up, is already very much of a question. What if it should be God's plan to people the world with better and finer material?"

113 *"Strong warned"*: ibid., p. 41.

113   *"It was 'foolish'"*: ibid., pp. vi–vii.

113   *"'the material splendor'"*: ibid., p. 165.

113   *"'one of the closing stages'"*: ibid., p. 254.

114   *"one of his later readers"*: See Theodore Roosevelt, *The Strenuous Life* (New York: Century, 1902). In 1900, Roosevelt thought enough of Josiah Strong to write him a letter of introduction to Albert Thayer Mahan, Roosevelt's fellow naval enthusiast and counselor. In the introduction to his subsequent book, *Expansion Under New World-Conditions* (New York: Baker and Taylor, 1900), Strong thanked Mahan for reading and criticizing several chapters. William H. Berge, "Voices for Imperialism: Josiah Strong and the Protestant Clergy," *Border States: Journal of the Kentucky-Tennessee American Studies Association* 1 (1973), spider.georgetowncollege.edu/htallant/border/bs1/berge.htm (accessed June 3, 2009).

114   *"Reverend Strong's dithyramb"*: Strong, *Our Country,* pp. 210, 211, 209, 212, 201, 213–14 (Strong's italics), 216–17, 216. For a valiant though unconvincing defense of Strong as a partisan of a "New Internationalism," see Dorothea R. Muller, "Josiah Strong and American Nationalism: A Reevaluation," *Journal of American History* 53, no. 3 (December 1966): 487–503 (the quote is on p. 503).

115   *"the younger TR"*: Speech of 1896, quoted in H. W. Brands, *T.R.: The Last Romantic* (New York: Basic, 1997), p. 298.

115   *"Social Darwinist vein"*: Thomas G. Dyer, *Theodore Roosevelt and the Idea of Race* (Baton Rouge: Louisiana State University Press, 1980), pp. 5–8.

115   *"drawn to big biological theory"*: Theodore Roosevelt, "National Life and Character," in *National Ideals,* vol. 2 (New York: G. P. Putnam's Sons, 1902 [1894]), p. 181.

115   *"fully fifteen years"*: Roosevelt, "National Life and Character," pp. 195, 206–207. As late as 1894, he still wrote unself-consciously of the "higher races," though without regarding "non-Aryan" races as threats.

115   *"Thomas G. Dyer"*: Roosevelt criticized "Anglo-Saxon" in 1905, "Aryan" in 1907 and 1910. Dyer, *Theodore Roosevelt,* pp. 46, 67, 68.

116   *"he read devotedly"*: ibid., pp. 12–18.

116   *"In his letters"*: ibid., p. 30.

116   *"In 1906"*: See Gary Gerstle, *American Crucible: Race and Nation in the Twentieth Century* (Princeton, NJ: Princeton University Press, 2001),

pp. 34, 62. Gerstle calls Roosevelt's belief in white superiority "beyond dispute" (p. 62).

116 *"Writing in 1889":* Theodore Roosevelt, *The Winning of the West,* vol. 1 (New York: G. P. Putnam's Sons, 1889), chap. 11, www. fullbooks.com/The-Winning-of-the-West-Volume-One5.html (accessed June 4, 2009). Roosevelt liked this story enough to extrapolate from it in volume 2: "Many of the best of the backwoodsmen were Bible-readers, but they were brought up in a creed that made much of the Old Testament, and laid slight stress on pity, truth, or mercy. They looked at their foes as the Hebrew prophets looked at the enemies of Israel. What were the abominations because of which the Canaanites were destroyed before Joshua, when compared with the abominations of the red savages whose lands they, another chosen people, should in their turn inherit?" *The Winning of the West,* vol. 2, chap. 5, www.fullbooks.com/The-Winning-of-the-West-Volume-Two3.html (accessed June 4, 2009).

116 *"Indians would be absorbed":* Dyer, *Theodore Roosevelt,* pp. 83–84, 123, 131–34. Israel Zangwill dedicated his play *The Melting Pot* to TR.

116 *"'race suicide'":* ibid., chap. 7.

116 *"he was convinced":* Gerstle, *American Crucible,* pp. 32–38.

116 *"he told the officers":* Roosevelt speech, June 1897, quoted in Brands, *T.R.,* p. 317. As late as December of that year, he expressed a preference for war with Germany—"but I am not particular, and I'd take even Spain if nothing better offered." Letter of December 23, 1897, quoted in Brands, *T.R.,* p. 323.

117 *"The Spanish-American war":* Roosevelt, "Expansion and Peace," *The Independent,* December 21, 1899, www.bartleby.com/58/2.html (accessed June 4, 2009).

117 *"Accepting the 1900":* Quoted in Brands, *T.R.,* pp. 401–402.

117 *"'The Philippines, like Cuba'":* Quoted in Frank Ninkovich, *The United States and Imperialism* (Malden, MA: Blackwell, 2001), pp. 39–40.

117 *"Woodrow Wilson":* Woodrow Wilson, "The Ideals of America," *Atlantic Monthly,* December 26, 1901, quoted in Walter McDougall, *Promised Land, Crusader State: The American Encounter with the World Since 1776* (Boston: Houghton Mifflin, 1997), p. 127.

118 *"'muscular Christianity'":* Joshua David Hawley, *Theodore Roosevelt: Preacher of Righteousness* (New Haven: Yale University Press, 2008), p. 18.

118 *"TR, who read the Bible"*: Gary Scott Smith, *Faith and the Presidency: From George Washington to George W. Bush* (New York: Oxford University Press, 2006), p. 131.

118 *"'Backward' peoples"*: Howard K. Beale, *Theodore Roosevelt and the Rise of America to World Power* (Baltimore: The Johns Hopkins University Press, 1956), pp. 72–73.

118 *"A 1900 Senate speech"*: Albert J. Beveridge, *Congressional Record,* 56th Cong., 1st sess., pp. 704–12, www.mtholyoke.edu/acad/intrel/ajb72 .htm (accessed December 6, 2009). Woodrow Wilson added Puerto Ricans to his list of "children" when he advocated their annexation: "They are children and we are men in these deep matters of government and justice." Quoted in McDougall, *Promised Land,* p. 127.

119 *"Bryan insisted"*: Bryan, "Imperialism," speech delivered in Indianapolis, August 8, 1900 (accessed March 7, 2009 at www.humanitiesweb .org.human.php?s=hop=c&a=p.ID=2309). In 1906, Bryan adjusted downward his idea of the American mission: "Each nation can give lessons to every other, and while our nation is in a position to make the largest contribution . . . to the education of the world, it ought to remain in the attitude of a pupil and be ever ready to profit by the experience of others." Quoted in Michael Kazin, *A Godly Hero: The Life of William Jennings Bryan* (New York: Knopf, 2006), p. 12.

119 *"William James"*: James to François Pillon, June 15, 1898, in *The Letters of William James* (Boston: Atlantic Monthly Press, 1920), p. 74. James concluded his letter: "I am going to a great popular meeting in Boston today where a lot of my friends are to protest against the new 'Imperialism.'"

120 *"Mark Twain"*: Mark Twain, "To the Person Sitting in Darkness," in Charles Neider, ed., *The Complete Essays of Mark Twain* (New York: Da Capo, 2000), pp. 286, 296. Twain, by his own account, began the Spanish-American War "a red-hot imperialist," believing the point of the war was to "relieve [the Filipinos] from Spanish tyranny to enable them to set up a government of their own," but by October 1900 wrote that he had thought we should act as the natives' "protector— not try to get them under our heel." Twain, "Returning Home," *New York World,* October 6, 1900, www.historywiz.com/primarysources/ marktwain-imperialism.htm (accessed June 8, 2009).

120 *"Charles Eliot Norton"*: Quoted in Robert Beisner, *Twelve Against Empire* (New York: McGraw-Hill, 1968), p. 83.

120 *"In 1907":* James to Henry L. Higginson, c. June 1, 1907, in *Letters,* p. 289.

120 *"ideological rupture":* Judis, *Folly of Empire,* p. 117.

120 *"By heritage":* William Roscoe Thayer, *Theodore Roosevelt: An Intimate Biography* (Boston: Houghton Mifflin, 1919), p. 129.

121 *"'in the heart'":* Woodrow Wilson, *Division and Reunion, 1829–1889* (New York: Longmans, Green, 1893), pp. 125, 268.

121 *"He was raised":* John Milton Cooper, Jr., *The Warrior and the Priest: Theodore Roosevelt and Woodrow Wilson* (Cambridge, MA: Harvard University Press, 1983), pp. 15–19.

121 *"divine mission":* Wilson, address delivered in Kansas City, Missouri, September 6, 1919, in Morris Edmund Speare and Walter Blake Norris, eds., *Vital Forces in Current Events: Readings on Present-Day Affairs from Contemporary Leaders and Thinkers* (New York: Ginn, 1920), p. 204. See also Judis, *Folly,* p. 79.

121 *"chosen, and prominently chosen":* Wilson, "A Campaign Address in Jersey City, New Jersey," May 25, 1912, in Arthur S. Link, ed., *The Papers of Woodrow Wilson,* vol. 24 (Princeton, NJ: Princeton University Press, 1978), p. 443, quoted in Judis, *Folly,* p. 78. The historian John Milton Cooper, Jr., maintains (*The Warrior and the Priest,* p. 171) that "despite a shared idealism in style and to some extent in content, Wilson did not adopt Roosevelt's brand of political evangelism." Given what Cooper calls "Wilson's intellectual approach to politics," his "restrained manner and belief in self-control," Wilson's public embraces of the Almighty are all the more striking.

121 *"Washington Gladden":* Washington Gladden, *The Nation and the Kingdom: Annual Sermon Before the American Board of Commissioners for Foreign Missions* (Boston, 1909), in Cherry, *God's New Israel,* pp. 255, 260.

122 *"He cited Ephesians":* Wilson cited this passage in 1873 and 1913, according to Adam Gómez, "We Wrestle Not Against Flesh and Blood: Themes of Civil Religion in Woodrow Wilson's Public Speech," n.d., p. 7, www.allacademic.com//meta/p_mla_apa_research_citation/2/3/8/2/4/pages238248/p238248-1.php (accessed June 9, 2009).

122 *"fiftieth anniversary":* Wilson address, www.ourcampaigns.com/InfoLinkDetail.html?InfoLinkID=3165 (accessed June 9, 2009).

122 *"Armed interventions":* G. John Ikenberry, "Woodrow Wilson, the Bush Administration, and the Future of Liberal Internationalism," in G.

John Ikenberry, Thomas J. Knock, Anne-Marie Slaughter, and Tony Smith, *The Crisis of American Foreign Policy: Wilsonianism in the Twenty-first Century* (Princeton, NJ: Princeton University Press, 2008), p. 14.

122 *"shifted to multilateralism"*: Thomas J. Knock, "'Playing for a Hundred Years Hence': Woodrow Wilson's Internationalism and His Would-Be Heirs," in Ikenberry et al., *Crisis,* p. 40.

123 *"Adam Gómez"*: Gómez, "We Wrestle Not," p. 17.

123 *"'the wrongs against'"*: Wilson, January 22, 1917, to the Senate, and April 6, 1918; quoted in ibid., pp. 17–20.

123 *"'Force, Force'"*: Wilson, April 6, 1918, quoted in Judis, *Folly,* p. 114.

123 *"Wilson often identified"*: Indeed, his head of the Committee on Public Information, George Creel, produced a 1918 movie called *Pershing's Crusaders.* The poster for the movie, reproduced on p. 26 of Adam Gómez's "We Wrestle Not," shows a ghostly crusader, a large cross conspicuous on his shield, in the background.

123 *"ex-president TR"*: Roosevelt, "Must We Be Brayed in a Mortar before Our Folly Depart from Us?" *Metropolitan* (September 1917), quoted in Cooper, *The Warrior and the Priest,* p. 327.

123 *"Wilson told the Senate"*: Quoted in Gómez, "We Wrestle Not," p. 30.

123 *"Although his explicit references"*: ibid., pp. 31–32.

123 *"In Boston"*: ibid., p. 32.

124 *"Adam Gómez"*: Gómez, p. 34.

124 *"The theme of divine favoritism"*: See Hughes, *Myths,* p. 38.

124 *"Franklin Roosevelt"*: See Smith, *Faith and the Presidency,* chap. 6.

124 *"'We are fighting'"*: Roosevelt, State of the Union Address, January 6, 1942, www.infoplease.com/t/hist/state-of-the-union/153.html (accessed June 16, 2009).

125 *"Reinhold Niebuhr"*: Reinhold Niebuhr, "Anglo-Saxon Destiny and Responsibility," *Christianity and Crisis,* October 4, 1943, in Cherry, *God's New Israel,* p. 304, citing Amos 3:2.

125 *"'Divine Providence has played a great part in our history'"*: Truman, speech delivered at the New York Avenue Presbyterian Church, Washington, DC, April 3, 1951, quoted in Merlin Gustafson, "Harry Truman as a Man of Faith," *Christian Century* (January 17, 1973), p. 77.

125 *"Clark Clifford"*: Clark Clifford, *Counsel to the President* (New York: Random House, 1991), p. 8. We elaborate on Truman's decision to recognize Israel in Part 4.

126   "Crusade in Europe": Dwight D. Eisenhower, *Crusade in Europe* (Garden City, NY: Doubleday, 1948), p. 157, quoted in Smith, *Faith and the Presidency,* p. 544, n. 70.

126   *"Ike quoted the Bible":* ibid., p. 229.

126   *"'In God We Trust'":* In 1907, President Theodore Roosevelt had proposed to remove the slogan from coins, convinced that such publicly displayed reverence "cheapened and trivialized the trust in God it was intended to promote" and amounted to "a sacrilegious association of God and mammon." Congress rebuffed him. Quoted in ibid., pp. 138–39.

126   *"'Judeo-Christian'":* Mark Silk, "Notes on the Judeo-Christian Tradition in America," *American Quarterly* 36, no. 1 (Spring 1984): 65–85.

126   *"Gary Scott Smith":* Smith, *Faith and the Presidency,* p. 242.

126   *"'the greatest force'":* Eisenhower, "Radio and Television Address . . . on the State of the Nation," April 5, 1954, quoted in ibid., p. 245.

127   *"'truly trying to follow'":* Eisenhower, "Remarks at the Annual Breakfast of the International Council for Christian Leadership," February 2, 1956, quoted in ibid., p. 245.

127   *"'the hand of Providence'":* Quoted in ibid., p. 229.

127   *"And was baptized":* Garry Wills, *Head and Heart: American Christianities* (New York: Penguin, 2007), p. 456, citing Martin Marty, *Modern American Religion,* vol. 3 (Chicago: University of Chicago Press, 1996), pp. 305–306.

127   *"A 1947 poll":* Wills, *Head and Heart,* pp. 452–53, citing Sydney Ahlstrom, *A Religious History of the American People,* 2nd ed. (New Haven: Yale University Press, 1972), p. 952.

127   *"'Our form of government'":* *New York Times,* December 23, 1952, p. 16, quoted in Smith, *Faith and the Presidency,* p. 254. On the difficulty of tracking down exactly what Eisenhower said on this occasion, and the frequent misinterpretations that have ensued, see Patrick Henry, "'And I Don't Care What It Is': The Tradition-History of a Civil Religion Proof-Text," *Journal of the American Academy of Religion* 49, no. 1 (March 1981): 35–49.

128   *"'The American covenant called on us'":* Lyndon B. Johnson, inaugural address, January 20, 1965, www.bartleby.com/124/pres57.html (accessed June 19, 2009).

128   *"Some historians detect":* Peter Stearns, *American Cool* (New York: NYU

Press, 1994), p. 186. See the discussion in Christina Kotchemidova, "From Good Cheer to 'Drive-By Smiling': A Social History
of Cheerfulness," paper presented to the 2004 Annual Conference of
the International Society for Research on Emotions, New York, July
7–11.

128 *"smiley face"*: Kotchemidova, "From Good Cheer," p. 20.

129 *"Bob Dylan"*: Bob Dylan, "With God on Our Side," first performed
April 12, 1963, lyrics at www.bobdylan.com/#/songs/god-our-side
(accessed June 19, 2009).

129 *"King told a prayer meeting"*: Rev. Martin Luther King, Jr., to Montgomery Improvement Association Mass Meeting, December 5, 1955,
Montgomery, Alabama, www.mlkonline.net/mia.html (accessed June
20, 2009).

130 *"1958 sermon in Detroit"*: Martin Luther King, Jr., sermon of March
12, 1958, in Detroit, in Clayborne Carson et al., eds., *The Papers of
Martin Luther King, Jr.,* vol. 6, *Advocate of the Social Gospel, Sept. 1948–
March 1963* (Berkeley: University of California Press, 2007), p. 337.
King foreshadowed George McGovern's 1972 motto, "Come home,
America."

130 *"'it may well be'"*: King, September 25, 1960, in Carson et al., eds., *The
Papers of Martin Luther King, Jr.,* vol. 5, *Threshold of a New Decade, January 1959–December 1960* (Berkeley: University of California Press,
2006), p. 509.

130 *"the luminous 1967 sermon"*: King, April 4, 1967, www.americanrhetoric
.com/speeches/mlkatimetobreaksilence.htm (accessed June 17, 2009).

131 *"America 'doomed'"*: Quoted in Frederick L. Downing, "Martin Luther King, Jr., as Public Theologian," *Theology Today* 44, no. 1 (April
1987), theologytoday.ptsem.edu/apr1987/v44-1-article2.htm#9 (accessed June 19, 2009).

131 *"His speeches on Vietnam"*: See Edwin O. Guthman and C. Richard
Allen, eds., *RFK: Collected Speeches* (New York: Viking, 1993), pp.
265–315.

132 *"He cited John Winthrop"*: Robert F. Kennedy, "Racial Problems in the
North," speech to the National Council of Christians and Jews, April
28, 1965, in ibid., p. 158.

132 *"'John Adams once said'"*: Kennedy didn't note that Adams wrote these
words in his diary but refrained from inserting them in the published

version of his 1765 "A Dissertation on the Canon and Feudal Law." See pp. 75–76 and 209 above.

132 *"Kennedy went on":* Kennedy, "Community, Compassion, and Involvement," April 20, 1968, in Guthman and Allen, eds., *RFK,* p. 372.

132 *"the camp of the enemy":* On this dynamic in the later New Left, see Todd Gitlin, *The Sixties: Years of Hope, Days of Rage* (New York: Bantam, 1987), chap. 11.

133 *"Jimmy Carter":* This was Micah 6:8: "He hath showed thee, O man, what is good; and what doth the Lord require of thee, but to do justly, and to love mercy, and to walk humbly with thy God." Inaugural address, January 20, 1977, www.bartleby.com/124/pres60.html (accessed October 31, 2009).

133 *"We are a purely idealistic Nation'":* Quoted in Smith, *Faith,* pp. 296–300.

134 *"even our great Nation has its recognized limits'":* Carter's inaugural address, January 20, 1977, avalon.law.yale.edu/20th_century/carter.asp (accessed December 10, 2009).

134 *"A Baptist televangelist":* Max Blumenthal, "Agent of Intolerance," *The Nation,* May 16, 2007, www.thenation.com/doc/20070528/blumenthal (accessed November 15, 2009).

134 *"Jerry Falwell had no doubt":* Jerry Falwell, *America Can Be Saved!* (Murfreesboro, TN: Sword of the Lord Publishers, 1979), quoted in Kevin Mattson, *"What the Heck Are You Up To, Mr. President?" Jimmy Carter, America's "Malaise," and the Speech That Should Have Changed the Country* (New York: Bloomsbury, 2009), p. 182.

134 *"Following Falwell":* On Carter, see Smith, *Faith,* chap. 9; on Reagan, see Smith, *Faith,* pp. 328, 334, 337, and a 1960 letter quoted in John Patrick Diggins, *Ronald Reagan: Fate, Freedom, and the Making of History* (New York: Norton, 2007), p. 195.

134 *"White House lawyer":* The lawyer was John G. Roberts, Jr., later Chief Justice of the Supreme Court. Todd S. Purdum and John M. Broder, "Nominee's Early Files Show Many Cautions for Top Officials, Including Reagan," *New York Times,* August 19, 2005, p. 12.

135 *"God has a plan for everyone'":* Reagan wrote that his mother had taught him that "God has a plan for everyone." *An American Life* (Norwalk, CT: Easton, 1990), pp. 20–21, quoted in Smith, *Faith,* p. 326.

135 *"God had 'intended'":* Cited in Rogers M. Smith, "Providentialism,

Foreign Policy, and the Ethics of Political Discourse" (2005), p. 18, web.mit.edu/polisci/research/wip/RogerSmith.pdf (accessed June 30, 2009).

135 *"I have always believed'":* Quoted in Godfrey Hodgson, *The Myth of American Exceptionalism* (New Haven: Yale University Press, 2009), p. 176.

135 *"Reagan liked to cite Emerson":* Reagan to the 1992 Republican National Convention, quoted in Diggins, *Ronald Reagan,* p. 41.

135 *"liked to cite the Deist":* On Reagan and Paine, see Diggins, *Ronald Reagan,* passim, and Harvey J. Kaye, *Thomas Paine and the Promise of America* (New York: Hill and Wang, 2005), p. 50.

135 *"The genius of Reagan'":* Diggins, *Ronald Reagan,* pp. 27, 51.

136 *"There's a wall around him'":* Quoted in James Mann, *The Rebellion of Ronald Reagan: A History of the End of the Cold War* (New York: Viking, 2009), p. 89.

136 *"Reagan's sunny persona":* Earlier, Reagan had no difficulty showing his anger. See, for example, his campaign commercial for Barry Goldwater in 1964 (www.livingroomcandidate.org/commercials/1964/ronald-reagan [accessed June 25, 2009]), and his on-camera reaction to left-wing University of California faculty during the People's Park battle in 1969 (footage in Mark Kitchell's film *Berkeley in the Sixties*).

137 *"disdained Puritanism":* On Reagan's disdain for the Puritans' idea of the covenant, see Diggins, *Ronald Reagan,* p. 31.

137 *"World Federalism":* His biographer Lou Cannon speaks of this as a "brief fling." Lou Cannon, *Governor Reagan: His Rise to Power* (New York: PublicAffairs, 2003), p. 93. Diggins writes of his having "advocated banning the atomic bomb" (*Ronald Reagan,* p. 100).

137 *"casual suggestion":* Goldwater on ABC-TV's *Issues and Answers,* May 1963, quoted in Bart Barnes, "Barry Goldwater, GOP Hero, Dies," *Washington Post,* May 30, 1998, p. A1, www.washingtonpost.com/wp-srv/politics/daily/may98/goldwater30.htm (accessed June 25, 2009).

137 *"one year later":* Mann, *Rebellion,* p. 42. On *The Day After,* see pp. 41–42. The "highest priority" quotation comes from Ann Landers, "Nuclear War Column Elicits Response from President Reagan," *St. Petersburg Times,* June 14, 1982, news.google.com/newspapers?nid=888&dat=19820614&id=tPONAAAAIBAJ&sjid=S3sDAAAAIBAJ&pg=4108.5874876 (accessed June 27, 2009).

137 *"he was sincere":* Arthur Miller once said that Reagan "disarmed his opponents by never showing the slightest sign of inner conflict about the truth of what he was saying"; his sincerity "implie[d] honesty, an absence of moral conflict in the mind of its possessor." Miller, "On Politics and the Art of Acting," Jefferson Lecture, 2001, quoted in Diggins, *Ronald Reagan,* p. 116.

138 *"'God is near'":* Text of President Bush's 2002 State of the Union Address, January 29, 2002, www.washingtonpost.com/wp-srv/onpolitics/transcripts/sou012902.htm (accessed June 29, 2009). Our discussion of George W. Bush benefited from a reading of the English-language version of Anders Stephanson's postscript to the Italian edition (2003) of his *Manifest Destiny,* kindly supplied by the author.

138 *"First Inaugural":* George W. Bush, First Inaugural, January 20, 2001, www.bartleby.com/124/pres66.html (accessed June 29, 2009).

139 *"Republicans ran away":* Geoffrey C. Layman and Laura S. Hussey, "George W. Bush and the Evangelicals: Religious Commitment and Partisan Change Among Evangelical Protestants, 1960–2004," paper originally prepared for "A Matter of Faith? Religion in the 2004 Election," Notre Dame, IN, December 2–3, 2005, www.bsos.umd.edu/gvpt/apworkshop/layman-hussey06.pdf (accessed August 17, 2009).

139 *"Three days after the attacks":* Peter Ford, "Europe Cringes at Bush 'Crusade' Against Terrorists," *Christian Science Monitor,* September 19, 2001, www.csmonitor.com/2001/0919/p12s2-woeu.html (accessed June 29, 2009).

139 *"'The liberty we prize'":* Bush's State of the Union speech, January 29, 2003, www.cnn.com/2003/ALLPOLITICS/01/28/sotu.transcript (accessed June 29, 2009).

139 *"'fix[ing] . . . the intelligence'":* "The Secret Downing Street Memo," *Sunday Times* (London), May 1, 2005, www.timesonline.co.uk/tol/news/uk/article387374.ece (accessed June 30, 2009).

139 *"accepting his second":* Bush, acceptance speech at the Republican National Convention, September 2, 2004, www.washingtonpost.com/wp-dyn/articles/A57466-2004Sep2.html (accessed June 30, 2009).

140 *"he was at pains":* George W. Bush, Second Inaugural, January 21, 2005, www.washingtonpost.com/wp-dyn/articles/A23747-2005Jan20.html (accessed June 29, 2009).

140 *"Bush repeatedly evoked":* Smith, "Providential," pp. 2, 15.

140   *"Once again'"*: Bush, State of the Union speech, January 29, 2003, www.cnn.com/2003/ALLPOLITICS/01/28/sotu.transcript (accessed June 29, 2009).

140   *"'Liberty is both the plan'"*: "President Bush Discusses Freedom in Iraq and Middle East," speech of November 6, 2003, www.ned.org/george-w-bush/remarks-by-president-george-w-bush-at-the-20th-anniversary (accessed March 7, 2010).

140   *"America was targeted"*: Bush, September 14, 2001, www.pbs.org/newshour/bb/military/terroristattack/bush_speech_9-14.html (accessed June 30, 2009).

140   *"Bush defended that war"*: Bush, November 6, 2003, quoted in Anthony Burke, *Beyond Security, Ethics and Violence: War Against the Other* (London: Routledge, 2006), p. 226.

141   *"A sense of messianic mission"*: See Todd Gitlin, *The Bulldozer and the Big Tent: Blind Republicans, Lame Democrats, and the Recovery of American Ideals* (Hoboken, NJ: Wiley, 2007), pp. 64–66.

142   *"A self-described 'mutt'"*: "Chewing Over Obama's 'Mutt' Reference," November 10, 2008, www.boston.com/news/politics/political intelligence/2008/11/chewing_over_ob.html (accessed June 29, 2009).

142   *"President Woodrow Wilson"*: Quoted in Saul K. Padover, *Wilson's Ideals* (Whitefish, MT: Kessinger, 2006), p. 132.

143   *"'We remain a young nation'"*: "Barack Obama's Inaugural Address," January 20, 2009, www.nytimes.com/2009/01/20/us/politics/20text-obama.html?pagewanted=all (accessed June 29, 2009).

3. THE UNCHOSEN

149   *"'This day'"*: Deuteronomy 2:25.

149   *"God even intervened"*: Deuteronomy 2:30–35.

149   *"'in threescore more cities'"*: Deuteronomy 3:6–7.

149   *"the Gibeonites, surrendered"*: Joshua 9:25–27. Joshua 12–17 consists largely of a list of the lands dispossessed as grants to the Israelites, as well as the names of a few unchosen peoples permitted to remain among them (Deuteronomy 2:19, Joshua 13:13, 15:63, 16:10, 17:12–13).

149   *"the Jews, who originated"*: Reuven Firestone, *Who Are the Real Chosen People? The Meaning of Chosenness in Judaism, Christianity and Islam* (Woodstock, VT: Skyline, 2008), p. 20.

151   *"The 1988 charter"*: "The Charter of Allah: The Platform of the Is-

lamic Resistance Movement (Hamas)," August 18, 1988, www.the
jerusalemfund.org/www.thejerusalemfund.org/carryover/documents/
charter (accessed December 6, 2009). This is the English translation
carried on the site of the Jerusalem Fund, a Palestinian organization.

152 *"the grand mufti"*: Shlomo Aronson, *Hitler, the Allies, and the Jews* (Cambridge, UK: Cambridge University Press, 2004), p. 60.

153 *"During the Vichy and Nazi occupations"*: Robert Satloff, *Among the Righteous: Lost Stories from the Holocaust's Long Reach into Arab Lands* (New
York: PublicAffairs, 2006), especially pp. 73, 160.

153 *"Sayyid Qutb"*: Sayyid Qutb, *In the Shade of the Qur'an,* vol. 1, trans.
M. A. Salahi and A. Shamis (Markfield, Leicester, UK, and Nairobi,
Kenya: The Islamic Foundation, 1999), vol. 4, pp. 127, 190, 197. First
published 1954.

153 *"unspeakable humiliation"*: Amin Malouf, *In the Name of Identity: Violence
and the Need to Belong,* trans. Barbara Bray (New York: Arcade, 2001),
p. 28; Neil MacFarquhar, *The Media Relations Department of Hizbollah
Wishes You a Happy Birthday: Unexpected Encounters in the Changing Middle East* (New York: PublicAffairs, 2009), pp. 6, 295; Lawrence Wright,
The Looming Tower: Al-Qaeda and the Road to 9/11 (New York: Vintage,
2007 [2006]), p. 98.

153 *"Ayman al-Zawahiri"*: quoted in Wright, *The Looming Tower,* p. 64.

153 *"Osama bin Laden"*: quoted in ibid., p. 171.

154 *"Thomas Jefferson"*: First Inaugural Address, March 4, 1801, www.bartleby
.com/124/pres16.html (accessed August 11, 2009).

154 *"converting the Indians"*: Harold Hellenbrand, "Not 'To Destroy But to
Fulfil': Jefferson, Indians, and Republican Dispensation," *Eighteenth-
Century Studies* 18, no. 4 (Autumn 1985): 524.

154 *"He also hoped"*: ibid., p. 547.

154 *"one of his supporters"*: David Ramsay, "An Oration on the Cession of
Louisiana to the United States" (Newport, RI: Farnsworth, 1804), p.
14, quoted in ibid., p. 546.

155 *"the Delawares"*: James Axtell, *After Columbus: Essays in the Ethnohistory
of Colonial North America* (New York: Oxford University Press, 1988),
p. 131.

156 *"The 'Indians' were awed"*: ibid., p. 135.

156 *"James Axtell"*: James Axtell, *Beyond 1492: Encounters in Colonial North
America* (New York: Oxford University Press, 1992), p. 58.

156   *"In New England"*: Axtell, *The European and the Indian: Essays in the Ethnohistory of Colonial North America* (New York: Oxford University Press, 1981), p. 135.

156   *"'prefabricated images'"*: Axtell, *Beyond 1492*, pp. 100–101.

156   *"the Europeans were inclined"*: Axtell, *The European and the Indian*, p. 44.

157   *"cheerfully content"*: Axtell, *Beyond 1492*, pp. 32–33.

157   *"Micmacs"*: ibid., p. 39.

157   *"John Lawson"*: Axtell, *After Columbus*, p. 243.

157   *"Another eighteenth-century Englishman"*: ibid., p. 142.

157   *"Crèvecœur"*: John Hector St. John de Crèvecœur, *Letters from an American Farmer* (1782), quoted in Axtell, *The European and the Indian*, p. 49. Axtell makes the apt point that the "ease of living" these captives found was the men's way of hunting, not the women's way of cultivating.

157   *"missionaries felt"*: Axtell, *The European and the Indians* pp. 45–46.

157   *"Axtell's summary"*: Axtell, ibid., p. 72.

157   *"natives were depleted"*: Axtell, *Beyond 1492*, p. 72.

158   *"As the Indians defended"*: ibid., p. 74.

158   *"The strongest among them fought"*: ibid., p. 100. They also crossed tribal lines to form alliances against the whites, playing some off against others. As early as 1641, Axtell writes (*The European and the Indian*, p. 113), "a Narragansett chief from Rhode Island . . . approached the Montauks on Long Island with plans for a coordinated attack upon all the English settlements of the region," proposing that

> we be one as [the English] are, otherwise we shall be all
> gone shortly, for you know our fathers had plenty of deer
> and skins, our plains were full of deer, as also our woods,
> and of turkies, and our coves full of fish and fowl. But
> these English having gotten our land, they with scythes
> cut down the grass, and with axes fell the trees; their cows
> and horses eat the grass, and their hogs spoil our clam
> banks, and we shall all be starved.

Therefore, he concluded, forty-one days hence they should "fall on and kill men, women, and children, but no cows, for they will serve to eat till our deer be increased again."

158   *"As the whites pushed"*: ibid., p. 113.

158   *"When the Indians went into debt"*: ibid., p. 111.

158   *"women's work"*: ibid., p. 114.

158 *"messianic cults"*: Anthony F. C. Wallace, "Revitalization Movements," *American Anthropologist* 58 (1956): 264–81.

158 *"Samoset"*: Dee Brown, *Bury My Heart at Wounded Knee* (New York: Holt, 2007 [1970]), p. 3.

159 *"Gershon Shafir"*: Gershon Shafir, *Land, Labor and the Origins of the Israeli-Palestinian Conflict, 1882–1914* (Berkeley: University of California Press, 1989, rev. 1996), p. 24.

159 *"Arab peasants"*: Rashid Khalidi, *Palestinian Identity: The Construction of Modern National Consciousness* (New York: Columbia University Press, 1997), p. 98.

159 *"Less than one-tenth of the land"*: Shafir, *Land, Labor,* p. 41.

160 *"Such collaboration"*: Shafir, *Land, Labor,* pp. 199–200.

160 *"A necessary condition"*: Quoted in Zeev Sternhell, *The Founding Myths of Israel* (Princeton, NJ: Princeton University Press, 1999), p. 75.

161 *"Tom Segev"*: Tom Segev, *One Palestine, Complete: Jews and Arabs Under the British Mandate* (New York: Metropolitan Books, 2000), p. 255.

162 *"Embattled, the Zionists organized"*: Khalidi, *Palestinian Identity,* p. 103.

162 *"The modern newcomers"*: Shafir, *Land, Labor,* p. 12.

162 *"hospitality rooms"*: ibid., p. 141.

162 "Altneuland": Theodor Herzl, *Old New Land* (*Altneuland*), trans. Lotta Levensohn (Princeton, NJ: Markus Wiener, 2000), p. 143.

162 *"'a people without a land'"*: Adam M. Garfinkle, "On the Origin, Meaning, Use and Abuse of a Phrase," *Middle Eastern Studies* 27, no. 4 (October 1991): 539–50.

163 *"scrupulously legal"*: Shafir, *Land, Labor,* p. 201.

163 *"If the Jews"*: ibid., p. 209.

163 *"Their agricultural successes"*: ibid., p. 215.

163 *"Rashid Khalidi"*: Khalidi, *Palestinian Identity,* p. 102.

164 *"Columbus's letter"*: *The Diario of Christopher Columbus's First Voyage to America, 1492–1493,* ed. and trans. Oliver Dunn and James E. Kelley, Jr. (Norman: University of Oklahoma Press, 1989), p. 281.

164 *"good for ordering about"*: Columbus, *Diario,* quoted in Bartolomeo de Las Casas, *Historia de las Indias,* as translated by Margaret Zamora, *Reading Columbus* (Berkeley: University of California Press, 1993), p. 90.

164 *"tales of combat"*: See Richard Slotkin, *Regeneration Through Violence: The Mythology of the American Frontier, 1600–1860* (Middletown, CT: Wesleyan University Press, 1973).

165 *"Werner Sollors"*: Werner Sollors, *Beyond Ethnicity: Consent and Descent in American Culture* (New York: Oxford University Press, 1987), p. 127.

165 *"'tales of lovers leaps'"*: ibid., p. 115.

165 *"'In the cult'"*: ibid., p. 117, quoting Cotton Mather, *The Life and Death of the Renown'd Mr. John Eliot. . . .* (London: John Dunton, 1691).

166 *"'I appeal to any white man'"*: Thomas Jefferson, "Notes on the State of Virginia," in *The Portable Thomas Jefferson,* ed. Merrill D. Peterson (New York: Penguin, 1977), p. 100.

166 *"Tecumseh's later"*: Tecumseh, October 1811, in Bob Blaisdell, ed., *Great Speeches by Native Americans* (Mineola, NY: Dover, 2000), p. 58.

167 *"A survey conducted"*: Public Opinion Polls, Jerusalem Media and Communication Centre, www.jmcc.org/publicpoll/results/2009/index.htm (accessed August 9, 2009).

168 *"'we remain like a wall'"*: Quoted in Adina Hoffman, *My Happiness Bears No Relation to Happiness: A Poet's Life in the Palestinian Century* (New Haven: Yale University Press, 2009), p. 311.

168 *"'Thrombosis in the Veins'"*: Taha Muhammad Ali, "Thrombosis in the Veins of Petroleum," in *So What: New and Selected Poems, 1971–2005,* trans. Peter Cole, Yahya Hijazi, and Gabriel Levin (Port Townsend, WA: Copper Canyon, 2006), pp. 13–17.

169 *"'The poem is angry'"*: Taha Muhammad Ali, quoted in Hoffman, *My Happiness,* p. 212. The story of the bombing of the village is told on pp. 122–34.

169 *"bitterness follows me"*: Taha Muhammad Ali, "The Bell at Forty: The Destruction of a Village," in *So What,* p. 107.

169 *"After we die'"*: Taha Muhammad Ali, "Twigs," in ibid., p. 119.

169 *"'I was a fool'"*: Taha Muhammad Ali, "Abd el Hadi the Fool," in ibid., pp. 129–35.

170 *"'I do not hate people'"*: Mahmoud Darwish, "Identity Card," www.ipoet.com/ARCHIVE/ORIGINAL/darwish/IdentityCard.html (accessed December 8, 2009).

170 *"Darwish wrote a poem"*: Mahmoud Darwish, "A Soldier Dreams of White Lilies," www.mahmoud-darwish.com/id/index.php?option=com_content&view=article&id=49:a-soldier-dreams-of-white-lilies-&catid=35:poetry&Itemid=6 8 (accessed August 11, 2009).

175 *"the year 1968"*: Let us not pretend an excessive precision. The singling out of the calendar year 1968 as opposed to say, 1967, is in many ways

conventional, and there is no reason to fuss over precise dates when we are speaking of upheavals that unfolded over a period of years.

175 *"Jean-Paul Sartre"*: Preface to Frantz Fanon, *Les Damnés de la Terre* (Paris: François Maspero, 1961), pp. 13, 17, 20, 26. Translations by Richard Philcox (*The Wretched of the Earth,* New York: Grove Press, 2004), modified by Todd Gitlin.

176 *"'a positive, formative'"*: ibid., pp. 69, 70.

176 *"'Now, comrades'"*: ibid., p. 240.

177 *"'The Third World today'"*: ibid., pp. 241, 242.

177 *"'The duty of every revolutionary'"*: Fidel Castro, Second Declaration of Havana, February 4, 1962, www.fordham.edu/halsall/mod/1962castro .html (accessed December 7, 2009).

178 *"The third leaflet"*: Ely Karmon, "Fatah and the Popular Front for the Liberation of Palestine: International Terrorism Strategies (1968–1990)," 212.150.54.123/articles/articledet.cfm?articleid=145 (accessed November 25, 2009).

178 *"Edward Said"*: Edward Said, *Culture and Imperialism* (New York: Random House, 1993), p. 327.

179 *"The Manichaean imagination"*: But did not Fanon, the patron saint of the Third World Revolution, abhor the nationalism into which it constantly threatened to degenerate? "If I have so often cited Fanon," Edward Said wrote (*Culture and Imperialism,* p. 268), "it is because more dramatically and decisively than anyone, I believe, he expresses the immense cultural shift from the terrain of nationalist independence to the theoretical domain of liberation." Without doubt, Fanon longed for that shift, but the prophet was not equipped to understand why nationalism possessed an unnerving and unaccountable staying power.

180 *"Hugo Chávez"*: "Israel Plans to 'Terminate the Palestinian People,'" *Ha'aretz,* November 28, 2008, www.haaretz.com/hasen/spages/1131227 .html (accessed January 31, 2010); and "Editing Chavez to Manufacture a Slur," FAIR, January 23, 2006, www.fair.org/index.php?page=2805, accessed March 7, 2010.

181 *"Noam Chomsky"*: To take one of many examples, in 2001, Chomsky surmised that the September 11 attacks, which he conceded were "major atrocities," might well have been vastly exceeded in scale by Bill Clinton's 1998 attack on a Sudanese pharmaceutical plant, after al-Qa-

eda's demolition of the U.S. embassies in Kenya and Tanzania (these attacks unremarked by Chomsky), in the mistaken belief that it belonged to bin Laden; and by a "silent genocide" that the United States was committing, or planning to commit, in Afghanistan. See Michael Bérubé's scrupulous discussion in *The Left at War* (New York: NYU Press, 2009), pp. 49, 76. For Chomsky and Edward S. Herman's slippery treatment of the Khmer Rouge, whose atrocities they regarded as (1) exaggerated, (2) pale in contrast to the American bombing of Cambodia that helped bring the Khmer Rouge to power, and (3) less sinister or interesting than early exaggerations of Khmer Rouge atrocities in the Western press—which turned out not to be exaggerated at all—see Chomsky and Herman, *After the Cataclysm: Postwar Indochina and the Reconstruction of Imperial Ideology* (Boston: South End Press, 1979), chap. 6. For an extensive, meticulous, and devastating summary of Chomsky's misrepresentations of the Khmer Rouge (for example, as conceivably "liberating" Cambodia in a manner comparable to the way France was liberated in 1944), as well as his misrepresentations of his own misrepresentations, and his charge that his critics are "depraved" and that in contrast to them "neo-Nazis and neo-Stalinists are on a far higher moral level," see Bruce Sharp, "Averaging Wrong Answers: Noam Chomsky and the Cambodia Controversy," www.mekong.net/cambodia/chomsky.htm (accessed January 30, 2010). For a recent examination of Chomsky's propensity to minimize the depredations of Slobodan Milosevic, see David Campbell, "Chomsky's Bosnian Shame," November 19, 2009, www.david-campbell.org/2009/11/14/chomskys-bosnian-shame/ (accessed January 30, 2010).

4. A SPECIAL FRIENDSHIP

183 *"'vital friend'"*: Yitzhak Benhorin, "US Poll: Israel Alone Named 'Vital Friend,'" *Ynet*, www.ynetnews.com/articles/0,7340,L-3368650,00.html (accessed December 10, 2009).

183 *"Pew Global Attitudes Project"*: See "Global Unease with Major World Powers," www.pewglobal.org/reports/display.php?ReportID=256 (accessed December 10, 2009).

184 *"'There are thirty million Arabs'"*: Quoted in John Acacia, *Clark Clifford: The Wise Man of Washington* (Lexington: The University of Kentucky Press, 2009), p. 95.

184 *"On May 12, Truman"*: This account of the White House meeting is taken from Warren Bass, *Support Any Friend: Kennedy's Middle East and the Making of the U.S.-Israel Alliance* (New York: Oxford University Press, 2003), pp. 30–32.

185 *"'I am sorry, gentlemen'"*: ibid., p. 24.

185 *"'You know I was elected by Jews'"*: ibid., p. 55. Bass quotes Richard Reeves, *President Kennedy: Profile of Power* (New York: Touchstone, 1993), p. 144, which sourced Kennedy's crude statement to journalist Charlie Bartlett, an old friend of JFK's. "The remark," Bass writes in his endnotes, "does not appear in the . . . meeting memcon"; still, its veracity was confirmed by the Kennedy Library oral history team, which confirmed the comment was made during a fifteen-minute interlude when both leaders were alone in the room.

185 *"And James Baker"*: See, for example, Anne E. Kornblut, "The Bushes and the Jews," *Slate,* April 17, 2002, www.slate.com/id/2064424/ (accessed January 18, 2010).

186 *"'major non-NATO ally'"*: ibid., p. 145.

186 *"'My concern in the Middle East'"*: Richard Nixon, *RN: The Memoirs of Richard Nixon* (New York: Grosset & Dunlap, 1978), p. 574.

186 *"Nixon and Henry Kissinger airlifted"*: See Capt. Chris J. Krisinger, "Operation Nickel Grass: Airlift in Support of National Policy," *Airpower Journal* (Spring 1989), www.au.af.mil/au/cadre/aspi/airchronicles/api/apj89/spr89/krisinger.html (accessed December 11, 2009).

188 *"Hal Lindsey"*: *The Late Great Planet Earth* (Grand Rapids: Zondervan, 1970), quoted in Goldman, *Zeal for Zion,* p. 292.

188 *"'To stand against Israel'"*: Ed Dobson, Jerry Falwell, and Edward E. Hindson, *The Fundamentalist Phenomenon: The Resurgence of Conservative Christianity* (New York: Doubleday, 1981), p. 215.

188 *"the Reverend John Hagee"*: The account of the CUFI summit is taken from Bill Moyers, "Christians United for Israel," *Bill Moyers Journal;* www.pbs.org/moyers/journal/10052007/profile.html (accessed December 10, 2009).

191 *"'the stranger must be made to feel at home in our midst'"*: Herzl, *Old New Land,* p. 111.

191 *"culture of victory"*: On the American side, see Tom Engelhardt, *The End of Victory Culture: Cold War America and the Disillusioning of a Generation* (New York: Basic, 1995).

Index

INDEX

INDEX

American, 41, 185–88
assimilating in Europe, 30–32
black Americans compared to,
110–11, 129
bound to God for eternity, 5–6,
18–19, 37
creation of, 24, 61
Diaspora of, 1, 31, 32–33, 41, 45–46,
163
emancipation of, 29–33, 43–44, 55
exile of, 1, 2, 25–29, 35, 40, 64, 67,
110
God's covenant with, 2, 3, 5–6, 12,
15, 16, 21, 24, 58, 61, 78, 98, 121,
150–51
identity of, 40, 43, 55, 58, 61, 63–64,
190
as "kingdom of priests and a holy
nation," 6, 16, 19, 20, 22, 90,
192
nationhood as goal of, 26, 33, 40–41,
47, 55, 163
non-Jews' hatred of, xvii, 32–33, 61,
150–54, 167
persecution of, 16–17, 32–33, 38,
56, 161
redemption of, 18–19, 33–35, 36–38,
41, 42, 80
secular, xv, xvii, 2, 29, 34, 36, 37, 38,
39, 40, 41, 42–43, 44, 46, 47, 55,
57, 58, 60, 61, 62, 64
as stiff-necked people, 6, 7, 15, 16,
21, 22, 24, 151
Johnson, Edward, 72
Johnson, Lyndon B., 127, 128, 131,
142, 186
Jones, Absalom, 110–11
Joshua, 17, 21, 80, 149, 154, 222, 231
Joshua Generation, 62
Judaism:
chosenness theme in, xv, 37, 39, 41
in Hebrew Bible, 1, 11, 25, 41, 149,
154

land, state, and religion joined in,
39–41, 42
messianism in, 23, 28, 31–32, 34–38,
40, 44
political vs. religious identity of, 30,
31, 36–37, 41, 43–44
rabbinical ideas in, 19, 27, 34–42
and Sabbath, 25, 37, 47
as theology of righteous separatism,
26, 29
traditional rituals in, 28, 64, 69
transformations of, 28–32
and Zionism, 33, 35
justice:
Abraham and, 13–14, 16, 20
Jews and, 8, 24–25, 29, 31, 57, 63,
64, 192
mission of, xvi, 129, 131
in the Promised Land, 45, 62, 63
racial, 110
as test of chosenness, 109

Kabbalah, 34
Kalischer, Zvi Hirsch, 34–35
Katz, Ya'akov, 59
Katznelson, Berl, 38
Kennedy, John F., 127–28, 185, 186, 238
Kennedy, Robert F., 131–32, 227
Khalidi, Rashid, 163
Khmer Rouge, 237
kibbutz movement, 55, 56, 162
Kierkegaard, Søren, 14
King, Rev. Martin Luther, Jr., 129–31,
132
Kipling, Rudyard, 99, 118
Kissinger, Henry A., 186
Kitchell, Mark, 229
Kivrot Ha'ta'avah (Graves of
Craving), 22
Kook, Rabbi Abraham Isaac, 35–38,
42, 43
Kook, Rabbi Zvi Yehuda, 39–40, 41–43,
46–47, 49, 54, 56, 62, 63

About the Authors

TODD GITLIN is the author of the bestseller *The Sixties: Years of Hope, Days of Rage* and eleven other books. A prominent social commentator and media analyst, as well as a novelist whose 1999 novel *Sacrifice* won the Harold U. Ribalow Prize for Jewish fiction, Gitlin is a professor of journalism and sociology at Columbia University, where he chairs the Ph.D. program in communications. He lives in New York City.

LIEL LEIBOVITZ, a former noncommissioned officer in the Israel Defense Forces, is the author of *Aliya: Three Generations of American-Jewish Immigration to Israel* and coauthor of *Lili Marlene: The Soldiers' Song of World War II*. He teaches communications at New York University. An editor at *Tablet,* an online magazine of Jewish life, politics, and culture, Leibovitz lives in New York City.